100 THINGS
OKLAHOMA
STATE FANS
SHOULD KNOW & DO
BEFORE THEY DIE

Robert Allen

TRIUMPH
B O O K S

Library of Congress Cataloging-in-Publication Data

Names: Allen, Robert, 1960– author.
Title: 100 things Oklahoma State fans should know & do before they die / Robert Allen.
Other titles: One hundred things Oklahoma State fans should know & do before they die
Description: Chicago, Illinois : Triumph Books, 2017. | Includes bibliographical references and index.
Identifiers: LCCN 2017015760 | ISBN 9781629374345 (paperback)
Subjects: LCSH: Oklahoma State Cowboys (Football team)—History. | Oklahoma State University—Football—History. | BISAC: SPORTS & RECREATION / Football. | TRAVEL / United States / South / West South Central (AR, LA, OK, TX).
Classification: LCC GV958.O54 A55 2017 | DDC 796.332/630976634—dc23 LC record available at https://lccn.loc.gov/2017015760

This book is available in quantity at special discounts for your group or organization. For further information, contact:
Triumph Books LLC
814 North Franklin Street
Chicago, Illinois 60610
(312) 337-0747
www.triumphbooks.com

Printed in U.S.A.
ISBN: 978-1-62937-434-5
Design by Patricia Frey
Photos courtesy of AP Images unless otherwise indicated

The newest Cowboy in the Allen family is Cash. He can choose his college to his wishes, with the wise counsel of his parents, Sam and Zach. He does need to know his Cowboy lore, and I hope this book from his "Pops" will help. I'm sure his Aunt Katy and soon-to-be Uncle Logan will help as well.

Contents

Foreword

When I first came to Oklahoma State, I thought it was the best opportunity for me. It was a very good decision based on the people here, my personality, and the environment and atmosphere, which were a great fit for me. Then, as I stayed here through my playing career, I became very attracted to the people here at the school and in the community. I was fortunate enough to have Coach (Pat) Jones hire me so that I could remain here. Then, after a period of time, you get addicted to living in this community and being involved with this university. Even today, with 26,000 students and 50,000 in the town of Stillwater, very seldom do you go anywhere that you don't know somebody. You can actually go into stores and if you forgot your wallet, they will let you take your item and come back and pay later. You have that small-town feeling, but there is so much to see and do.

Something I've always said, and I'm proud of, is that we have 50,000 people who watch our football games in Boone Pickens Stadium, and 40,000 of them are students or graduates of Oklahoma State University or a legacy of Oklahoma State in some way. It's that way for all sports, and I think that is something that makes us special. I've always been repetitive in what I like to do, and I've always thought that as a coach here I hope I am doing something that will help Oklahoma State for a long time. That is why I've stayed. Like I've said in the last year, Oklahoma State has become a part of me and a part of my wife, Kristen, and our three boys. I would say that I have become a part of the people and part of the university, as well. It will be that way forever. I'm always hesitant to use comparisons, but it is almost like what Frank Beamer did at Virginia Tech. When you sit and look at it, I almost think that is where I am right now.

I'm very close with the Sutton family. I've stayed in touch with Coach (Eddie) Sutton and Sean for years, and even today. Gary Ward—I don't think people understand the legacy he had. I think it was 16 straight Big Eight championships in baseball. We all know baseball—one good pitcher can beat you on any given day. What John Smith has been able to accomplish—I didn't realize that John has been here 26 years as the head coach. It goes by so fast.

What Mike Holder, our athletic director, did in golf as coach—are you kidding me? He coached 32 years. He won all those conference championships and eight national championships.

There is just an unbelievable legacy in athletics here that we have, and until the advent of social media I'm not sure people really knew about it. As Robert points out at the beginning of this book, for us to compete for as many national championships and do it for so long with a pretty moderate athletic department budget is rare. I didn't even mention Edward C. Gallagher and Henry Iba; you go to the Suttons and the Wards and Tommy Chesbro. You can go back to Pat Jones and Jimmy Johnson. I think Jimmy Johnson had three guys working here on his staff who became NFL head coaches. The people who have come through here are pretty amazing. When you start to look at it, the people and the accomplishments at this school are incredible.

It's really kind of neat with Coach (Tom) Holliday's son, Josh, here now in baseball; it's the next generation. You just don't see things like that at other schools. I have a relationship with Coach Ward through today. He will work with my sons on hitting. People don't understand what he brought to the game as a hitting coach. He was way ahead of his time with that. What I'm saying is here at Oklahoma State it is a pretty neat setup. Just look at all the Olympic champions we have in wrestling.

It's nice we can add to it in football. I've always said that we've started a tradition in football here and it's running on about year eight. It takes 20 years, maybe, in football to establish tradition.

Over the last eight years, we've started to establish some tradition like they've had in wrestling, golf, baseball, and basketball. Hopefully, we can keep this going and have in football the tradition they've had in all of these other sports. It just takes time, and it is not something that you can do overnight. I think we've made some headway.

When you tie all of that together for the Gundys, I have three boys: one has graduated from high school, one is in high school, and the other is going into middle school. It is just a lasting effect and a comfortable feeling that we have here. Oklahoma State can offer a lot more to coaches and to students than many of the Power Five schools when you count the university and the community. You can read about some of those things and some of the reasons why in this book.

—Mike Gundy
Head football coach
2005–present

Acknowledgments

I want to thank my wife, Lynne, a constant partner in all projects and a wise advisor and initial editor.

I also want to thank head coach Mike Gundy for writing the foreword, as well as Kevin Klintworth, Matt "the Chief" Davis, Gavin Lang, Ryan Cameron, Wade McWhorter, and Larry Reece from Oklahoma State for their time, advice, and encouragement. To my broadcast partners, Dave Hunziker and John Holcomb, for the same. Thanks to all the coaches, athletes, and fans at Oklahoma State for making it a very special place.

Introduction

I'm going to make this as brief as possible, because I want you to get to reading and enjoy the spark of these memories and the joy of these accomplishments you may have seen in person or only heard about. Perhaps the championships or victories in the following pages were won while you were a student, someone in your family was a student, or you were just enjoying Oklahoma State as an alum or a longtime fan. A lot of schools talk about family or, the latest word, *nation*. I know there are other Cowboys out there, but Cowboy Nation really stands for something and there is a unity in supporting the Orange and Black. My good friend and the subject of a chapter in this book, Larry Reece, the stadium and arena voice of the Cowboys, has a saying: "Sometimes it's tough to be us." He uses those words not in the aftermath of defeat. At Oklahoma State, the student-athletes, coaches, and fans can take losing—not like it, but take it like competitors and learn from it and use it to improve. Larry's saying comes from some of the real tough times we've had.

Those are in the book, too. We've had horrific losses at our school, such as a plane crash that took the lives of 10 fine men involved in the Cowboys basketball program, and another crash that cost us four more cherished lives, including a beloved basketball coach and one of his brightest assistant coaches. At Oklahoma State, we mourn, we remember, and we always move on stronger. There is a camaraderie in the stands that I don't think you will find just anyplace in America. That is what this school and the community of Stillwater are—a special place imbued with the love of school, athletics, and life.

Now, as to the organization of this book: Chapter 1 is the proof that Oklahoma State is more than worthy to be a part of this fun series of books in the Triumph Books family. Those national championships are hard earned and top all but a trio of West Coast schools that offer many more sports than Oklahoma State.

The next 12 chapters form unofficial Mount Rushmores. The categories here are the most important or most relevant individuals in Oklahoma State University's athletic history. I have three representing the deep past, prior to 1970; the era of 1970 to 2000; and then the foursome that has had the most recent impact up to the present.

Edward Gallagher, Henry Iba, Bob Kurland, and Bob Fenimore represent the most historic era of (primarily) Oklahoma A&M. Eddie Sutton, Barry Sanders, Gary Ward, and Mike Holder represent the era from 1970 to 2000, although Holder is still very relevant, as his role as an administrator and the athletic director carries right through to the present. Then you have Mike Gundy, John Smith, Josh Holliday, and Rickie Fowler.

The trio of Gundy, Smith, and Holliday are all crossovers, as their playing careers came earlier. Gundy quarterbacked some of the school's best football teams ever prior to his coaching the most successful era of Cowboys football, which started during his tenure and continues today. Smith won two Olympic gold medals as a wrestler, but is now the school's all-time winningest coach. Holliday was one of the top student-athletes in school history as a player, and he woke up the echoes of OSU baseball success as a head coach, getting the program back to the College World Series in Omaha. Then there is Fowler, who is in the group because there may not be a more recognized former Oklahoma State athlete on the planet today than the very popular PGA golfer.

I also want to warn you—this book is vastly different from some of the other books in the 100 Things series. Many of the books stick to primarily one, two, or three sports. In this book, 10 sports are prominently mentioned or the subjects of chapters. There is a country music megastar, one of the richest men in the history of the United States, several UFC champions, and the home of the most famous cheese fries ever consumed by a sitting president of the United States.

That is Oklahoma State: a great athletic tradition, albeit a very diverse one.

1 National Championships

Outside of schools in California, Oklahoma State has more NCAA National Championships than any other Division I college or university. Oklahoma State at one time was the overall leader in NCAA championships, but the program cannot match the number of sports offered by schools on the West Coast and across the country. Oklahoma State's athletic budget (based on *USA Today* 2014–15 financial figures) is the second lowest of the schools ranking in the top 10 all-time in NCAA championship wins.

Oklahoma State has won 52 NCAA championships, which ranks fourth all-time as of 2017. The Cowboys have claimed all 52 of those championships; the school is still looking for its first national championship in an NCAA-accredited women's sport. Once dubbed the Princeton of the Plains, Oklahoma State has more than held up its end of the bargain when it comes to collegiate athletics, as the school has maximized its success based on how much has been spent over the years on athletics.

The Oklahoma State breakdown of championships is as follows: 34 in wrestling, 10 in golf, four in men's cross country, two in basketball, one in football, and one in baseball.

Below is an interesting chart featuring the top 10 schools with NCAA Division I championships won, the number of sports they offer, and their annual athletic expenditures based on the figures published by *USA Today* for the 2014–15 academic year.

1. UCLA   113 NCAA championships (74 men/39 women)
                 23 sports offered/$96,918,767
2. Stanford   111 NCAA championships (63 men/48 women)
                 35 sports offered/Private school—no figures available

1

3. USC   103 NCAA championships (84 men/19 women)
                  20 sports offered/Private school—no figures available
4. Oklahoma State 52 NCAA championships (52 men)
                  13 sports offered/$93,144,396
5. Penn State   48 NCAA championships (24 men/11 women/13 coed)
                  29 sports offered/$122,271,407
6. Texas   44 NCAA championships (21 men/23 women)
                  18 sports offered/$173,248,133
7. Arkansas   44 NCAA championships (42 men/2 women)
                  17 sports offered/$114,172,847
8. L.S.U.   43 NCAA championships (18 men/25 women)
                  16 sports offered/$121,947,775
9. North Carolina 42 NCAA championships (12 men/30 women)
                  26 sports offered/$89,080,843
10. Michigan   36 NCAA championships (34 men/2 women)
                  27 sports offered/$151,144,964

2 Edward C. Gallagher

Former Oklahoma State basketball coach Eddie Sutton—who, by the way, was a pretty good basketball player before he moved into coaching the sport—once said that a good coach could coach any sport. The philosophy of coaching can be the same for any sport; the subject and technique are what differ.

One of the greatest coaches in the history of college athletics and of wrestling didn't actually wrestle. Edward C. Gallagher was never involved in amateur wrestling in his athletic career, yet, when he was done after 23 years as Oklahoma A&M's wrestling coach, Gallagher had a record of 138 wins, just five losses, and four ties.

Gallagher's teams won 11 NCAA team championships. He coached 32 individual national champions, and the Aggies also won six AAU team championships.

How does a man who never wrestled competitively coach that much success?

A native of Perth, Kansas, Gallagher's parents had their family in Oklahoma, which allowed Gallagher to attend Oklahoma A&M College, a land-grant university. He was an outstanding athlete, a track star who once was said to have run a 100-yard dash in 9.8 seconds in a Southwest Conference meet. Gallagher had the longest run from scrimmage in school history—99 yards in 1908 against Kansas State. He was the captain of the track and football teams at Oklahoma A&M and the senior class president. Gallagher was awarded a degree in engineering, which would later prove to be very important.

He was so impressive that he stayed on after graduation as the school's track coach for four years. Gallagher married and started a family, having six children: three boys and three girls. Then Baker College came calling as Gallagher coached football, basketball, baseball, and track. After two years at Baker, Oklahoma A&M brought Gallagher back as its athletic director. His return is considered the launching point for the school into big-time college athletics.

At the time, Oklahoma A&M had no wrestling program. The first matches were more like exhibitions, and Gallagher admitted he had no idea how to coach the sport. The school's early champions won on their pure physical ability. The coach called on his engineering training and his coaching gene to put together a series of successful techniques and moves. Gallagher became enthralled with the sport and went on to write a book, *Amateur Wrestling*, which became somewhat of a textbook on the sport. His second book, titled simply *Wrestling*, documented more than 400 moves and holds that he knew and developed. Gallagher expected his wrestlers to know at least 200 of these. His coaching blended training on toughness and competition with technique and leverage, as well as psychology. Gallagher coached on positives and positive thinking.

His saying, which is mounted over the training room in the building that bears his name, Gallagher-Iba Arena, says it all:

IF YOU DO NOT HAVE TO SACRIFICE, THEN YOU WILL NOT CARE WHETHER YOU WIN OR NOT.

Gallagher may never have wrestled himself, but he trained so many great champions not only collegiately, but also in the Olympic Games. He trained 17 Olympians, including gold medal winners Jack VanBebber and Robert Pearce in 1932. In 1936 Gallagher was named the honorary coach of the USA team and in those Berlin Olympics Frank Lewis took the gold, while Ross Flood won silver.

Gallagher had developed Parkinson's disease and it was affecting his health. He resigned as the athletic director at Oklahoma A&M in 1938, but stayed on as the wrestling coach. In 1939, *Life* magazine devoted three pages to a story on him and called him the "Gibraltar of Grappling." Gallagher died in the summer of 1940, and the funeral was held in Gallagher Hall, the new fieldhouse finished in 1938 that would become Gallagher-Iba Arena.

The *New York Times* eulogized him as "the Dean of Collegiate Wrestling."

3 Henry Iba, the "Iron Duke"

If you truly want to know how important an individual is to a community, you should take roll at his funeral or memorial service. For Henry Iba, that came in January of 1993. It was miserable Oklahoma weather with sleet and ice on the roads and snow coming, but attending the service held in Gallagher-Iba Arena were all of the Oklahoma dignitaries, including players Iba had coached like Bob Kurland, Bob Mattick, Eddie Sutton, and so many more. From the coaching community there was Mike Krzyzewski of Duke, who came into Stillwater on a Lear jet that had to be towed after it slid off the runway; Don Haskins of UTEP, who skipped a trip and a game in Hawaii with his team; Norm Stewart, whose plane couldn't land in Stillwater but did in Tulsa, prompting the

Oklahoma State legend Henry Iba is one of the most influential coaches in the history of college athletics.

Missouri coach to rent a car and drive into Stillwater; Gene Keady of Purdue; Lon Kruger, then of Florida; Nolan Richardson of Arkansas; future Kansas head coach (and then-Cowboys assistant coach) Bill Self; and many more.

It was a who's who of basketball. Bob Knight, who had Iba sit on the bench as an honorary coach for Team USA in the 1984 Olympic Games in Los Angeles, couldn't get there and was as frustrated as he has ever been. Now that's frustrated.

There were media dignitaries in attendance, too, as well as leaders from the world of politics.

Henry Iba is one of the most influential coaches in the history of college athletics. He touched college basketball as firmly as Phog Allen, Adolph Rupp, and John Wooden. Next to James Naismith, who invented the sport, there was no other person out there with as profound and positive effect on the game of basketball as Iba. That was how he was known. Until several years after he was gone, I'd always heard him referred to as "Mr. Iba." To this day, most people in the Oklahoma State and the Stillwater community still refer to him as Mr. Iba.

It was the greatest sportswriter the state of Oklahoma has ever known, Bill Connors, who was chosen to speak at the service, and he eulogized Iba exceptionally well. His words are reprinted every year in the Oklahoma State University Basketball Media Guide:

> This is personal. Mr. Henry Iba was the most principled, modest, loyal, gracious, dignified, and considerate man I ever met. It was no contest. Knowing him was the greatest privilege I have experienced in 40 years of reporting on the people who shaped the athletic landscape.
>
> From Tobacco Road to Bloomington, Indiana, from Los Angeles to the U.S. Senate, the old lions and the new lions of basketball said much the same thing while he was alive.

Whether Iba coached them at Oklahoma State or in the Olympics or counseled them at clinics or at his home in retirement, they knew him as John Wooden described him: "Basketball's greatest friend and finest gentleman."

I knew there would come a day when God would say we had enjoyed Mr. Iba long enough and He needed him in another place to install a delay game or improve a defense.

If Iba could hear the tributes, he would surely say, "Cut that foolishness out." Those are the words he used countless times to erring players and to those who praised him in public.

Iba never talked about his accomplishments. Never. He did not talk much about the past or how he became known as the high priest of defense. Even in his 23 years of retirement, he was preoccupied with today and his protégés' next games, not his national championships, not the past. He did not seek the spotlight but he could not avoid it; he was too successful, too influential, too innovative, too involved in landmark events.

Iba was no saint. He was a salty man's man who liked Scotch in moderation and had a wonderful wit that cracked up audiences of cronies on fishing trips or associates on plane flights or players during pregame talks.

He was a tough soul. They did not call him the Iron Duke for nothing. He was the quintessential taskmaster whose passion for discipline had no limit. He could deliver the most searing of tongue lashings during four-hour practices and burn the ears of a referee with whom he disagreed. His booming voice added to his intimidating presence.

But, when a game ended, his game face was put away and the ferocious rival was once again a friend who took legendary opponents like Ray Meyer and Clair Bee to dinner. He was so fair, so supportive, as quick to praise players as he was to reprimand them that he was held with ultimate respect and affection.

There was never a hint of scandal about him in his professional or personal life. Except in the most casual of situations, he always wore a coat and tie in public. His conduct in mixed company was exemplary. His unflagging spirit and concern for others made you feel better for merely being in his presence.

He always ended every telephone conversation by saying, "Thank you for calling." He never seemed to grasp that it was the callers who should have offered thanks.

But Iba did one awful thing: he succeeded in making us think for the longest time that he was not special. Hence, we expect other coaching giants to walk on the same unsullied pedestal and were disappointed when they did not. That was unfair to them. There was only one Henry Payne Iba.

How did he rank as a coach? Coaching giants who competed against him and observed him were as captivated as those with subjective roots to Iba's coaching tree. A favorite assessment of Iba came in a 1991 letter from Duke's Mike Krzyzewski, who said:

"Coach Iba, in my estimation, is the greatest coach in the history of the game of basketball. He epitomizes what a coach must do on and off the court, and the manner in which it should be done. Everything he did and continues to do, from the way he handled people to the way he dressed, was an example of how things should be done on this level."

In a guest column in 1987, Bob Knight said he considered Iba to be among the "four or five coaches who made great innovative contributions to basketball. Mr. Iba did it before there was anyone for him to copy. He was the first to run the motion offense. He was the first to incorporate the 'help' principles of zone defenses with man-to-man defense. He opened up the game for the big man."

U.S. Sen. Bill Bradley of New Jersey, who was a member of the 1964 U.S. Olympic team that Iba coached to a gold medal in Tokyo, said in a letter to the coach:

"...More inspiring and more important to me than the basketball instruction were the hints on how to live a more worthwhile life, which were sprinkled throughout practice sessions, team meetings, and casual remarks. Now I understand why men are always proud when they say, 'Mr. Iba was my coach.' So am I."

What endeared Iba to his players was the countless favors he did on their behalf after their eligibility was completed. Whether it was Bob Kurland, superstar of his 1945 and '46 national champions, or the lowliest reserve on one of the losing teams that marred his final years, Iba treated them like sons.

Iba transcended the coaching box. When OSU honored him with a distinguished service award, Mickey Holmes, executive director of the Sugar Bowl, who formerly worked in the Big Eight Conference office, captured the essence of the day when he said, "An institution is honoring its institution."

What made Iba so popular with coaches was his devotion to basketball. In retirement, he worked to improve the game, to encourage coaches with integrity to remain in the profession and to help any coach, regardless of philosophy, who sought a better job or advice or encouragement. More than any of the legends of his generation, Iba was perceived as basketball's godfather; the giant to whom giants bowed.

The surest way to increase turnout at a coaching function was to honor Iba. Sponsors of the All-College Tournament in Oklahoma City never attracted more than participating coaches for their promotional golf tournaments until they staged it around a dinner for Iba in 1988. Suddenly, Dean Smith and Bobby Knight flew in.

At a Final Four press conference in 1967, UCLA's Wooden explained why he delayed endorsing a shot clock, even though he favored such legislation. He waited until studies convinced him, Wooden said, "that a shot clock would not hurt Mr. Iba. I would never be a part of anything that hurt Mr. Iba. He is basketball's greatest friend and finest gentleman."

Until failing health grounded him, VIP coaches and obscure coaches flocked to Stillwater to talk shop and brought him to their campuses to critique their teams. They did not go merely to pay their respects.

"I love being around him because he is such a great guy and so much fun," Knight said. "But the main reason I talk basketball with him is that I get so much out of it."

A coach did not need to be a protege or have VIP credentials to enjoy Iba's counsel. Toledo's Larry Gipson had never met Iba when he left high school coaching in Ohio to become an assistant at Tulsa in the mid-80s. Gipson asked and received Iba's permission to come to Stillwater and talk basketball. "He treated me like I was Bobby Knight," Gipson said.

The only thing Iba would not do for coaches who sought his help was—and he told them up front—help them in any competition they might have with OSU.

Oh, how he loved the school whose payroll he graced for 36 years. "Our school," and "our place," he would say of OSU. Anyone who played at OSU, no matter what sport, was in favor with Mr. Iba.

The late Sparky Stallcup, who played for Iba at Maryville (Missouri) and became coach at Missouri, was scolded by Iba when he asked why Iba tried to secure a job for a former player who had lost a job because of unbecoming conduct.

"Why, he went to school at our place," Iba said.

The affection Iba felt for OSU and his class were illustrated when he was asked to speak to a group of freshmen during orientation week in 1949. Iba was at the peak of his career. OSU had been '49 runner-up for the national championship that it won in '45 and '46.

Iba did not mention himself or his team or athletics. Instead, he told the freshmen how fortunate they were to attend college, that they should make the most of their opportunities and to remember their parents by writing them at least once a week.

Even an 18-year-old freshman recognized this was more than a Hall of Fame coach.

Iba was so much more than numbers, but the numbers were impressive. In 41 years as a college basketball coach, 36 of those seasons at Oklahoma A&M and then Oklahoma State, Henry Iba won 767 games and lost 338. His teams won two national championships and were runners-up one other time, and went to four NCAA Final Fours, three NIT Final Fours, eight NCAA Tournaments, and four NIT Tournaments.

Iba coached 12 All-Americans, and five players he coached went on to become Division I head coaches. Fourteen current coaches are second generation on the Iba coaching tree; another six, including Bill Self at Kansas, are third generation. Two more are fourth generation, and two are fifth generation.

Iba was first selected to coach the United States Olympic basketball team in 1964 in Tokyo, and the Americans won the gold medal. He was the first coach to be chosen to coach the team a second time, and in 1968 and despite many college players boycotting the games in protest to the Vietnam War and civil rights the USA won in Mexico City. Two years after he had retired from Oklahoma State, Iba was again chosen to coach the USA team in the 1972 games in Munich. Those games were marred by the terrorist attack on the Israeli team in the Olympic Village. On the court the Americans saw their chance to win taken away by controversial officiating. Russia took advantage of the second controversial call to hit a shot after time had run out to be declared the gold medal winners. The American team chose not to accept their silver medals. It was his greatest coaching disappointment. Later, when serving as an honorary coach and consultant for the 1984 team under Bob Knight, Iba was carried off the floor after winning the gold medal in Los Angeles.

Iba is in the Naismith Basketball Hall of Fame in Springfield, Massachusetts, and the Helms Foundation Hall of Fame, and he is one of three American coaches in the FIBA Hall of Fame. There are two awards named for the great Oklahoma State coach and one, the Iba Award, goes to the top coach in the country as voted on by the United States Basketball Writers Association. The other is the Henry P. Iba Citizen Athlete Awards presented annually in Tulsa by the Tulsa Rotary Club. These awards go to a male and female athlete who have displayed great humanitarian efforts.

Of all the great things said about Mr. Iba, one of the most simple is in my opinion the very best.

"Of all the shadows cast over the game of basketball, his was biggest." —Bob Knight

4 Bob Fenimore, the "Blond Bomber"

When the American Football Coaches Association (AFCA) informed Oklahoma State in October 2016 that it had actually won a football national championship—as the AFCA Blue Ribbon Panel convened to analyze and name schools to be awarded national championships by the coaches from the start of the association in 1922 to 1949, all the years prior to the start of the coaches' poll—the image that had to come to mind for many Cowboys fans familiar with that era was a photo of standout players Bob Fenimore of Woodward and Neill Armstrong of Tishomingo. The two All-American Oklahoma players and best friends are pictured shaking hands before a game, Fenimore in his now-retired No. 55 jersey and Armstrong in his No. 56. They made a tradition of shaking hands before every game.

It is a memory frozen in the minds of many Oklahoma State fans and college football historians. The school was known as Oklahoma A&M at the time, and Fenimore would go on to own some 60 school records and many conference and national marks.

Armstrong will tell you that Fenimore was usually first in everything; he even beat his good friend to the gates of heaven.

Playing tailback in the Aggies' single-wing offense, Fenimore accumulated 1,758 yards to lead the nation in total offense in 1944 while also finishing in the top 10 in rushing (899 yards), passing (997 yards), and scoring (77 points). Nicknamed the "Blond Bomber," he finished ninth in the Heisman voting that season.

During the Aggies' undefeated season in 1945, Fenimore was the nation's leader with 1,119 yards rushing and 1,641 yards of total offense. He ran for two touchdowns and threw for another in the Sugar Bowl, which pitted Fenimore, third in the Heisman voting, against Herman Wedemeyer of Saint Mary's, who finished fourth for the Heisman. Army's vaunted duo of Doc Blanchard and Glenn Davis finished first and second that year.

"He's just a great part of Oklahoma State, just the best of all time," Armstrong said of Fenimore after his good friend had passed away. "I was talking with one of my sons yesterday and telling him about Bob passing away and he said, 'Well, he didn't have a big ego.' Everybody was always happy to see Bob get the accolades that he got because he didn't wear it on his sleeve and everybody had a lot of respect for him."

Fenimore was always happy to talk, but much preferred discussing others, especially Oklahoma State greats such as Terry Miller, Thurmas Thomas, and the school's lone Heisman Trophy winner, Barry Sanders. On a rare occasion, he admitted one of his fondest memories was the 46–40 win in 1944 over Tulsa in T-town.

"It was sophomore year," Fenimore said in a 1988 interview with the *Tulsa World*. "That game gave us national recognition. Tulsa was a powerhouse and going to bowl games then. We played them in Tulsa and it was a wild game.

"We scored on the first play, 70-some yards off tackle, and were never behind," Fenimore continued. "The game was offense and I intercepted a pass at the 5-yard line to stop Tulsa's last drive. From that point on, newspapers and writers started looking at Oklahoma A&M. We ended up going to the Cotton Bowl that year and beat TCU."

Fenimore led his team in pass interceptions each of the four years he played. He also led OSU in punt and kickoff returns. He was all over the field.

"He was," agreed Armstrong. "He returned punts, too, and punted. I think some of those records may not ever be broken. Of course, his running records have been broken, but Bob did everything. He threw the ball and he ran, and he was a good forward passer. He would say he wasn't a good passer, but he was. I caught

All-American Oklahoma football players and best friends Neill Armstrong and Bob Fenimore shake hands before a game. (Photo courtesy of OSU Athletics.)

a few of them and I always thought they were good. At times, he made me look good. He always told me I made him look good because I would go up high and catch them one-handed. It was always there or I wouldn't have been able to catch them at all."

Many say Fenimore and others of his era got away with facing and being compared with lesser competition, because those were the war years and many of America's best athletes were called to duty in the Army, Navy, and Marines. Players began playing both ways and, because squads were smaller, did more, like Fenimore. But when those servicemen returned, Fenimore was still regarded as one of the best. In an era where an average running back weighed in at around 175 pounds, the Blond Bomber was 190 pounds and ran on the football field with track speed.

Those Aggies teams dominated most opponents, and especially Oklahoma, as the Fenimore–led team in 1944 beat OU 28–6 and then the national championship team of 1945 handed OU its worst loss in school history, shutting the Sooners out 47–0.

The Chicago Bears selected Fenimore in the first round of the draft in 1947. He played for legendary NFL co-founder and then Bears head coach George Halas.

"I was never successful at all," said Fenimore, who had been injured in 1946. "I played left halfback in the T formation, and I wasn't used to wearing a brace. I didn't have a chance to get accustomed to it. I came from the single wing in college to the T formation. It was quite a change, and I was never one to have a quick start. I didn't hit the holes quick enough.

"I had a three-year contract, and I could have continued to play," he added. "But it wasn't fun and I decided to call it quits. It was a disappointing way to finish. Sure, I wonder how things might have turned out if I hadn't been hurt, but that's life."

Fenimore and his bride, childhood sweetheart Veta Jo, settled in Stillwater, where Fenimore worked for Massachusetts Mutual Life Insurance Co. and continued to do so until retirement. He was a great supporter of his alma mater, and even though he was extremely humble he would take pictures and share stories when fans would ask him about those great teams and his many talented teammates. It always seemed in his stories that Fenimore would take a backseat role to some great catch or block by a teammate.

Movies in those days would describe leading men as the strong, silent type. That is a great way to describe Bob Fenimore. Hall of Famer is also appropriate, as he has been named to four: the Cotton Bowl Hall of Fame, Oklahoma Sports Hall of Fame, OSU Hall of Fame, and College Football Hall of Fame.

5 Bob Kurland

Bob Kurland was credited with being one of basketball's first seven-footers, but truth be known, the Aggies' giant star of the 1945 and 1946 NCAA Tournament Championship team was actually 6'10½". It didn't matter, as Kurland towered over his competition and was athletic enough in an age when tall players were considered oddities, goons, kind of a basketball freak show. Instead, Kurland had skill and, in Henry Iba, a coach who knew how to blend his talents into his teammates' and bring a more-than-formidable game against competition. Kurland caused the rules of basketball to change, especially those on defense, as he was able to block shots with virtual ease. Many of those blocks under today's rules would be considered goaltending. He made it into a skill, and most basketball experts believe he had more to do with the rules that created defensive goaltending than any other player of that time.

Kurland was a dominant rebounder and he also had some touch with his shot—maybe not quite like Bryant Reeves, the Cowboys' later seven-footer, but Kurland could score.

Born in St. Louis, Missouri, Kurland graduated from high school in Jennings, Missouri, and was recruited to Oklahoma A&M by Iba. He was a three-time All-American because in those days, even during the war years, freshmen were ineligible in basketball. In his first season of varsity basketball, Kurland earned first- and second-team All-American honors, but from that point on it was nothing but first-team honors.

In the 1944–45 season Kurland led the team in scoring and was voted the Outstanding Player of the NCAA Tournament as Oklahoma A&M defeated Utah 62–37 in the semifinal of the Western Regionals in Kansas City. It finished off the Western

Regional with a 68–41 win over Arkansas. It was the fourth game Oklahoma A&M played that season against Arkansas, winning three of the four.

The NCAA Championship Game was in New York's Madison Square Garden against NYU. Not only were the Violets at home—or nearly home—but they were favored over the Aggies. Kurland scored 22 points and his teammate Cecil Hankins added 15 as the Aggies won 49–45 in a more defense-oriented game, which played right into Kurland's big hands.

Right after the NCAA win, the Aggies stayed in New York to face DePaul and their big man George Mikan (actually 6'10") in a showdown of "seven-footers" and tournament champions, as DePaul had won the NIT. The game benefitted the Red Cross, and A&M and Kurland won 52–44 as Hankins was the leading scorer with 20 points. Kurland averaged 17.1 points for the season and outplayed Mikan in the final contest of the year.

The 1945–46 season was a testament to Kurland's dominance as he finished the season with 643 points to lead the nation, averaging 19.5 points a game. Kurland wasn't always the Aggies' leading scorer, focusing in many games on rebounding and defense. But on February 22 of that season he was encouraged by Iba to score, and he finished with a career-high 58 points. Kurland did it against the Saint Louis Billikins' Ed MacCauley, who would go on to a Hall of Fame career with the Boston Celtics and St. Louis Hawks. MacCauley said he kept a copy of a story on that game.

"Every time I thought I needed to be humble," he told the Tulsa *World*, "I would look at that box score and remember that I was the guy who held Bob Kurland to 58 points."

The team went back to Kansas City for the Western Regionals and swept Baylor 44–29 and then California with a 52–35 verdict. It was back to Madison Square Garden, where Kurland was impressive as usual, scoring a game-high 23 points in the Aggies' 43–40 win over the Tar Heels. For the second straight season, Kurland was named the Most Outstanding Player in the NCAA Tournament.

Not only did Kurland lead the nation in scoring, but he also helped A&M lead the nation in team defense as they held their opponents to an average of 32.1 points per game.

Back then there was no NBA, as that would later be created with the merging of the National Basketball League and the Basketball Association of America. Instead, Kurland focused on playing for his country in the Olympics and other international competition. He played on the U.S. Olympic teams in the 1948 games in London and then in the 1952 Olympics in Helsinki, Finland. In 1952 he was the second leading scorer behind Alex Groza as the USA defeated France for the gold medal 65–21. It was gold again for Kurland and the USA in Helsinki as they defeated the Soviet Union 36–25.

Kurland continued to play the sport he loved with the AAU Phillips 66ers. Kurland obtained some additional education at Stanford University and became an executive with the Phillips Petrolium Company, where he was very successful. He retired from the company in the mid-'80s to Sanibel Island in Florida. Always humble, Kurland often returned to his alma mater but was never comfortable being celebrated for his career.

Kurland would often tell the story of how Iba recruited him, without a lot of fanfare.

"He said: 'I've never seen anyone like you before,'" Kurland recalled Iba saying in a story in the *Tulsa World*. "'I don't know if you can play basketball or not, but if you come to school here, enroll, and stay eligible, I'll see that you get a college education.'"

Turned out that he really could play basketball, so well that he changed the game and is remembered as one of the 25 greatest basketball players of all time. Kurland passed away at the age of 88, still living in Sanibel Island.

6 Eddie Sutton

It was a sunny day outside Gallagher-Iba Arena, but it was brighter inside the arena in the varsity room on the second floor of the building, as a man who wasn't often known for an ear-to-ear smile was grinning as broadly as his facial features would let him. The "Iron Duke" of Oklahoma A&M and Oklahoma State basketball, known to all but his closest contemporaries as "Mr. Iba," wore a smile that could light all of Oklahoma as his protégé, Eddie Sutton, took over as head coach of his school. You could tell by Mr. Iba's face that all was finally right again in his world.

Eddie Sutton had come from tiny Bucklin, Kansas, to Stillwater to play for Henry Iba, turning down the likes of Kansas head coach Phog Allen in the process. Sutton was that "coach on the floor" type of player. He loved the intricacies of Iba's offense and the toughness of the old man's defense. Iba saw some of himself in Sutton. The wiry Kansan wasn't a great player, as he averaged 8.3 points per game in his career, but he was dependable, with a career free-throw percentage of over 80 percent. In the famous 56–54 win in Gallagher Hall over No. 2–ranked Kansas and All-American seven-footer Wilt Chamberlain—a game where Mr. Iba was carried off the floor—Sutton scored 18 points.

Sutton graduated with a bachelor's degree and then served as a graduate assistant for Iba and earned his master's from Oklahoma State. Then Sutton went off on his Hall of Fame coaching career, which would eventually lead him back to that sunny day in Stillwater.

He started out in high school at Tulsa Central, where he coached not only basketball but also the golf team. In his seven years at Central the basketball team went 118–52 and the golf team was one of the best in the state.

'I've always believed that if a man can coach, he can coach," Sutton said. "Give me a book that shows me what my athletes need to do, and I'll absorb the book and coach them up. It helps if you've played the sport, but it's not absolute. If you can teach and communicate, that is what coaching is. You have to relate to that athlete and get them to understand the technique and the intensity."

Sutton's meteoric rise started in college at Southern Idaho Junior College, where in three years his teams won 84 games to just 14 losses. From there it was on to Creighton, where the Blue Jays had gone three years without a winning record. Sutton wasted no time with five consecutive winning seasons, leading Creighton in 1974 to a 23–7 record and a berth in the NCAA Tournament. This was coming out of the Missouri Valley when only 32 teams advanced to the NCAA.

Arkansas and its legendary head football coach and athletic director, Frank Broyles, needed a fix for Razorback basketball. Sutton came into Arkansas and often joked that he was always sweeping up over at Barnhill Fieldhouse, where there were still some dirt floors in areas of the building. Broyles knew a coach when he saw one, and when Sutton took over in the Ozarks in the 1974–75 season he got a program that had not been to the NCAA Tournament since 1958. After back-to-back seasons of 17–9 and 19–9, Arkansas went on a nine-season run in the NCAA Tournament and at least 21 wins each season. The Razorbacks dominated the old Southwest Conference and Sutton was a two-time National Coach of the Year (USBWA in 1976–77) (AP, UPI in 1977–78).

In 1977–78, Sutton's team finished with a 32–4 record after advancing to the Final Four and losing to North Carolina State. Sutton stayed at Arkansas through the 1985 season and finished with a record at Arkansas of 260–75. Sutton left Arkansas for the bluegrass of Lexington and the University of Kentucky.

"It's the only job I would leave Arkansas for," Sutton said of going to Kentucky. There was certainly some truth to that statement, as his alma mater at Oklahoma State had tried to lure Sutton back to Stillwater several times. Little did anyone know that the move to Kentucky would eventually lead back to Stillwater. Sutton took off at UK like he would be there the rest of his coaching career. He led the Wildcats to a 32–4 record in 1985–86 and a top-three ranking in the polls, and he got the Wildcats into the NCAA Elite Eight. The Associated Press and the NABC named him National Coach of the Year.

Just two years after that successful first run, the Kentucky term for Sutton started to unravel when one of his assistants, Dwane Casey, was alleged to have sent $1,000 to big-time recruit Chris Mills of Los Angeles. The money was discovered spilling out of an Emery Air Freight envelope. The NCAA investigated that and other reported violations against the Kentucky program and in May of 1988 placed UK on three years' probation for recruiting and academic rules violations with a two-year ban on postseason play. The NCAA report showed no violations committed by Eddie Sutton. Just 10 months later, after a 13–19 season—the first losing season in 61 years at Kentucky—Sutton resigned.

After a year out of coaching and broadcasting college basketball, which he was very good at doing, Sutton did come home to Oklahoma State. A very long period of mediocrity interrupted only by one Big Eight Tournament championship and one trip to the NCAA Tournament under Paul Hanson came to an end. Is it any surprise that in his first season as Cowboys head coach, with his mentor, Mr. Iba, watching in his regular seat up in the corner of Gallagher Hall, Sutton led Oklahoma State to a 24–8 record, a Big Eight title, and a Sweet 16 NCAA Tournament appearance?

Sutton never led Oklahoma State to an NCAA National Championship like Iba did, but in his era it was so much more difficult to do so. Sutton did lead the Cowboys to two Final Fours with seven-footer Bryant Reeves, sweet-shooting guard Randy Rutherford, garbageman Chianti Roberts, and "toothless in Seattle" reserve Scott Pierce. In Seattle, Reeves shattered a backboard in the Kingdome and Pierce had a tooth knocked out earlier in the NCAA Tournament, sparking the "toothless" identity.

The late Bill Teegins had the call for the winning moments in East Rutherford, New Jersey, where the Cowboys triumphed over UMass after beating Wake Forest and future NBA Hall of Fame big man Tim Duncan. UCLA beat the Cowboys 74–61 in the national semifinal.

Sutton was known as the first coach to take four different schools to the NCAA Tournament in Creighton, Arkansas, Kentucky, and Oklahoma State. Sutton also took two different teams to the Final Four—Oklahoma State and Arkansas. He finished at Oklahoma State with 368 wins and 151 losses. He would end with 806 wins overall, adding a few more coaching stops, including the University of San Francisco.

Sutton has always been a prolific letter writer. Long before Kansas State football coach Bill Snyder became famous for writing opposing players to congratulate them on a performance or comfort them in tragedy or strife, Sutton would read the newspaper or watch the news on television, see somebody in need, and write him or her a letter. He'd even send that person something to help and encourage them. The legendary head coach often talked about how that "valentine" was a key ingredient to some of his best players, such as Byron Houston, Bryant Reeves, Randy Rutherford, Desmond Mason, Doug Gottlieb, Maurice Baker, Tony Allen, John Lucas, and Joey Graham. A player had to have physical gifts but also a big heart inside.

Sutton needed a big heart repair on the night of January 27, 2001, as he had to deal with the worst moment of his coaching career. To make better use of travel time, Oklahoma State, like many schools at the time, would take a fleet of private aircraft. The Cowboys were traveling back from a game at Colorado on two small jets and a King Air propeller engine plane. The King Air went down on the Colorado tundra, and all 10 men on board lost their lives.

It was an event that tore apart Sutton's heart down to his core. He called every one of the men's next of kin. He held up like a boulder, but there is no doubt that it took a lot out of him. Sutton never forgot a player and he never forgot any of the family members of the group that would come to be known as "Remember the Ten."

Sutton took the Cowboys to another NCAA Final Four in 2003–04. The combination of big-time defender Tony Allen at guard, point guard John Lucas, brothers Joey and Stephen Graham, Ivan McFarland, and Terrence Crawford, along with a supporting cast, led the Pokes to San Antonio with a win over a vaunted St. Joseph's team in East Rutherford, New Jersey. It was not lost on new play-by-play voice Dave Hunziker that he was in the same arena and was calling the same team in the regional final that the late Bill Teegins had called to an NCAA Final Four. Hunziker paid homage to his predecessor after calling one of his greatest moments as a broadcaster. The Cowboys lost to Georgia Tech 67–65 in an exciting national semifinal.

Sutton still lives in Tulsa and, even at age 80 and with his physical health declining, he still makes it over to Oklahoma State for games. He always receives a standing ovation when he enters the arena or is recognized by public address announcer Larry Reece. Unfortunately, on January 28, 2017, the Cowboys hosted Arkansas in the Big 12/SEC Challenge and Sutton, who had planned to make it, didn't feel up to the trip that day from Tulsa. However, during the second half in a timeout, Sutton's career was honored. His tremendous influence on both schools playing in the game—having reached Final Fours with both programs—was described, and fans of both teams, with a large number of red-clad Razorbacks in the building, all rose and gave Sutton an ovation.

If you make your way into either Gallagher-Iba Arena or the auxiliary gym during a Cowboys practice and you shut your eyes, you can hear the echoes of coaching through the years.

7 Barry Sanders and the Heisman

There are two things a school that wants to claim football prowess at the Division I level needs to have to be credible. The first necessity is a national championship and, although it was retroactively rewarded, thanks to the American Football Coaches Association the Cowboys have that. The other requirement is a Heisman Trophy, and thanks to a little-known and lightly recruited-out-of-high-school running back from Wichita, Kansas, Oklahoma State had that in 1988.

There are 31 schools in history that have both a national championship and a Heisman in their trophy case, and 28 of them are still competing in Division I FBS. There are 11 schools that won a championship and had a player win the Heisman in the same season. That did not happen in Stillwater, but the Cowboys weren't far from it.

Barry Sanders was playing cornerback and wingback at Wichita North High School when in his senior season his coach, Dale Burkholder, had an idea: maybe he should try Sanders, who had dominated in Pop Warner as a running back, in the backfield.

"The fourth game [of the season] I started at running back, and it was one of the greatest football years of my life, not just because of earning a scholarship to Oklahoma State, but from being around Coach Burkholder, who absolutely loved being around high school kids, coaching football, and just being there on the field, getting ready for Friday nights," Sanders said at his Pro Football Hall of

Fame induction. "He is the type of guy that I would hope my son could grow up to play for, someone like him."

Sanders did earn that scholarship as he rushed for 1,417 yards and averaged 10.2 yards per carry over those last seven games in earning All-State honors. Still, there weren't a lot of colleges knocking down the door. Tulsa, Iowa State, and Oklahoma State were the primary trio, and recruiting Sanders for OSU was longtime defensive line coach and assistant head coach George Walstead. Walstead was a crafty recruiter; so was the running backs coach at the time, Bill Shimek. They knew there were only seven games of tape of Sanders at running back and Shimek, according to then–head coach Pat Jones, managed to keep most of them in his possession between the end of the Wichita North season and signing day. To this day, former Oklahoma head coach Barry Switzer claims his staff never got to see any of it despite recruiting the Wichita area.

When Sanders arrived, he was not really ballyhooed that much. On media day his freshman year, the picture in which he was featured was one with future television and movie actor, and now deceased, Jaime Cardriche. The two were both in the freshman class. Sanders was 5'8", 180 pounds, and Cardriche was 7'0", 360 pounds, making for quite a contrast. Cardriche would later switch to basketball and then make his way back to California and get into acting. Sanders made his way to the weight room, increased his explosiveness with a powerful core and thighs, and became a runner few defenders could get their hands on or get to the ground.

Sanders was not a practice player. It wasn't that he loafed or didn't do what he was supposed to, he just didn't go all gung-ho in practice. His immediate predecessor at the position, Thurman Thomas, was a practice monster. Sanders was seemingly happy playing pickup basketball at the Colvin Center on campus and sleeping as much as he could get away with. Sanders still proved his abilities, as he was an All-American in his sophomore season returning kickoffs and punts and showing his skills backing up Thomas.

In one game against Nebraska, the Huskers defense held Thomas to next to nothing for three quarters as it built up a decisive advantage, winning the game 35–0. But Sanders came in during the fourth quarter and threatened the shutout, rushing for 60 yards in the final frame. It prompted Switzer to give this warning to his defense before the Bedlam game that season in Norman.

"Whatever you do, don't hurt Thurman. You don't want to play against this freshman [actually sophomore] back they have

Barry Sanders is one of Oklahoma State's most accomplished athletes. While at Oklahoma State, he received the Walter Camp award, given annually to the collegiate American football player of the year, the Maxwell Award for the college player of the year, and the 1988 Heisman Trophy. In the NFL, he was named the Offensive Rookie of the Year in 1989 and the co–NFL Most Valuable Player in 1997.

named Barry Sanders," Switzer told his defense before the 1987 Bedlam game, which Oklahoma won 29–10.

The next season, Sanders exploded. He opened the season taking back the opening kickoff of the year against Miami (Ohio) for a 100-yard touchdown. He then proceeded to rush for 178 yards against the Redskins, 157 versus Texas A&M, 304 versus Tulsa, 174 on the road with *Sports Illustrated* doing a feature story at Colorado, 189 yards in a loss to Nebraska, 154 against Missouri, 320 yards playing just over a half at Kansas State, 215 yards in a close loss in Bedlam, 312 yards against Kansas, and 293 at Iowa State.

That sewed up the Heisman, because Sanders and his offensive line, nicknamed the War Pigs; his fullback, Garrett Limbrick; and his head coach, Pat Jones, were in the CBS News Bureau in Tokyo, Japan, the morning that Oklahoma State would go on to beat Texas Tech 45–42. Sanders would run for 332 yards. He then finished with 222 yards and five touchdowns in the Holiday Bowl win over Wyoming.

Sanders' season was one that we will almost certainly never see the likes of again. He established 34 NCAA records with 2,850 yards rushing, 42 touchdowns, 7.6 yards per carry, 237.5 yards per game, four games with 300 yards or more rushing, seven games of 200 yards or more rushing, and a complete season of 100 yards or more rushing in every game.

"It still takes my breath away," Pat Jones said to *Oklahoman* reporter John Helsley on the 25th anniversary of Sanders' record-breaking Heisman season. "He'd score, turn around and hand the ball to the official, and go over to our groups who were huddled up for the extra point; patting every one of the offensive linemen and the fullback on the head. Then he'd trot to the bench. Every time.

"Aside from the sheer numbers, he set an unbelievable mark and did it with more class and dignity than you've ever seen before," concluded Jones.

Sanders declared early for the NFL Draft after the Holiday Bowl; in fact, he was kind of the guy who started that precedent. He went on to become one of the all-time rushing leaders in the NFL despite retiring after just 10 years, all with Detroit. Sanders helped the Lions make the playoffs five times, but after advancing to the NFC Championship and losing to Washington, the Lions never made it further. Sanders never played in a Super Bowl despite rushing for 15,269 yards, catching passes for 2,921 yards, and scoring 109 touchdowns (99 rushing and 10 receiving). Sanders was a first-ballot inductee into the Pro Football Hall of Fame, as he was for the College Football Hall of Fame. He later had the joy of watching his oldest son, Barry J. Sanders, play his final season in college at Oklahoma State.

Mike Holder

How should Oklahoma State fans think of Mike Holder? There are at least three distinct roles Holder has played in helping Oklahoma State to some form of success. You could go chronologically, but let's go by maximum impact.

Mike Holder the athletic director started as the vice president for athletic programs and athletic director in 2005. He immediately took advantage of the contacts he had made while raising money for the golf program as head coach and for the building of Karsten Creek. Holder had always had the idea of building a first-class, world-class golf course to be the home of Oklahoma State golf. That dream came true when in 1994 *Golf Digest* magazine named the course that was cut into the Payne County countryside west of Stillwater the Best New Public Course in America. Holder was the visionary, fund raiser, business manager, and creator of Karsten Creek.

When trying to decide if he was going to give up the golf program and take over as the head of the department he was pushed by one of his biggest benefactors in T. Boone Pickens. Holder knew that for Oklahoma State athletics to grow and prosper and for his vision of an athletic village with state-of-the-art facilities to take shape, Pickens would need to step up to a level that even Pickens had not conceived of at that point. Pickens had already given his first big donation, and the stadium project was under way. To finish the project, Holder persuaded Pickens to go all-in with $165 million and then, in 2008, another $63 million to complete the west end zone.

The expansion included the new track and field facility, the completion of the Sherman E. Smith Training Center, and maybe the very best facility in collegiate tennis in the Malone and Amy Mitchell Tennis Center.

In 2013, Holder was recognized as a finalist for the National Athletic Director of the Year in the Sports Business Awards by *SportsBusiness Journal* and SportsBusiness Daily.

Holder has a plan, and he has a strong business acumen to execute that plan. On deck to go with the other facilities are a new baseball stadium to be built across the street from the new tennis center and a soccer stadium to replace the bleachers up on the hill where the Cowgirls play soccer.

Holder is a hands-on athletic director who sits not in the suites on game days; he and his wife, Robbie, sit in the seats they've had for a long time right behind the Oklahoma State bench. On the road, Holder and Robbie will be on the sidelines watching from the field, never using the box that all schools have reserved upstairs for the visiting athletic director and guests.

Holder has recognized coaching ability when he sees it and made some excellent hires, such as promoting Jim Littell after the

As athletic director, Mike Holder has been responsible for much of the Cowboys' recent success, especially when it comes to improving the university's athletic facilities.

death of Kurt Budke to head coach of the Cowgirls basketball team. Dave Smith has been awesome as the head of cross country and track, and the same goes for Josh Holliday as baseball coach. Most recently, Kenny Gajewski has excelled as the softball coach. Holder smartly executed a buyout on basketball coach Travis Ford.

The Holders donated $500,000 for the first fully endowed scholarship for Oklahoma State football. That program has grown by leaps and bounds under Holder as many of the scholarships in all sports across the board are now either fully or partially endowed.

For 32 years Holder was the head of the golf program at Oklahoma State. He took over from his mentor, Labron Harris, in July 1973. His accomplishments are unparalleled at the Division I level, as he coached eight NCAA team championships, 25 Big Eight or Big 12 Conference championships, six individual NCAA champions, 12 National Players of the Year, 112 All-Americans, 20 conference individual champions, and 21 academic All-Americans. He had three Ben Hogan Award winners, an award based on academic and golf excellence; Kevin Wentworth won it in 1990, Trip Kuehne in 1995, and Hunter Mahan in 2003.

Holder has also had a strong impact on the sport as the head of the NCAA golf committee on a couple of occasions.

The native of Ardmore started as a student-athlete. He was an honorable mention All-American as a sophomore, a third-team All-American as a junior, and then again as a senior. That senior season he was the Big Eight Individual Champion and was also the Oklahoma State Amateur Champion as a sophomore. He graduated from Oklahoma State with a degree in marketing and then completed work on his MBA in 1973.

Athlete; coach; administrator; there are few who can say they contributed and excelled at all three, but Mike Holder can.

9 Gary Ward and Decade of Dominance

It's interesting that the chapters for Mike Holder and Gary Ward are right next to each other, because when those two were coaching their sports at Oklahoma State under then–athletic director Myron Roderick, the former wrestling coach often had to officiate fund-raising rivalries between the two coaches. Not until women's tennis coach Chris Young came along did the Oklahoma State campus see another active and aggressive fund-raising coach.

Ward came in and, in a very short time, got a stadium built by going out and getting the funding himself. Of course, Holder was able to fully endow the scholarships in his program and then built one of the great golf courses in America right outside Stillwater. Their fundraising rivalry is the stuff of legends, according to some of the old-timers who have followed Oklahoma State athletics.

The greatest example I know of to truly illustrate what Gary Ward was like came when the Cowboys' head baseball coach hired me to help him put together a series of instructional videos called *The Hitting Machine*. The first location we used for taping was the Seretean Center at Oklahoma State University. Ward was dressed in full Oklahoma State baseball uniform and had set up on the stage of the performing arts building all the props he needed. He proceeded for close to an hour straight to preach into the Ikegami video camera on the art and discipline of hitting a baseball. Change the topic to religion and put Ward in a robe and he would rival the most spirited of Southern Baptist preachers. Ward knows how to teach hitters and he knows how to motivate young men—and at Oklahoma State he did just that, to the tune of 16 consecutive Big Eight Conference championships, 17 NCAA Regional appearances, and 10 appearances in Omaha at the NCAA College World Series.

Later, a video was created marking Ward's success at Oklahoma State titled *Decade of Dominance*. That is great, but most people think of a decade as 10 years. Ward and his Cowboys were the league's baseball power for 19 years and champions for 16 consecutive years. When Ward retired in 1996, he was the second winningest baseball coach in the country. His 19-year record at Oklahoma State was 953–313, which equates to a win percentage of .759. Not only did Ward coach winning baseball, but he marched into Stillwater from little Yavapai Junior College with assistant coaches Tom and Dave Holliday and recruited talented players and wealthy alumni. The players on the early Ward teams like outfielder Bill Ireland, first baseman Duane Evans, and pitcher Rick Kranitz helped turn the program around, while the boosters helped Ward build Allie Reynolds Stadium, which opened in April of the 1981 season. One of the advantages of the new stadium, which was considered the best college baseball facility in the Midwest, was that Oklahoma State got into the business of hosting NCAA Regionals, and the Cowboys hosted eight of them during Ward's tenure.

A product of Ramona, Oklahoma, where he excelled in baseball, basketball, and track, Ward had wanted to come to Oklahoma State and play basketball for Henry Iba. Instead, he played baseball and basketball for one year at Phillips University, one year in both sports and Northeastern Oklahoma A&M Junior College, and then two years of baseball and basketball at New Mexico State University.

Ward's ascension through the coaching ranks was similar to his college experience. He started out as the graduate assistant coach in baseball and freshman basketball at New Mexico State while he earned his master's degree. He came back to Oklahoma as the head baseball and basketball coach and assistant football coach at Collinsville High School, and then he went to Yavapai, where he was the head baseball coach and assistant basketball coach. In seven seasons he dominated junior college baseball with a record of 240–83, winning two NJCAA national championships on the diamond.

Oklahoma State made a wise choice. Ward came in and taught an aggressive style of baseball that was ultradisciplined at the plate. His hitters played mind games with pitchers and forced them to throw a lot of pitches, taking them deep into counts and eventually exploding and knocking them off the mound and to the showers. Those Oklahoma State teams set all kinds of records for runs scored, home runs, and extra-base hits. They also showed up and played with an attitude. Ward's teams did not shake hands after ball games. They didn't incite fights, but they definitely did not back away from them. It was an us-against-them mentality, and it seemed the majority of the players recruited into the program had an easy time buying into Ward's mind-set toward competition.

In his 19 seasons, Ward's teams won at least 45 games in all but three campaigns. He sent 108 of his players on to professional baseball, including major league stars Robin Ventura, Pete Incaviglia, Mickey Tettleton, Monty Fariss, Mike Henneman, Dave Mlicki, and Jeromy Burnitz.

Ward had nine first-team All-Americans in his years at Oklahoma State in pitchers Jason Bell and Dennis Linvingston, outfielders Jeff Guiel and Pete Incaviglia, third baseman Robin Ventura, shortstop Monty Fariss, catcher Robbie Wine, and designated hitters Jim Ifland and Michael Daniel. Players were named first-team All–Big Eight while playing for Ward 76 times.

Two of Ward's players went on to play for Team USA in the Olympic Games; Gary Green was a member of the 1984 Olympic team in Los Angeles, and Robin Ventura was a gold medalist with the 1988 U.S. Olympic Team.

Ward trusted his chief recruiter and assistant, Tom Holliday, to go anywhere for players. Oklahoma State recruited California, where it found the likes of Ventura and Incaviglia and Canada, where it landed several players, and Ward and his staff also went to the East Coast. The Cowboys recruited nationally for baseball, another similarity to Mike Holder and his golf program, which also recruited on a national basis.

The two hallmark players under Ward were Incaviglia and Ventura, as both demolished college records that were publicized nationally and made huge news. In 1985, Incaviglia was crushing baseballs out of Allie Reynolds Stadium and hitting the roofs of houses across Duck Street. It wasn't just home games in the stadium, which opposing coaches and pitchers labeled a "band box;" Incaviglia was hitting the ball out of every ballpark he played in. "Pistol Pete" hit an NCAA-record 48 home runs that season.

Two years later, Ventura was making national news and was on ESPN's *SportsCenter* as he made a run at one of the most iconic records in baseball. Just about any baseball fan knows the number 56—as in Joe DiMaggio and his record 56-game hitting streak. That was with the Yankees and in the big leagues, but as Ventura's collegiate streak kept climbing so did the attention. Ventura took it all the way in the postseason to Omaha and Rosenblatt Stadium, where he passed 56 and went two better to 58 before the streak ended in the College World Series against Stanford. Ventura would rebound later in the championship loss to Stanford with four hits, including two doubles. Ventura hit .364 in that CWS. The next season, in 1988, Ventura was named the Golden Spikes Award winner as the top player in collegiate baseball.

Ventura and Incaviglia have joined their head coach Gary Ward in the College Baseball Hall of Fame. Later, that trio was joined by an earlier Cowboy hero, Tom Borland, a 1955 All-American pitcher who played in the major leagues for the Boston Red Sox. All four of those men have their Oklahoma State numbers retired—including the No. 20 that was always worn by the hitting evangelist Gary Ward.

10 Mike Gundy

There are a lot of sides to Oklahoma State head football coach Mike Gundy.

There is the loyalty passed down from his dad, Ray, and mom, Judy. The Gundys are a loyal family—to each other and to their friends. Mike's younger brother Cale was a standout quarterback at the other Bedlam school in Oklahoma and has coached there for 18 seasons and counting. Now, there is rivalry between the two brothers, but I have often noted that if fans from either Oklahoma State or the University of Oklahoma were to take a slam at the other brother, their next move should be to duck because there is likely a clenched fist coming their way. Bedlam is bedlam, but brothers are blood.

There is exuberance, as Gundy is well known for his unique, almost limboesque dance moves in the locker room after a win over a ranked opponent. The players will circle around Gundy as he performs the move, dropping his hips and getting as low as he can. Gundy has a history of some back issues, and those celebratory dances almost always ignite a new round of trips to the athletic trainer.

There is defiance, as the former Oklahoma State quarterback loves to be told there is something he can't do, prides himself and his teams in situations where they are doubted, and loves to prove critics wrong. That goes for his sons, as his youngest, Gage, told his dad in the summer to go get his hair cut following a long baseball vacation where Gundy and his wife, Kristen, followed the two youngest sons on baseball tournament trips. After being antagonized about needing a haircut, Gundy told his son that he'd just let it grow out. He wasn't kidding; the coach with the mullet became national news and even sparked a T-shirt design featuring Gundy's profile on gameday with his mullet and a visor.

That is harmless defiance, but that part of Gundy's personality can have a stronger bite to it.

During Oklahoma State's run through the Big 12 in 2011 and within a few votes of playing for a national championship, Gundy, aware of a new 10-year contract for then–basketball coach Travis Ford, hired agent to football coaches (including Alabama's Nick Saban) Jimmy Sexton to negotiate his new contract. It rubbed Oklahoma State megadonor Boone Pickens and athletic director Mike Holder the wrong way, but Gundy got the contract he was looking for. That may not have been Gundy's most golden moment with his administration, but there is a reason that Gundy is the school's all-time winningest coach, the only coach in the school's history to win more than 100 games in his career, and the longest-tenured football coach in Oklahoma State history. Gundy understands Oklahoma State. The school and its former quarterback and current head coach have a lot in common.

Gundy came up in Midwest City as a promising athlete. He was talented, but he wasn't the biggest, the strongest, or the fastest. Gundy was crafty, dedicated, and determined. If he had to outwork an opponent, he would. If he had to outsmart an opponent, he could. Watching the 5'10", 165 pound Gundy play quarterback for the Bombers teams coached by Dick Evans, I once described him as playing like a surgeon who was so skilled he would have opposing defenses carved up and bleeding before they ever felt the first cut. He did the same thing in college.

In the third game of the 1986 season, Gundy's freshman year, head coach Pat Jones walked toward the ramp in the southeast corner of Lewis Field at halftime, his team trailing Houston with starting quarterback Ronnie Williams spraying the ball all over the field, into the stands, and into the hands of Houston defenders. He looked into this reporter's face and said, "You want to see a fresh-man quarterback play, do you?"

I thought that Jones might have lost it, so I scrambled up the ramp to see what was going on and found the baby-faced Gundy in the equipment room getting pads snapped into his helmet, as he didn't have any up to that point. After taking some practice snaps with the center, Gundy got some last-minute advice from offensive coordinator Larry Coker and went out and quarterbacked the second half. He became an instant star, as he set the then–NCAA record for most attempts to start a career without an interception with 138 passes before his first pass was picked. Gundy would go on to have a 29–14 record as quarterback at Oklahoma State. He handed the ball off to the likes of Thurman Thomas and Barry Sanders and threw many of his completions to another All-American in Hart Lee Dykes.

Gundy ended his career as the Big Eight's all-time leading passer and all-time leader in total offense. His name is still listed among the leaders in several categories in the Oklahoma State media guide.

"The four years that I was at Oklahoma State in college were the most enjoyable years of my life," Gundy said in the 2012 book he cowrote with this author. "I think everybody when they look at where they are in life they have to take away certain things. There are some things you don't compare to, but back then as far as living life there wasn't much that went on here that I wasn't involved in. I was just smart enough to realize that Coach Jones just didn't want you to throw interceptions and that if you didn't throw interceptions then you were going to get to play. I wanted to play."

Gundy came straight out of school and, in a very rare move, was hired immediately by Jones as a full-time assistant coach. That simply doesn't happen, rarely then and almost never in today's college coaching world.

"Mike was different," Jones said. "He knew a lot of football and he knew a lot of coaching. He just was much further along than anybody at his age. I knew the recruiting would be tough, but he had that it-factor that got older players like Thurman and Hart, even Ronnie [Williams] after a while to follow him even though they were initially mad that I put him in there. I knew that would be what would get him by on recruiting. He could get kids to join him and that is what recruiting is."

Gundy coached for Jones through some tough probation years, stayed on at the start of Bob Simmons' tenure, and then left. Gundy was at Baylor for a year under Chuck Reedy, but it was assistants he worked with there like Larry Fedora and Darrell Wyatt who made the bigger impact, then and later. After Reedy and that staff was let go, Gundy landed in Maryland as the wide receivers coach and passing-game coordinator for Ron Vanderlinden.

The Oklahoma State job opened again when Simmons was fired. Another former OSU assistant in Les Miles, who had gone to coach with the Dallas Cowboys, edged out Gundy for the job, but at the request of athletic director Terry Don Phillips, Miles hired Gundy as his offensive coordinator and assistant head coach. The two had worked together under Simmons, had stayed close, and made a good team. Gundy would later say that Miles let him in on virtually everything that was crossing the head coach's desk, often saying, "This is going to be your job someday."

Someday was January 3, 2005, when Gundy was named head coach at Oklahoma State University. Gundy called it that day his "New York Yankees job." He came armed with a plan. All of his experience as a recruit, a player, an assistant coach, and the assistant head coach, and from his life growing up in Oklahoma had taught him that Oklahoma State was different. *Good* different, but you had to know the nuances you were dealing with. It started with the kind of people who would fit Oklahoma State and the way an OSU team needed to be put together. It is almost like that great pie recipe. Bring in 10 bakers and give them that same recipe, and nine of them may mess it up, but one will do it just right. For Oklahoma State, Gundy knew how to do it just right. He knew the kinds of assistants he wanted, the kinds of players he wanted them to recruit, and the way those players needed to be developed. He knew he needed a cutting edge and taskmaster of a strength, conditioning, and speed coach in Rob Glass to be maybe the most important part of the recipe.

"You know I coached 11 years before I ever had a winning record as an assistant coach," Gundy said. "We had some really tough times here during the probation era when I first started coaching. At Baylor we were really close and at Maryland we started to turn the corner and they fired [Ron] Vanderlinden. As I look back I think that was maybe the best thing that could have happened to me as a coach because I learned a lot of things not to do. I also learned how to handle adversity and how not to handle it in a negative way that only made everything worse. I learned to appreciate what we have now. I combined that with knowing the landscape of Oklahoma State, what you could get done here and what you couldn't. More important, how to go about doing it."

The first thing Gundy did was let 13 players go—players who had off-the-field issues, either with the law or academics, or both. He began recruiting the kind of character players he wanted in his program and he built from a 4–7 team his first season to bowl teams every year from that point on, starting with the 2006 Independence Bowl Champions. That team finished its 7–6 season with a field goal in the final minute to beat Alabama 34–31.

Gundy labels the 2008 season as the breakthrough year, with a 28–23 upset win on the road at No. 3–ranked Missouri as the game that changed the destiny of the program. The team finished 9–4 that season despite losing to a very good Oregon team in the Holiday Bowl 42–31.

After another 9–4 season in 2009 and an 11–2 campaign in 2010, the 2011 Cowboys, with quarterback Brandon Weeden and receiver Justin Blackmon returning, were sitting at 10–0 and just two games away from the BCS National Championship when the season hit a huge bump on a cold Friday night in Ames, Iowa. The No. 2–ranked Cowboys lost in overtime 37–31 after leading

Since 2005, Mike Gundy has overseen a Oklahoma State football renaissance, including leading the Cowboys to a 9–4 2008 season that earned the head coach a seven-year contract extension. In 2011, Gundy's Cowboys finished first in the Big 12.

the entire contest. It was a sobering loss coming just more than 24 hours after the school's popular women's basketball coach Kurt Budke and one of his assistants, Miranda Serna, had perished in a plane crash recruiting in Arkansas. Gundy took his team, players only, into the locker room that night and carefully explained to them that they were not to publicly or privately blame the loss on the deaths of the two coaches that most of them knew. They were to give credit to Iowa State and learn from the Cyclones, who had used an open week prior to the game to prepare for a huge effort. You see, he reminded his team, you have an open week to prepare for the most important game of your life.

The 2011 Cowboys came out on a chilly night and erased the disappointment of the Iowa State loss with a rousing 44–10 win over Bedlam rival Oklahoma. The BCS did not see fit to put Oklahoma State in the championship game, but the Cowboys won a showdown of the No. 3 and No. 4–ranked teams in the Fiesta Bowl as they beat Stanford and Andrew Luck 41–38 in overtime.

The bowl streak continues at 11 straight, and so does the pursuit of Big 12 Championships and national championships. Oklahoma State fans have higher expectations than ever, meaning more pressure on Gundy and those in the program to deliver. Gundy understands, but he also knows why he is in the coaching business. He prides his program on building future husbands, fathers, and productive citizens. He treats his players much like he treats his three sons. He knows that winning is part of it, but the journey is also.

Another part of Gundy's success is staying new—reinventing himself in certain ways. There is a lot of Gundy's coaching philosophy that is unbending and won't change, but in Xs and Os and in his approach to recruiting he stays fresh through his own experiences as a father to his three boys, his relationship with his players, and his relationship with his coaches and staff. He has always said the hardest part of his job is replacing coaches, but he has had to do it often, and he has done it well.

"I'm always trying to hire coaches and people smarter than I am to be on this staff and in this program," Gundy has said. "If I do that then it comes back to me and this program reaps the benefits."

He has been through four offensive coordinators, not including the three seasons where he called the plays himself. Larry Fedora was his first, and he went on to become the head coach at Southern Miss and is now at North Carolina. Dana Holgerson was brought in to lend the Hal Mumme/Mike Leach influence to the offense, and is now head coach at West Virginia. Todd Monken succeeded Holgorsen and helped coach the Cowboys to the 2011 Big 12 Championship and he is now offensive coordinator at Tampa Bay in the NFL. Gundy's former defensive coordinator Tim Beckman left to become head coach at Toledo and later at Illinois.

"I learn from every coach that comes through this program because they've been places I haven't and worked for coaches I don't know that well," Gundy explained. "I can take their ideas and know how to apply them to this situation because Oklahoma State is what I know."

Gundy is more relaxed than he has ever been because he has the program in the best place it has ever been. Can it get better? Absolutely, but as Gundy communicated in the middle of the 2016 season, you have to come at it with a definite degree of confidence that comes as a result of the serious building and shaping that has gone on for a decade in putting the program on the same solid ground as the facilities and infrastructure of the program.

The 2016 season was another double-digit win campaign for Gundy—his fifth at Oklahoma State, the program's third in the last four seasons, and its fifth in the last seven years. His team was fired up to win the 100th for Gundy as head coach in a critical 37–20 win at home over then-unbeaten and No. 9–ranked West Virginia. The Cowboys beat three ranked teams in 2016, including two in the top 10, as they finished with a dominant 38–8 win over No. 10—ranked

Colorado in the Alamo Bowl. In his first 12 seasons, Gundy is now 104–50 as head coach.

"I'm comfortable with where we are. We've played pretty well at times, and if we didn't we were able to identify why...and find a solution," Gundy said. "If there's a solution to the issues we have in every phase of the game, then I'm okay with that because we can coach and teach it, and the players are committing themselves to getting better. I'm not very relaxed when I don't have an answer for what would be football that's not quite up to par. We've got young men who are committed and we've been able to identify our problems at times and we have answers for it. That's coaching, and I enjoy that part of the game."

That quote really sums up Gundy as a coach these days. There is always that fierce loyalty and, sometimes, that controversial defiance, for which he was known for so many of his years in coaching because of his famous rant after a win over Texas Tech and discovery that one of his players had been embarrassed in a sports column in that morning's paper. Gundy is still complex; he's now way past "I'm a man, I'm 40," as he turns 50 about the time this book is released. Gundy is comfortable, but still hungry, and that is the way Oklahoma State fans should want him to be.

11 John Smith

In the summer of 2016, the sports world saw John Smith in a role it never had before. A two-time Olympic gold medalist, six-time world champion, first-ever wrestler to win the James E. Sullivan Award and America's Top Amateur Athlete (1990), and the winningest head coach at the all-time-winningest collegiate wrestling program at

Oklahoma State, Smith went back to the Olympic Games in Rio de Janeiro wearing an NBC polo shirt and a broadcaster's headset. Smith brought the same work and determination he put in at the Olympic Games in Barcelona, Spain, and Seoul, South Korea, and the same intensity he brought to coaching the USA Olympic wrestlers in 2000 and 2012 to making his debut as a wrestling broadcaster. Smith was a combination of teacher and entertainer as he informed the audience on the interesting aspects of freestyle and Greco-Roman wrestling alike. He knew the participants and he knew their techniques, for men's and women's wrestling.

Smith had been a major player in the marketing and public relations fight that wrestling staged when the International Olympic Committee put wrestling on the list of sports considered for exclusion from the games. Smith knew his role in Rio of educating about and drawing fans' interest to his sport would be important, and he excelled, as he has in every other aspect of his career in wrestling. He studied and he practiced as a broadcaster, and by the time the Olympic Games began, Smith was a star and very popular with viewers, even those completely new to watching wrestling.

"I don't know if I was that good; I'll leave the broadcasting to you guys that do it for a living," Smith said after returning home from Rio. "I enjoyed it and it was important to help grow more fans. You know, explain the sport to them so they could enjoy it. Besides, what other sport would feature two coaches stripping down to their skivvies to protest?"

Smith actually said it was an embarrassing moment for wrestling when two Mongolian coaches stripped to their underwear in protest moments after officials took two penalty points from Mongolian wrestler Mandakhnaran Ganzorig's 7–6 win to give the bronze medal to his opponent from Uzbekistan.

"That is another problem in our sport that we have to fix," Smith said after the Olympics. "We need to become more consistent and more simple in our scoring and officiating."

Smith should know; he has been participating in wrestling almost since he was old enough to walk.

"It's funny; when we would take the boys around the country in the summer to wrestling events, you just knew John was going to win," said Gundy's father, Ray. "We would take those boys to tournaments in Oklahoma, Kansas, and Colorado. John would walk into the gym and right away he would be sizing up the competition. You could see some of those kids would take John for granted, but a few seconds into the match they would be on their back. It got to the point at some events that nobody would want to wrestle John."

That attitude never stopped. Smith rose through the ranks of amateur wrestling beginning at Del City High School, where there is now a statue of Smith from his Olympic days in front of the John W. Smith Fieldhouse. Smith was 105–5 in his prep career.

At Oklahoma State, Smith won two NCAA individual National Championships in 1987 and 1988 and was a three-time All-American, adding to his championship years with that honor in 1985. He finished his collegiate career with a 152–8–2 record.

Then it was on to international competition and the Olympics and world championships. No wrestler has ever put together a streak like Smith, who won the world championship from 1987 to '92, the Olympic Gold Medal in 1988 and 1992, gold at the Pan American Games in 1987 and 1991, and gold at the Goodwill Games in 1986–90. Smith faced wrestlers from Iran, Turkey, Japan, Bulgaria, and many of the Slavic countries, but he was always fired up to face the Russian wrestlers. It was the Russians that always could inspire his competitive juices.

"I get up in the middle of the night and train," Smith once said as he prepared for his final Olympic Games. "I do it because that is when the Russian wrestlers are training in their country. I can't stand the thought that I am lying on my back sleeping when they are working out."

Of course, Smith was also working out during the day with his training hours in Stillwater.

In 1990, Smith was honored with the FILA Master of Technique Award, becoming the first American to win the honor symbolic of the best amateur wrestler in the world. In 1997, Smith went into the United States Wrestling Hall of Fame, a stone's throw from Gallagher-Iba Arena, where he wrestled in college and trained through his international career. He finished with a record of 100–5 in international sanctioned wrestling matches.

There are some sports greats who can compete, but for some reason can't pass on their technique, attitude, or the attributes that made them successful as competitors; Smith, however, was instantly able to do that. He retired from wrestling after his final Olympic Games in Barcelona in 1992, and shortly after a victory parade held in Oklahoma City that led from the state capitol to his high school in Del City, Smith took over as the wrestling coach at Oklahoma State.

He is the all-time-winningest coach at Oklahoma State in wrestling. He started with a bang as Smith led the Cowboys to an NCAA team National Championship in 1994 and then later put a string together with titles in 2003 through '06. Smith has coached the Cowboys to 16 Big Eight or Big 12 Conference Championships and he is the 15-time conference coach of the year.

When Smith travels to the Far East, the Middle East, or Europe for international competitions, he is easily recognized and is treated like a rock star. In the wrestling world, John Smith is royalty. Not a big man, as he wrestled primarily at 134 pounds in college (he has vowed never to step on scales again after his final Olympic match), but he stays in excellent shape and routinely drills with his team. In the Cowboy world, Smith is Oklahoma State's John Wayne. Nobody in his smart mind is going to mess with John Smith—no wrestlers, no opposing wrestling coaches, not even the snakes he routinely kills on his land outside Stillwater. Smith may only be about 5'10", but in the sport of wrestling, no one stands taller.

12 Rickie Fowler

There may not be a more popular Oklahoma State athlete alum worldwide than PGA Tour golfer and pop culture trendsetter Rickie Fowler. Whether it is on the golf course, off the golf course, or back in Stillwater attending a football game, Fowler is always the object of attention. Fowler was a multisport athlete in high school, but it was not your typical combination as the self-taught golfer who mainly played in his developmental years on a driving range was also a serious competitor on the dirt-bike circuit. His talent was enough to draw the attention of Oklahoma State and then–head coach Mike McGraw. After Oklahoma State—and the multiple awards he earned there, including two-time All-American honors and the 2008 Ben Hogan Award—Fowler started his PGA career and has gone on to win seven tournaments and play well in some of golf's majors.

Growing up in Murietta, California, Fowler was a very successful youth racer in dirt bikes, and his father, Rod, actually won the 1986 Baja 1000 while racing for a Yamaha-sponsored team. He continued to race dirt bikes until an accident prior to his freshman year in high school left him with a couple of broken bones in his foot. Fowler, who gets his middle name of Yutaka from his grandfather Taka Tanaka, started playing golf at age three, but he found his swing and his technique from countless hours working on his own at the local driving range. As he progressed through high school, he gained attention with his abilities. He led Murietta Valley High School through the SW League with scores of 64 and 69 and on to the California State Championship.

At Oklahoma State, Fowler wasted no time in making history as he became the first freshman to receive the Ben Hogan Award.

This was presented to him as the top male collegiate golfer out of all divisions, taking into account all of his collegiate and amateur competitions over the calendar year. He was ranked at the top of NCAA Division I most of his freshman year, as he finished in the top 10 in 10 of his 12 starts that season. In fact, he started on fire, finishing in the top 10 in his first nine tournaments in college. He won twice and finished in the top five in six of the events. He won his second collegiate tournament, the Fighting Illini Invitational. His one-shot victory included a round of 63 to match the court record at famed Olympia Fields that was held by Vijay Singh. His second collegiate win was in the Big 12 Championship over team-mate Kevin Tway. He was named the Big 12 Player of the Year and the Newcomer of the Year.

As an amateur that year, he won the Sunnehanna Amateur and the Players Amateur before he even set foot on the Oklahoma State campus and home course of Karsten Creek. He had already earned a berth on the U.S. Walker Cup squad. Fowler finished that fabulous first year in college finishing fourth individually in the NCAA Championship and making the cut in the U.S. Open at Torrey Pines in San Diego, where he finished 60th.

Fowler concluded his two years as a collegian with seven top-10 finishes in 12 tournaments, including winning the Aggie Invitational, finishing fourth in the Ping/Golfweek Preview, and tying for third in the 2009 NCAA Championship.

The Cowboys teams Fowler was on won the Big 12 Championship and finished fourth in the 2008 NCAA Championship, and then won the 2009 NCAA Championship medal play before losing in the quarterfinal match to Georgia under the new format, which called for the top eight teams to play a match-play bracket for the title.

Fowler has won four PGA Tournaments, including the 2017 Honda Classic and the prestigious Players Championship in 2015, an event many consider golf's fifth major. He also won the

Rickie Fowler is one of Oklahoma State's most recognized alums across the world. He has four PGA Tour wins and two in the European Tour.

2015 Deutsche Bank Championship and the 2012 Wells Fargo Championship. On the European PGA Tour, Fowler has won the 2015 Aberdeen Asset Management Scottish Open that leads into The Open Championship and the 2016 Abu Dhabi HSBC Golf Championship. Over in Asia in that PGA tour he won the 2011 Kolon Korea Open.

He has also played for his country in the Ryder Cup in 2010, 2014, and 2016.

Fowler has a number of sponsors and endorsements, including Farmers Insurance and Crowne Plaza Hotels for commercials. His clothing and shoe sponsor is Puma, and he has put that brand back into the mix with major sports fashion monsters Nike and Adidas.

Fowler and three of his close fellow PGA Tour competitors, Ben Crane, Bubba Watson, and Hunter Mahan, recorded two music videos as the Golf Boys. The first video was "Oh, Oh, Oh" and the second was "2 Oh." The videos have been immensely popular and, because of donations from Farmers Insurance, have made a lot of money for charities.

Fowler has incredible potential, is an electric personality, and will continue to represent Oklahoma State in a strong way well into the future.

13 Josh Holliday

It's a little less than an hour before the first pitch at Allie Reynolds Stadium in the far northeast corner of the sprawling Oklahoma State campus, and the Cowboys have just taken the bright-green and-brown-dirt diamond for infield. It's a little sultry as spring starts to definitely turn toward summer, and as the Cowboys take the infield, some of the reserve pitchers throw the baseball off the screen at home plate at all kinds of crazy angles and a little kid dressed in a miniature OSU baseball uniform dives to make circus catches as the ball comes off the screen. He watches where the ball hits on the screen and seems to have memorized where it will go. He spins his little legs and gets his glove in position to make the catch. Fans are paying more attention to the show behind home plate than the Cowboys in the field. The little highlight maker is Brady Holliday, son of Cowboys baseball coach Josh Holliday.

If you went back 30 years, you would still find a youngster back behind home plate making catches off the screen, and his name also would have been Holliday—Brady's dad, Josh. Josh had a partner, too. At the time he was smaller, but little brother Matt Holliday would overtake Josh and end up at 6'4", 240 pounds, his most recent listed dimensions from 2017 in the outfield for the New York Yankees. The two Holliday boys grew up at Allie Reynolds Stadium, on the Oklahoma State campus, and throughout the family-oriented college town of Stillwater.

Their father, Tom Holliday, came along with Gary Ward and completely turned the Oklahoma State Cowboys baseball team into a juggernaut—the Decade of Dominance. Oklahoma State won 16 consecutive Big Eight Championships, going to the NCAA Tournament each of those years and to the College World Series in Omaha on seven occasions.

"I didn't realize how special that was," Josh Holliday said late in the 2016 season. He was preparing to take his team to Omaha, breaking a Cowboys College World Series drought that had lasted since 1999, his senior season as he was playing for his dad, who was then the Cowboys' head coach. "When we were kids we went to Omaha it seemed every summer. We just thought that was where everybody vacationed. I remember asking if we could go somewhere else."

Holliday and his younger brother were standouts on the local diamonds all the way through high school and both played quarterback at Stillwater High School.

"My dad was always very busy with his job [back then] and never got to see me play much baseball," Josh Holliday remembered. "One thing my parents always did was be there to watch me play football, and Matt too, on Friday nights. That time of the year cooperated, and I think my mom was just hoping we wouldn't get hurt, but my dad really enjoyed watching those games and when your buddies are at your house spending the night and then they are out on the field there with you, that became an important part of our childhood. You learn things in high school football that stay with you forever."

Josh went on to Oklahoma State and played catcher and some third base. He was a four-time All-Academic Big 12 performer who was on the President's Honor Roll. He was also an All–Big 12 performer who finished with a career average of .311, 53 home runs, 62 doubles, and 237 RBIs. He is in the Cowboys Baseball Hall of Fame and is still in the top five all-time career lists in games played, at bats, runs, hits, doubles, and total bases.

After a couple seasons chasing the pro dream in the Toronto Blue Jays organization, he came back to Stillwater and started out as a student coach for his dad. Matt Holliday would sign a letter of intent to play both football and baseball at Oklahoma State, but when drafted by the Colorado Rockies he opted to go to professional baseball. Not long after, Tom Holliday was dismissed. There were ill feelings as Tom went to Texas as a pitching coach. Josh got his education and more serving as an assistant at strong programs North Carolina State, Georgia Tech, Arizona State, and Vanderbilt. Josh was bitter about his dad's exit, but still had fond feelings for his hometown and alma mater. He had married Jenny Moore, who was from Stillwater. They both knew how neat it would be if Brady and his sister, Olivia, could grow up in that same community.

There were other candidates for the position, even other former Oklahoma State players, but senior associate athletic director Larry Reece thought Holliday would knock it out of the park, much like his younger brother often did for the Cardinals. Holliday came into interview and athletic director Mike Holder asked him to stay in town for a few days and maybe invest in an orange tie.

On June 8, 2012, Josh Holliday came full circle from the kid who grew into an Oklahoma State baseball hero and OSU Male Student-Athlete of the Year as a senior to being the man in charge of guiding current college baseball players and recruiting high school talent to work toward their dreams on the Allie P. diamond.

He has not let anybody down so far, with four NCAA Tournament appearances in his first four seasons and a 2016 five-game run through the state of South Carolina that included regional wins at Clemson of 6–0 over Nebraska and 12–2 and 9–2 over the host Tigers. Then in the best of three Super Regional at University of South Carolina, he guided the Cowboys to back-to-back 5–1 and 3–1 wins over the Gamecocks to head to Omaha.

There were two wins there, including a stellar 1–0 shutout of Arizona, before the Wildcats came back for two wins to eliminate the Pokes. Holliday finished his first four seasons with a record of 170 wins and 77 losses. He is proving to be as reliable a coach as he was a player in Orange and Black. He had taken the program and its fans back to the vacation spot they missed in middle America at the College World Series.

"We had a special year, a special group of kids, and as I told them, Oklahoma State hasn't been playing at this time of year since 1990, and a 26-year gap between then and now is something these kids should really hold their heads really high about," Holliday related of what he told his players after they were eliminated. "They brought the 'OS' to a place of importance in college baseball."

Just like Brady putting on a catching exhibition before games and being a trustworthy bat boy during the games, his father stands for family with his players and his coaches, which includes former Cowboys pitcher, Holliday's pitching coach, and trusted confidant and advisor Rob Walton. Walton played for Josh's dad and brought his son Donovan—an All–Big 12 shortstop for three seasons—into the fold. It is about family. It has made Oklahoma State baseball unique and special. The players get it, and now Brady Holliday has some 35 big brothers and, in turn, all of those Cowboy players have more than a coach—a family away from family at Oklahoma State. It was the same way for Josh and Matt when they grew up with big brothers like Pete Incaviglia, Robin Ventura, Jim Ifland, Rob Walton, and many more

The one member of the Holliday family who never wore the Orange and Black still may someday soon. Josh has had Matt's back and been there to help during his All-Star major league career, pitching to him in home-run-hitting contests, helping work on his swing when needed, and just lending all-around moral support. As Matt's career winds down, he aspires to come back to Stillwater and help Josh make more trips to Omaha. Matt is married, and he and his wife have five children whom they could see growing up in Stillwater. Dad Tom is back as a color analyst on Cowboys baseball telecasts and was recently inducted into the Cowboy Baseball Hall of Fame. Mom Kathy is the pillar of this baseball family and always a strong and loving presence.

Once again, at Oklahoma State and in Stillwater, you can always come home—especially for the Hollidays.

14 T. Boone Pickens

You definitely want to stay on T. Boone Pickens' good side. For those who do, well, good things generally happen. Pickens has been linked permanently to his alma mater for all time through a series of generous donations that have improved academics on the campus, but he received the most notoriety by making Oklahoma State football a genuine force and top-20 program in the past decade. Pickens, who grew up in Holdenville, Oklahoma, and started his life in business with an ever-expanding paper route as a 12-year-old, has joked that it could have been Texas A&M that would have benefitted from his collegiate generosity had it not been for his losing his scholarship at that school. Pickens started out at Texas A&M on a basketball scholarship, but then returned to his home state and attended and graduated from Oklahoma State.

He often said that his money might have found its way to Oklahoma State earlier if Henry Iba had recognized Pickens' basketball talents. It found its way to Oklahoma State primarily through the cultivation of a strong friendship between Pickens and longtime Cowboys golf coach Mike Holder. Several of Pickens' friends and fraternity brothers, such as the late Sherman Smith, whose name is on the Sherman Smith Training Center across from Boone Pickens Stadium, and the late Jerry Walsh, who helped to get Pickens and Smith acquainted with Holder through his OSU golf fundraisers, were instrumental in bringing Pickens and Holder in touch. The trio were in business together on different ventures as Walsh was involved in mud, Smith was in the drilling end of the industry, and Pickens was a geologist. As Holder built the Oklahoma State golf program into an even greater dynasty and the three men helped fund it, they all drew closer. Holder built Karsten

Creek and included cabins on the grounds, where the friends often stayed on trips to Stillwater.

Then Holder took a greater interest in the overall welfare of Oklahoma State athletics and came at it with the understanding that an underfunded and underachieving football program needed to be fortified for the greater good of the entire athletic program—and Pickens was the man to bring the facilities up to speed. Pickens had given money to the School of Geology, which bears his name, but now there was a succession of gifts, with the catalyst being a $165 million gift in 2005 to the athletic department that came after an earlier gift of $70 million in 2003. It is hard to know the exact value of those gifts, as they were almost immediately placed in the O.S.U. Cowboy Golf Inc. fund and were managed as investments through Pickens' hedge-fund company, BP Capital Management. The funds invested took roller-coaster rides to great heights but were also subject to major losses. In all, the funds were used to turn what was an old, rust-covered stadium in Lewis Field into the shining home that it is today for Oklahoma State football in Boone Pickens Stadium. Also, boosted by a later contribution of $20 million, came the Sherman E. Smith Training Center across Hall of Fame Avenue on the north side of the stadium.

The best estimate is that Pickens has donated more than $500 million to Oklahoma State, as there was a later $100 million donation that was part of Oklahoma State President Burns Hargis' billion-dollar campaign Branding Success. The last donation was strictly for academics and was matched by the State of Oklahoma. The campaign, due in large part to Pickens' donation, raised a reported $1.2 billion.

Pickens has never been shy about making comments—and what could loosely be interpreted as demands—about the results he would like to see in the athletics department and primarily in football. It has caused controversy and a strained relationship between two of the major reasons for Oklahoma State's success in college football: Pickens and Oklahoma State's winningest head football coach, Mike Gundy.

Through his business career that was often well documented in newspapers and trade publications, Pickens not only got rich, but did so in some captivating ways. After graduating from Oklahoma State with a degree in geology, he went to work for Phillips Petroleum for three years. Then, after nearly two years as a wildcatter—a term used for an oilman or geologist who drills exploratory oil wells looking to strike big—Pickens formed the company that would become his cherished Mesa Petroleum.

In the 1980s, Pickens and Mesa began taking over other companies in the oil and gas industry. He started with taking over Hugoton Production Company, which was 30 times the size of Mesa Petroleum. He had attempted buyouts of Cities Service (a Tulsa-based company), Gulf Oil, Phillips Petroleum, and Unocal. He did lead successful acquisitions of Pioneer Petroleum and mid-continent assets of Tenneco. His success in takeovers earned him the reputation of a corporate raider and put him on the cover of *Time* magazine. There was even a consideration of running for president in 1988.

Instead, Pickens chose to help fund political candidates and issues as a big supporter of President George W. Bush and later former New York City Mayor Rudy Giuliani. He has funded many causes and is the author of "The Pickens Plan," a well-written and methodical outline for the United States to achieve energy independence and alleviate the need for and dependence on foreign energy sources.

Pickens also sold Mesa Petroleum and has centered his business interest and acumen for the last 20 years in BP Capital Management, a company he founded that manages hedge funds involving energy and commodities. Pickens has always taken great interest in energy sources, but is now interested in various other resources, especially water. He owns 46 percent of BP Capital and as of late 2016 his overall net worth was estimated at $500 million.

As one would imagine, Pickens has a suite in the stadium that bears his name on the 50-yard line and he is donor No. 1, with his name in capital letters, when it comes to Oklahoma State University athletics. He flies in his private jet from the air strip on his Mesa Vista Ranch in the panhandle of Texas to Stillwater for home games and will often fly and attend Cowboys games on the road. His relationship with Oklahoma State University vice president of athletics and athletics director Mike Holder is closer to father and son than business partners.

There is no doubt that when you attend an Oklahoma State athletics event, especially for football, you are seeing a lot of what was created with the financial backing of T. Boone Pickens.

15 Boone Pickens Stadium

Originally known as the athletic field, wooden bleachers and a dirt and cinder track were the early elements of the site that is now Boone Pickens Stadium. It has seen many additions and changes, but nothing like the metamorphosis that took place between 2002 and 2009 as the stadium received one of the most extensive make-overs in modern American sports-venue history.

The stadium had its birth in 1913 and in 1914 was named Lewis Field, in honor of the former Dean of Veterinary Medicine and of Science and Literature. Laymon Lowery Lewis was one of the most popular figures in Oklahoma A&M history at that time, and was said to be an avid supporter of athletics. Lewis also served as the acting president of the university in 1914, the year it was

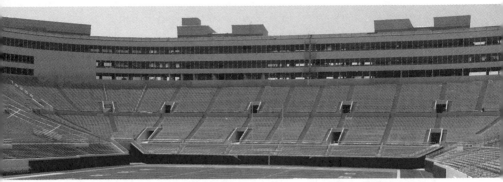

*Oklahoma State fans have athletic director Mike Holder and alumnus donor
T. Boone Pickens to thank for their sprawling, state-of-the-art football home.*

named for him. Wooden bleachers with a cover were the early
makings of Lewis Field, but in 1924 permanent south-side stands
were built. The stadium originally had a north-south perspective,
like most stadiums in the country, but was changed to run east and
west in order to avoid the strong prevailing winds in the region,
which run north and south. This change would later cause swirl-
ing wind currents in the stadium that tend to give the Oklahoma
State punters and kickers with local knowledge and practice a solid
home-field advantage on Saturdays.

Permanent north-side stands were built in 1929. At that time
the goal was to build a horseshoe-shaped stadium similar to the one
at Ohio State University. That idea was shelved for some reason,
possibly cost. Following World War II in 1947, the south-side
seating was renovated to a capacity of 30,000 overall, and then the
north-side renovation in 1950 brought capacity to 39,000.

Until 1971 the stadium, with its row of hedge bushes sur-
rounding the track and field, remained the same. In 1971 the
track was eliminated, the field was lowered, and artificial turf—the
original AstroTurf—was put down as the playing surface. The
changes and lowering of the field created enough extra seat room

to expand capacity to 51,000. Later, in 1978, a coaches' building was completed between the stadium and Gallagher Hall in the east end zone and a new press box was constructed, replacing the tin structure that had been there.

In 1984, ESPN brought in portable lights from the Iowa sports lighting company MUSCO to light the stadium for a night game with Missouri. It was a success, and Oklahoma State added a permanent lighting system in time for the 1985 season.

Honestly, the old stadium had its faults. In many cases, the metal beams had developed rust. They were painted over, but the rust continued to show up. It was antiquated in some ways, but every seat was a good one. It had an intimacy about it, and with that lowering of the stadium and field in 1971, fans were right on top of the action. The drawback was that the sidelines and the walls were, in places, dangerously close to the field.

Boone Pickens was brought to the table by longtime golf coach and future athletic director Mike Holder. With Pickens' generosity and Holder's direction, the old stadium—actually the oldest west of the Mississippi River—got a facelift that may be one of the all-timers when it comes to sports venues. In 2004, a new south side was opened with a beautiful brick exterior and new suites and club levels, concourses, and revamped seating topped by a new broadcast, photo, and coaches' level on the roof. The traditional press box was built into the suite level on the far southeast end. The north side was completed in 2006 and matched the south side. The stadium was finally in the horseshoe form that had been envisioned back in its early days in 2009 with the construction of the west end zone.

The newest part of the stadium included coaches' offices and meeting rooms, a training-table area, and a beautiful lobby and trophy room, all on the lower club level. Down below on the field level was a locker room, equipment room, team meeting room, and sports medicine area complete with huge temperature-controlled pools for rehab purposes. Everything was state of the art and marveled at by other schools and NFL teams alike. Dallas Cowboys owner Jerry Jones came in to survey the facility before building AT&T Stadium and his more recent Star Training Center in Frisco, Texas.

How good is Boone Pickens Stadium? How much of an improvement is it over the older, rusting Lewis Field? George Schroeder of *USA Today* put it this way:

> The easy comparison is to the way things used to be in Stillwater. Anyone who remembers the aging stadium that was can't help but be overwhelmed by the changes. But the better comparison is to Oklahoma State's peers in the top 25 football programs. Put simply, there is not a better facility anywhere. Plenty of new facilities have been built, and many are filled with bells, whistles, and the latest gizmos and gadgetry. Very few are designed as well from top to bottom—literally, from the coaches' offices to the locker room and the other player areas. It is fabulous but very functional. Those terms don't always go together; in Stillwater, they mesh seamlessly.

16 Gallagher-Iba Arena

Originally finished in 1938 and named the 4H Club and Student Activities Building, the facility that would become Gallagher-Iba Arena did not take long to get its second name: Gallagher Hall. The building, which cost $1.5 million to construct, was so named to honor the founding father of the proud wrestling tradition at

Oklahoma A&M, Edward Gallagher. At the time, the seating capacity was just more than 6,000 and the original maple floor, still used today, was one of the most expensive of its kind in the country.

The first basketball game played in the building was on December 9, 1938, when Mr. Iba's team beat Phog Allen's Kansas Jayhawks in a defensive struggle 21–15.

Gallagher's first wrestling match in the house named after him was on January 27, 1939, as the Aggie grapplers defeated Indiana 18–6. On February 3, 1989, the Hoosier wrestlers returned to what was by then Gallagher-Iba Arena, and the Cowboys celebrated the 50th anniversary of the building with a 28–6 dual victory.

Old-time wrestling fans will tell you the grand lady that is the arena was at her best for the home team during the 1978 Big Eight Wrestling Championships. There is no telling how many fans packed the building, causing the fire marshal to shut the doors to any more fans. Unranked Oklahoma State wrestler Daryl Monasmith beat defending national champion Frank Santana of Iowa State in a match that helped decide the team champion and win it for Oklahoma State. It got so loud that light bulbs in the arena's powerful lights exploded, much like the scene in the baseball movie *The Natural*. It was the loudest Oklahoma State fans say that it ever got inside the building. Others will say that extraordinary decibel level had to be matched in two wrestling matches a few years later, when unsung Oklahoma State heavyweights David Hille and Mitch Shelton both defeated Oklahoma All-American Steve "Dr. Death" Williams.

Hille was a 197-pound wrestler whom Cowboys coach Tommy Chesbro moved up to face Williams. It should have been a rout, but at one point Williams began slugging Hille and claiming the Cowboy wrestler bit him on the arm. Williams and his coach, Stan Abel, were showing the official the bite marks, but after the fracas on the mat, the official called a double disqualification and that left Oklahoma State the winner of the dual. The noise during the match was deafening. The same took place in another Bedlam dual when 400-pound Cowboys heavyweight Mitch Shelton was able to take Williams down, and then basically jumped on top of him and used every ounce of his 400 pounds to pin the Sooner to the mat and clinch the win.

The spirit of what longtime public address voice Larry Reece calls proudly "the rowdiest arena in the country" has been there for Cowboys basketball over the years. As of this writing, Oklahoma State basketball had a record of 783–222 in the building, with 10 unbeaten seasons at home in that time. The Cowboys' 80-game home-court nonconference winning streak that ran from 1987 through 1998 ranks fifth all-time in NCAA Division I history.

A renovation in 2000 brought Gallagher-Iba Arena into the 21ˢᵗ century, but the building has existed in some form since its original construction in 1938.

Oklahoma State has lost just seven regular season conference home games since 1987. That's 29 years.

Back to the building and its design. It made history again in 2000 when the new Gallagher-Iba Arena was unveiled. Then–athletic director Terry Don Phillips, a former football player for Frank Broyles at Arkansas and the point man for Arkansas on the building of the Bud Walton Arena, was looking for a way to capitalize on the success of basketball at Oklahoma State under Eddie Sutton. He knew he needed to find a way to improve facilities, and basketball was a logical program to start with. However, Phillips was aware that no Oklahoma State enthusiast wanted to lose the coziness and the tradition of Gallagher Hall. Phillips challenged architects and settled on a plan that called for the arena size to be more than doubled, with a building being constructed above and around the current structure and the roof to be basically peeled off the old building. It sounded crazy, and as the project advanced and the people of Stillwater and Oklahoma State watched it still seemed far-fetched, but it worked like a charm. They were even able to save the original maplewood playing floor.

The new arena seated 13,611 and was still as cozy and as loud and rowdy as ever. It is considered by most basketball experts to be one of the best home-court venues in all of college basketball. It is a must-see for enthusiasts of two sports: basketball and wrestling. While most basketball teams have to be hoodwinked into scheduling their teams into the building because of that legendary home-court prowess, wrestling teams are begging to come and wrestle the Cowboys so their wrestlers can say they competed in one of the sport's most historic venues. It is a must-see for any college sports fan.

17 Sherman Smith Center

Shortly after the Sherman E. Smith Training Center opened, an NFL scout was being shown around the new facility. He toured its two full 100-yard natural-grass practice fields, one running north-south and the other running east-west, and two FieldTurf practice fields—one outside, but shaded in the afternoon by the indoor facility, and the other indoors with three large, heavy-duty fabric roll-up doors.

"There is nothing like this anywhere else I've been," said the longtime scout. "I don't know of a single NFL team that wouldn't love to have a facility exactly like this one. This could very well be the best football practice facility in the nation."

It took some time to get completed, thanks to the downturn in energy and several financial crashes in the markets that adversely affected the original donation for the facility after it had been invested, but once it was completed it was one of a kind. The roll-up fabric doors allow head coach Mike Gundy and his staff to work in secrecy and do it in a building where they can duplicate about any weather condition they choose. In order to get direct sunlight, you do have to go outside, but the ability to vary the doors can change the lighting inside. It can do more to affect the temperature and the humidity. Doors all the way down on a warm summer or early-fall day can create a greenhouse effect that turns up the heat and humidity. On the same day, rolling up the doors to catch the predominant west-to-east flow of air and wind can get you varying degrees of cool. There are also turbines in the building that can assist in generating airflow. The only condition you can't totally change is a frigid winter day. You can keep the wind out and make it more comfortable, but it is still going to be colder inside on those days.

Named after longtime Oklahoma State donor Sherman E. Smith, the indoor building is just short of 94,000 square feet and has an indoor clearance of 65 feet above the playing field. There are regulation goal posts that hang on either end, allowing for field goals and point-after attempts. There are also three platforms for video or coaching access.

With few exceptions, Oklahoma State football uses the facility for its practices and off-season workouts. There is a decorative, shorter turf field in front of the building, where kids often play on game days. Other organizations ranging from ROTC to intramural teams use that field for activities.

Baseball, softball, soccer, and track and field use the facility for work as well, especially when the weather is unfit to be outside.

18 Allie Reynolds Stadium

In the 2014 college baseball season, Allie Reynolds Stadium welcomed back an old friend who grew up running around the grandstands; the field; and the hallways, offices, and storage rooms underneath. The cry was and continues to be for funding to build a new baseball stadium. Believe me: Josh Holliday is on board with that. However, the little kid who grew up running around with his brother, Matt, and then playing third base and catcher on its diamond, and now coaching in the dugout and making the stadium his business home every day also understands the history and how special the stadium is.

Josh's dad was there working alongside the legendary Gary Ward as they built what was a struggling but proud baseball program into one of the most dominant teams in the history of the sport. University Park was on that corner and was the home of Cowboys baseball when Ward and Holliday arrived, but Ward, much like then–golf coach and now athletic director Mike Holder, knew how to go out and fund-raise for his program—and he did. Ward had Allie Reynolds Stadium built, and when it was finished it was the baseball showplace in the Big Eight and throughout the Midwest.

The stadium opened in 1981 and was officially dedicated on April 24, 1982, in a ceremony attended by the namesake Allie Reynolds and his New York Yankees teammates (and Oklahoma natives) Mickey Mantle and Warren Spahn and Louisiana native Bill Dickey. The Cowboys had won their first game in Reynolds Stadium the year before on April 5 against Big Eight rival Missouri.

Reynolds began his baseball career at Oklahoma A&M on a track scholarship. He was watching baseball practice one afternoon when he was asked by legendary coach Henry Iba if he could help out and throw some batting practice. Without as much as a warm-up pitch, Reynolds struck out the first four batters he faced. The legend began, and Reynolds began his professional career with the Cleveland Indians, where he won 51 games over his first five seasons and then went on to star for the Yankees from 1947 to 1954 before an accident cut his career short.

The five-time All-Star appeared in 15 World Series games, winning five of his nine starts and picking up four saves and two wins in six relief appearances. Reynolds was an integral part of six world championship teams while in New York.

His most memorable season came in 1951 when, in spite of fighting bone chips, he became only the third player in major league history to hurl two no-hit games in a single season. All told,

Reynolds compiled a 182–107 record with 48 saves and 1,423 strikeouts during his 13-year career.

On August 26, 1989, Reynolds was given the highest honor for any New York Yankee when he received a plaque in Monument Park beyond the center-field fence at Yankee Stadium.

Reynolds Stadium, which opponents have always claimed is a band box, allowing power hitters like Pete Incaviglia, Jim Ifland, Robin Ventura, Monty Farris, and others over time to take aim at the short fences, now plays very fair with the new restrictions on the bats. The predominant winds are out of the north and the south, so early in the season it can be a pitcher's friend and later in the season a hitter's helper.

The stadium includes 1,000 chairback seats, 2,000 bleacher seats in the main grandstand, and another 1,000 bleacher seats on the left-field line, seating approximately 4,000. The Cowboys have won close to 82 percent of their home games over the 36 years it has served as home of the Pokes. The stadium has hosted 12 NCAA regionals over the years and one Super Regional in 2014.

The stadium has been remodeled and expanded several times, but one facet of it that ranks among the very best in all of baseball— professional and college—is the field itself. It is considered one of the finest playing surfaces in baseball. Opposing coaches and major league scouts have often complimented the field for its fair play and ability to hold up to some rough conditions. Todd Tribble is the field superintendent at Oklahoma State, and he does a masterful job with all facilities.

Soon, Oklahoma State will have the funding to build a new baseball stadium and the plot of land is already selected at the corner of McElroy and Washington Streets, but the little boy who grew up at Allie P. and who will coach at the new stadium doesn't sound like he is in a hurry.

"I realize what a new stadium will do for the program and it will primarily show the department's intentions of doing what it takes to be successful in baseball," Holliday said when asked about the new stadium. "I will never complain about Allie Reynolds Stadium, because I know how special this place can be and what a great home it can be for a team that cares for each other and loves to play the game of baseball. It was that way for me and has been that way for many years."

19 Karsten Creek

The first line of the description that the Oklahoma State athletic department website uses to describe the school's world-class golf course reads as follows:

Conceived in the mind of one man and brought to life through the efforts of many over a period of 15 years, Karsten Creek now serves as a daily reminder of the commitment to excellence of the OSU golf program.

That one man is longtime golf coach and current Oklahoma State athletic director Mike Holder. Holder put together the project with the purchase of land that he claims he could see would be suitable for the layout of an elite golf course. Holder then convinced famed golf course architect Tom Fazio to design the course into the rolling hills of the land he purchased outside of Stillwater. Holder did not envision a course that would host PGA Tour events and be surrounded by a huge, elite residential development. This was not a project of profit, but a project of commitment for a long, long future of success for Oklahoma State golf. It is not unlike the projects the athletic department has on campus with Boone Pickens Stadium, Sherman Smith Training Center, the Michael and Ann Greenwood Tennis Center, and the future baseball stadium. Projects like those show commitment to the sport and to its success.

Karsten Creek is the most elite home to any collegiate golf program in the country. PGA touring professionals, and not just former Oklahoma State golfers, have routinely made their way into Stillwater to play the 7,400 yards of tight, rolling fairways that wind through the native blackjack oak trees and other natural vegetation. A 110-acre lake, Lake Louise, comes into play on many holes on the back nine of the course. The course itself is named in honor of Karsten Solheim, the founder of Karsten Manufacturing—the maker of PING golf clubs—and Lake Louise is named in honor of his wife. It is easily one of the most challenging courses in North America and was named by *Golf Digest* as the Best New Public Course for 1994. The track was honored by the famed publication again in 1998, and this time with its first five-star rating. Karsten Creek is one of only 10 courses in the United States to have that distinction.

A modest but homey $4.5 million clubhouse was completed in 2001 and houses a complete pro shop; a grill and restaurant that also serves as the training table for Cowboys and Cowgirls golfers; locker rooms and offices; and an extensive display honoring the history, championships, and great individuals and All-Americans in the men's and women's golf programs.

The facility hosted the NCAA Men's Golf Championship in 2003 and 2011. For a fairly decent-sized green fee, one can play the course, and it should be experienced at least once. It will chew up even a talented golfer, but you will find the bent-grass greens and especially the Zoysia fairways to be as luscious as any carpet you have ever walked on. Every Oklahoma State fan who appreciates the school's athletic history should at least walk the course that pros like Rickie Fowler and Hunter Mahan once played every day in college.

Oddly enough, Oklahoma State has yet to win a national championship on its own course.

20 Michael and Anne Greenwood Tennis Center

Oklahoma State has a proud tennis heritage built by one of the school's great coaches in James Wadley and the late Ike Groce, who had some tremendous Big Eight Championship teams and coached Wimbledon singles semifinalist and Oklahoma State Hall of Famer Lori McNeil. However, tennis has not won a national championship, though that could soon change—and it almost did in one of the most exciting sporting events involving Oklahoma State in the 2015–16 season. Chris Young has made a huge difference in the Cowgirls tennis program. It's not just his recruiting and coaching abilities, but his fund-raising, as he became close with Michael and Anne Greenwood and let them know there was a need for the school to build a tennis facility. Prior to the Michael and Anne Greenwood Tennis Center, built on the corner of Washington and McElroy, the two tennis teams at Oklahoma State had been competing on courts at the Colvin Center, where the priority was first to classes taught on the courts and, second, to student play and intramurals. You don't find that pecking order in most athletic departments.

Since the project was mostly completed in 2014, the Michael and Anne Greenwood Tennis Center has already provided Oklahoma State's men's and women's tennis programs with an unbelievable home-field advantage and a major recruiting advantage as one of the best facilities of its kind in the nation. The center was launched with the indoor portion of the complex hosting the first varsity matches, and then competition continued later that year on the 12 outdoor courts, two rows of six with stands and ample, comfortable seating.

The 50,000-square-foot tennis center is located just north of Boone Pickens Stadium. The indoor facility houses six tennis courts, along with coaches' offices, locker rooms, and a sports-medicine hub complete with a hydrotherapy center. The indoor facilities seat at least 350 spectators.

Another exciting feature is the webcams installed on every court of the facility with fiber-optic cables that feed the pictures and sound to the west end zone and Orange Power Studios. The aforementioned exciting event from the 2015–16 sports calendar was the finals of the NCAA Women's Tennis Championships hosted at the University of Tulsa. Oklahoma State knocked off No. 5–ranked Georgia, No. 4–ranked Ohio State, and top-ranked California on its way to playing Stanford for the title and it came down to the last set, last point, as Stanford's Taylor Davidson finally outlasted the Cowgirls' Vladica Babic in No. 2 singles 3–6, 7–5, 7–5, and Stanford won 4–3.

"I'll remember this week for the rest of my life," Young said. "I'm not at all disappointed in the outcome; I'm just so proud of these kids because how could you not be? I'm proud of Oklahoma State, I'm proud of our fans, and I'm proud of tennis in the state of Oklahoma and what we could do," Young said.

I'm a firm believer that championships are won with blood, sweat, and tears, but finding the right people with the right blood is recruiting, and a spacious, gorgeous facility goes a long way in drawing in the right players with the right talents.

The center includes 12 lighted outdoor tennis courts in two sets of six courts. The courts are set up to allow fan viewing of each match being played in both the indoor and outdoor venues.

The facility has caught the attention of both NCAA and United States Tennis Association officials, and in 2016 it was honored as one of the outstanding tennis facilities in the country by the USTA. Oklahoma State has already hosted a slew of tournaments, both collegiately and even a professional satellite tour stop, which is unheard of for a community like Stillwater. More tournaments being hosted on the Oklahoma State campus are in the offing, and both Chris Young and athletic director Mike Holder are confident that the Greenwood Center will someday soon host the NCAA Tennis Championships.

"Through every stage of building the facility we have been able to talk to those selection committees, we ask them what things they are looking for to make sure we are including things that are going to be the most important when hosting championship events," Young said.

The Greenwoods took to the idea of being involved in contributing the lead gift in getting the facility done quickly. Upon hearing the tennis teams were third-call on the courts they practiced and played on and how many times the teams had to get in vans and go to Oklahoma City or Tulsa because they did not have a facility to practice or compete in, the couple was all in.

"Our OSU tennis coaches and players have had to practice and play in extreme heat, bitter cold, and gale-force winds," Michael Greenwood said. "And whenever rain is involved, the teams have to leave Stillwater and find an indoor alternative or cancel the scheduled event. This has provided an unfair playing field for our dedicated student-athletes for over 40 years, and we decided the time to correct this situation was long overdue."

There is no doubt that it puts Oklahoma State in a great position in tennis and it has done so in a hurry.

21 Chris' University Spirit

On any game day or night in Stillwater, you can always expect to run into a traffic jam and find it difficult to park in the bend around the University Fire Station known as Campus Corner. For one, Hideaway Pizza is on the corner across from the fire station, and word is, firefighters over the years have done a good job of keeping the popular pizza joint in business. But about 20 yards farther down from the pizza and fried mushrooms is Chris' University Spirit. Starting as a small college store that featured everything from Cowboys souvenirs to any item fit for Greek lettering from the fraternities and sororities on the Oklahoma State campus, the store has grown into 5,000 square feet and become the place to go for Oklahoma State fans for that special polo, T-shirt, sweatshirt, or hoodie to commemorate a huge Oklahoma State accomplishment or to support the team at the game.

The store owner, Chris Norris, grew up in a family that ran department stores in southeastern Oklahoma. He grew up playing sports and actually played defensive back at another school with a Cowboy mascot—the University of Wyoming—before transferring and finishing his education at Oklahoma State. Chris' University Spirit recently celebrated its 30th anniversary of being the place to go for Orange and Black.

"Honestly, the store started because I was so miserable at what I was doing," Norris said of the beginning of the store. "I was in corporate business and just didn't enjoy it at all. My family had been in the department store business, and I knew something about it and had great built-in advisors in my parents. This started like a little-bitty college department store, but we expanded I discovered I really liked selling the college stuff more. I learned quickly that an

Oklahoma State Cowboy sweatshirt was going to sell quicker than a bumper sticker with Greek letters on it."

Oklahoma State fans are lucky to have choices, and I'm not just pointing out the major sporting-goods stores and larger department stores found in Oklahoma City and Tulsa. In Stillwater you can find O-State gear at the End Zone over on Elm Street next to Eskimo Joes; Hall of Fame Booktrader, a bookstore over by Gallagher-Iba Arena and Boone Pickens Stadium on the northeast corner of campus; and, down on the Washington Street Strip, long-time mom-and-pop sporting goods store DuPree's Sporting Goods. All of those stores have their own niche, but it is Chris' that has grown the largest.

One of the largest buying groups for independent college stores is University Spirit of America, and Chris' now ranks third in square footage of that group of stores, trailing only University Spirit of Purdue and the Lodge, located right off campus at Mississippi State. Chris' University Spirit is one of the top 10 stores catering to college clothing and souvenirs in the United States.

If it features Oklahoma State, Pistol Pete, or the brand logo on it, you can find it in aisles of the wood-floored store on Campus Corner. They also have their own screen-printing shop, so immediately after major wins and championships Chris' staff, many of whom have been with him for much of the 30 years the store has been in business, can put out shirts to honor the accomplishment.

"I've had some great luck with that and some not-so-great luck," Norris said. "You know this year when Josh's team went to the College World Series, so many fans were thirsty for that and we had a shirt with a great design that one of our people came up with and I could have printed more and I should have. I think the all-time sales topper was the first time Eddie Sutton took the basketball team to the Final Four in 1995. Until that time, Oklahoma State had struggled some and it wasn't as hot a school, but when that happened I knew we were moving into something special with the future of Oklahoma State athletics."

Speaking of Coach Sutton, Chris said he would often open the store up on Christmas Eve, as Coach Sutton would routinely come down and do his holiday shopping in the empty store as Chris personally handled the legendary coach's checkout.

It was during the Sutton era that the athletic director Terry Don Phillips put a boost in business for Chris and all the others in the business of outfitting Oklahoma State fans. OSU had used black as a dominant color, or sometimes orange—for a decade they had used the burnt or "Texas" orange used by the Longhorns. You would find Oklahoma State merchandise and clothing in all of those colors, and then Phillips put out the decree for fans to wear orange—bright orange. Fans flocked to stock up on "America's brightest orange" and became the "sea of orange" at games. It was a big boost to clothing sales and still is.

On the week of the football opener in 2016, the store celebrated its 30th anniversary and among the attendees were head football coach Mike Gundy, head baseball coach Josh Holliday, associate athletic director Larry Reece, voice of the Cowboys Dave Hunziker, head soccer coach Colin Carmichael, and head women's basketball coach Jim Littel.

"I'll bet the store at Ohio State or Alabama can't draw that kind of lineup to their anniversary," said a proud Chris Norris.

"Hey, I know that Kristen [his wife] and I are in here all the time buying things for family and friends," Gundy said at the anniversary celebration. "I was in here the other day buying a Stillwater High School shirt because now I have a son playing quarterback there."

"My mom was always in here and we were always happy to go," Holliday said. "A big part of the wardrobe for any kid who had a dad coaching here would come from Chris.'"

"I know this: I walked into my office when I first took the job and there was a gift basket there from Chris' and that got me started," former head basketball coach Underwood said. "Our family didn't have a lot of orange in the closet coming from Stephen F. Austin and having been at Kansas State. A lot of purple, but Chris' gives your whole family a chance to do a color makeover."

It's a must-do for any Oklahoma State fan or even one considering a conversion to the orange: you have to make a stop at Chris' University Spirit.

22 Hideaway Pizza

Every college town needs a place where you can go get a slice—and not the kind with crusts that taste like the cardboard box it is placed in. The place in Stillwater is right across the street from Oklahoma State University and, actually, across the street from one of the original buildings on campus in Old Central. Now on any given night—weeknight or Saturday during football and Big 12 Conference basketball season—before and after the start time down the street at Boone Pickens Stadium or Gallagher Iba Arena you will see a line outside the door and tables will be tough to come by. The modern-day Hideaway features pizza as good as it has always been, but over the years they have developed some interesting pies. There are the Supreme and the Veggie Supreme, but then there is the Little Kahuna, named for Hideaway owner Richard Dermer. It has their original olive-oil-and-garlic sauce with mozzarella, provolone, chicken, bacon, sun-dried tomato, and feta cheese.

Another original Hideaway recipe is Pizza of the Gods, which has the olive-oil-and-garlic sauce with mozzarella, fresh tomato, artichoke hearts, mushrooms, and extra cheese. The Big Country is named after basketball seven-footer and Cowboy great Bryant

Reeves. It's a meaty delight and includes pepperoni, Italian sausage, Canadian bacon, applewood smoked bacon, and cheddar cheese.

The Hideaway is now known for its various salads ranging from the Just-A-Beginner, which is a dinner salad, to the Big Salad, which lives up to its name. There are sandwiches, including the Dagwood, Hideaway Submarine, and Meatball. They have great pasta, including a delicious sausage lasagna.

Besides the pizza, the most famous menu item at the Hideaway is the Famous Fried Mushrooms. They are breaded to order with a unique and flaky batter and come with the dressing of your choice. Most folks opt for the ranch or the parmesan peppercorn ranch.

The original Hideaway Pizza opened in Stillwater in 1957 on Campus Corner, but over on the southeastern portion of the block. It was a tiny little place with mural collages of pop culture icons on the walls. You could find pictures of Steve McQueen, Ali McGraw, Twiggy, Andy Warhol, and the Pope. The best thing was the pizza. The crust was somewhere between thick and medium, with an original sauce and very fresh ingredients, from the fabulous pepperoni, Canadian bacon, and smoked oysters to the vegetables, such as onions, spinach, broccoli, fresh tomatoes, and green peppers. No Oklahoma State student could really put his or her finger on it, but it was just different and better than any pizza he or she had ever had before.

Hideaway offered delivery, as well, and you could always spot a delivery in progress because of the fleet of Volkswagen Beetles that made them. You saw one of those cars in front of a friend's dorm or house, and you had to check and see if they had some pizza. It was too good not to.

In 1960, lifelong Stillwater residents and Oklahoma State students Richard and Marti Dermer, in partnership with Richard's brother-in-law, bought the Hideaway for $10,000. The original restaurant seated only 90 people, but in 1980 they moved to the current location, where a theatre and dance club had been located.

The new seating capacity was doubled in 2002 and is now at 348 seats.

Richard passed away in 2016, but he saw the restaurant become an Oklahoma landmark and celebrate its 50th anniversary in 2007. Going to the Hideaway is still a pizza delight, but also an experience, ranging from the tie-dyed T-shirts as souvenirs to the relaxed attitude of the wait staff. It's all easygoing and the pop culture collages from the late 50s and 60s still decorate the walls, along with some interesting artwork.

As for the pizza, there are now Hideaways in Oklahoma City, Edmond, Tulsa, Owasso, and Bartlesville. However, connoisseurs will tell you there is nothing like the pizza at the original in Stillwater. The secret, many of us believe, its the old ovens that go back to the original restaurant and were moved over to the new location. It's all in the ovens.

23 Eskimo Joe's

On any football or basketball game day, take a hike just a couple of blocks from Boone Pickens Stadium or Gallagher-Iba Arena south to Elm Street and you will find one of the most historic college hangouts in the nation. There are plenty of folks who may not know who Pistol Pete is, but they know Eskimo Joe and his husky sidekick, Buffy. The cartoon Eskimo with the toothy grin was at one time the object of the second-most-popular restaurant/ bar T-shirt franchise, behind Hard Rock Cafe. On any given day in Stillwater, there is likely a line outside the door or hungry fans of hamburgers and cheese fries waiting in Joe's Clothes store next door for a table.

Eskimo Joe's was the dream of a couple of childhood friends in Tulsa, Steve File and Stan Clark. In May of 1975, both were young and ready to conquer the world as entrepreneurs.

"I'm going to open a bar," proclaimed File.

"I know where there's a two-story building for rent. I'll go in as partners with you," responded Clark.

Later that day the building at 501 West Elm was rented. File came up with the name Eskimo Joe's. Bill Thompson, a freshman commercial art student, drew the famous Eskimo Joe's logo with a magic marker.

"I loved it the second I saw it," Clark said, not realizing what great marketing taste and business savvy he was actually showing at the time.

On July 21, 1975, Eskimo Joe's opened for business, serving up ice-cold beer, featuring local musicians for entertainment, and selling 72 first-edition Eskimo Joe's T-shirts at the bar. By the end of the first week, a lot of beer had been sold and so had every one of the T-shirts. Clark, who is now an inductee into the Oklahoma Hall of Fame and has won several business, restaurant, and service honors and awards, bought out his original partner in 1978, and with Clark's enthusiasm and penchant for pushing the smiles aspect of the business, Joe's grew. Known and marketed as Stillwater's jumpin' little juke joint, the bar adapted to the times and when the legal drinking age in Oklahoma was raised from 18 to 21, food service was added and Eskimo Joe's became a restaurant.

The combination of burgers (Joe's Special), chicken sandwiches (Fowl Things), and cheese fries (served plain and with bacon, sweet pepper bacon, chili, and peppers), along with the overwhelming popularity of the clothes (from T-shirts to sweatshirts and pants to socks) and the souvenir plastic cups, Eskimo Joe's was a one-stop restaurant equivalent of Disney World. The customer service and overwhelmingly friendly attitude were there to match.

President George H.W. Bush came in and spoke at the Oklahoma State University commencement in 1990—and as part of his speech, he endorsed the cheese fries at Eskimo Joe's. Now, with a presidential endorsement, Stan Clark had was an unstoppable force. Joe's popularity has led to two other restaurants—Mexico Joe's and Mojo's. Joe's clothes are sent all over the world and are printed in the Joe's Clothes screen-printing plant. They are sold retail over the internet, at the Joe's Clothes World Headquarters adjacent to Eskimo Joe's, and in Joe's Clothes stores in Oklahoma City and Tulsa.

The bar/restaurant, once fairly tiny in that two-story building, is still there, but that building has been expanded several times and now has a retractable-dome roof over part of it that can be opened on pleasant days and evenings. Right next to it on the second story is a permanent outdoor patio that overlooks Gallagher-Iba Arena and Boone Pickens Stadium to the north.

Stan welcomes many guests annually, and the Eskimo Joe's summer anniversary week is the second-most-well-attended event in Stillwater behind Cowboys football games. As many as 65,000 people have crammed Elm Street for the celebration, which went from a weekend to a full week just to space out the crowds. All Stan Clark asks is that patrons follow Joe's lead and "come with a smile."

24 Garth Brooks

There is a wide debate over when the loudest moment was in the history of Gallagher Hall and Gallagher-Iba Arena. Wrestling enthusiasts offer up several options, including the win by underdog Daryl Monasmith over Iowa State's All-American Frank Santana in the 1978 Big Eight Championship. There are those who were there that night who swear some of the lights in Gallagher Hall exploded because of the noise of the crowd. I know from personal experience; my eardrums were in danger during the Bedlam wrestling matches in 1981 and 1982. In 1981, Tommy Chesbro sent out a little-known 190-pounder, David Hille, to take on OU standout heavyweight and football offensive guard Steve "Dr. Death" Williams. The outmatched Hille bit Williams, who in turn started slugging Hille, and the double disqualification allowed Oklahoma State to escape with a dual win. The next year the place was just as noisy for nearly-400-pound Mitch Shelton as he was battling Dr. Death and somehow managed to fall on Williams. The Sooner wrestler landed on his back and was almost instantly pinned by the underdog, Shelton. Basketball fans will claim the roof almost came off the arena when seven-footer Bryant "Big Country" Reeves hit a half-court shot at the buzzer to force overtime against Missouri in a game the Cowboys dominated in the extra five minutes.

All good answers, but many swear the arena was loudest when Oklahoma State graduate-turned-country-music-superstar Garth Brooks came back for two nights on his award-winning Ropin' the Wind Tour and the second night, just after the first Gulf War, came out for the start of the show waving a big American flag. Garth has always known how to bring down the house, and he learned his early lessons as a showman at Oklahoma State University.

When I first agreed to write this book, I had discussions with the good decision makers at Triumph Books on the breakdown of the 100 chapters herein. When Garth Brooks came up in the conversation, there was a long pause. I knew that they were thinking, *What does Garth Brooks have to do with Oklahoma State sports?* He graduated with a degree in advertising in 1984 and then later earned his MBA, walking the stage in 2011 to accept his master's degree in the same building in which he had performed for sold-out crowds on several occasions. That still doesn't qualify him for inclusion in a book on Oklahoma State and subjects connected to Cowboys sports. In 2009, Garth Brooks shared the honor as Grand Marshal for the Oklahoma State University Homecoming with baseball star, and most recently, Chicago White Sox manager Robin Ventura and Heisman Trophy winner and College and Pro Football Hall of Fame member Barry Sanders. Okay, that's closer. Garth Brooks is in this book because the eventual bestselling solo artist in the United States—selling even more units than Elvis Presley and trailing only the Beatles—came to Oklahoma State on an athletic scholarship in track and field and threw the javelin for the Cowboys.

Born in Tulsa, Oklahoma, on February 7, 1962, and raised in Yukon, Oklahoma, Brooks learned to play the guitar and the banjo following his mother, who recorded as a country singer in the 1950s. Sports were Brooks' first love in high school as he played football and baseball, and ran track for the Yukon High School Millers. Brooks was at one time the starting quarterback at Yukon. At Oklahoma State, he roomed with his older brother Kelly, who was also on a track scholarship. Brooks went from running to throwing the javelin and even managed to medal once at the famous Kansas Relays, a major track-and-field event in the spring hosted by the University of Kansas.

As he progressed through college, the javelin and track became less important to Brooks and his music and performing in front of audiences became paramount. Brooks performed in a lot of little clubs and bars in the college town and became a regular on the corner of Washington Street and Fourth Street at Willie's Saloon. Brooks would perform country and then break into some James Taylor, Dan Fogelberg, and Billy Joel. Brooks got a job, and also made a connection that would help him with his early marketing of souvenirs and his lounging wardrobe for himself and his band on concert tours. Eddie Watkins and his wife, then the owners of DuPree's Sporting Goods right across the street from Willie's, became early fans of Garth's music and the relationship led Brooks to a job there while he was in school. To this day, it is not unusual when he is in Stillwater to see Garth Brooks stop at DuPree's.

Brooks also met his good friend, and later, longtime lead guitar player in his band, Ty England, in Stillwater. The two of them often performed on amateur nights and they would also take their act to the children's ward at Stillwater Medical Center. His senior year at Oklahoma State he took a job as a bouncer at Tumbleweeds Ballroom. It was there that he heard a lot of musical acts and also saw firsthand how the business worked at that level: a level he started at, but didn't stay around long before rising up the ladder of stardom.

Little did anybody know at the time that Brooks would go on to win multiple Grammy and American Music Awards—17 of the AMAs, including the Artist of the 90s Award. Brooks has released 21 records in all and has sold more than 160 million records as of 2016. He has toured the world multiple times and had a residency show, Garth at Wynn, that has packed it out performance after performance in Las Vegas. In 2012 he was inducted into the Country Music Hall of Fame.

Now married to fellow country superstar Trisha Yearwood, Brooks is a frequent visitor to Oklahoma State and comes back for football games and other events. His daughter was a goalie on the Oklahoma State soccer team for part of her time in school there.

His impact on his alma mater is evident at the start of the fourth quarter of every football game in Boone Pickens Stadium, as a kind of unofficial anthem, "Friends in Low Places," is played over the stadium speaker system and sung along with in every corner of the stadium—sometimes the visitors' sections as well.

It is certainly not as well known as his prowess on stage or in a recording studio in places like Nashville, but Garth Brooks is a part of the athletic and campus landscape and history at Oklahoma State. Drive through Stillwater today and just off campus you will find at 227 Duck Street a hand-painted sign over the porch of the house proclaiming that Garth Brooks lived there in 1987–88.

25 Walt Garrison

Walt Garrison will forever be known as the Cowboys' Cowboy. Many might think that is because Garrison went from a stellar career at Oklahoma State to a career as a fullback in the NFL with the Dallas Cowboys. The truth is Garrison, who grew up and was raised in a tight-knit but modest family in Lewisville, Texas, was and is a true Cowboy who to this day still competes as a team roper and has also competed in steer wrestling and roping events. His major at Oklahoma State was preveterinary medicine. If you want real proof of his Cowboy status, just like the school's mascot Pistol Pete, Garrison was a tobacco-chewing-and-spitting Cowboy who later became the chief spokesman for United States Tobacco and its Skoal brand. Garrison accepted, as his signing bonus with the Dallas Cowboys after the 1966 NFL Draft, a Pontiac Grand Prix convertible and an inline horse trailer. The trailer he kept; the convertible was traded in six months later for a pickup.

Garrison is a storyteller deluxe who also whittles, and that again puts him on par with his school's mascot.

"Everything that has happened to me started at Oklahoma State," Garrison has often said.

The Lewisville, Texas, high school linebacker was working Friday nights after high school games and Saturday nights at the American Nut Company at a factory that produced peanut butter for the military and those on welfare. He loaded gallon cans of peanut butter on boxcars. His boss at the factory, Zan Burroughs, told Garrison's father that Walt needed to go to school, that his brother was the lieutenant governor in New Mexico and that he would call him and have him get Walt a scholarship to New Mexico State, a land-grant school. The only problem was New Mexico State was on probation and didn't have a scholarship available, so Burroughs' brother called the governor of Oklahoma and had him pitch the name to Oklahoma State.

Cowboys great Neill Armstrong, from the 1945 football National Championship team, was dispatched to Lewisville to look Garrison over and recruit him. He did, Garrison made an official visit, and history was about to be made.

"I came up there on my visit and got my first introduction to pool halls and beer joints," Garrison said of his visit, noting that his host wasn't even at Oklahoma State as a player by the time Garrison arrived as a freshman. "I also saw all the horses, cattle barns, and fields, and I thought I really liked this place. The fact that Oklahoma State was kind of out in the middle of nowhere, that really appealed to me."

Garrison came in as a linebacker and started the two freshman games at the position, one against Arkansas and a win over the OU freshmen in Norman. The NFL Hall of Famer Sammy Baugh was the freshman coach.

Then, before Garrison's sophomore season, Phil Cutchin arrived as the new head coach coming from Alabama, and Texas A&M before that, where he had become a coaching disciple of Paul "Bear" Bryant's. Cutchin had every linebacker also play on offense, either as a fullback or a center. Considering Garrison was just under 6'0" and back then weighed around 185 pounds, he wasn't a center. He was going to be a survivor—as Garrison points out, that Cuchin team started with around 120 players and many were cut during the spring. Even after reloading with new bodies in the freshman class, Garrison said there were maybe about 30 players suiting up by the end of the season.

"I didn't like it," Garrison said of the fullback position. "I'd never carried the ball in my life. I will say this about Coach Cutchin in that he brought us closer together because there weren't many of us left."

He may not have liked it, but it liked him, and the tough-as-rawhide Garrison began running through Big Eight defenses. As a sophomore, he was the second leading rusher on the team with 387 yards. In his junior and senior seasons he flourished with 730 yards and 924 yards, respectively, the most yards a Cowboy had gained since Bob Fenimore rushed for 1,048 yards on the 1945 National Championship Oklahoma A&M squad. Garrison and his teammates made good on a promise they had pledged to each other as freshmen—to go back to Norman and beat Oklahoma, which they did that season 17–16.

Garrison earned All–Big Eight honors and represented Oklahoma State in the East-West Shrine Game, the Senior Bowl, the Coaches All-America Game, and the College All-Star Game in Chicago, where he and his teammates played against the World Champion Green Bay Packers.

Garrison went on to play nine seasons in the NFL. He played the 1971 NFL Championship Game with the San Francisco 49ers with a broken bone in his leg. He was as tough as a football player could be. In his NFL career he rushed for 3,886 yards and 30 touchdowns on 899 carries. He also caught 182 passes for 1,794 yards and 9 touchdowns.

"If it was third down, and you needed four yards, if you'd get the ball to Walt Garrison, he'd get you five," Garrison's teammate and famous humorist quarterback Don Meredith once said. "And if it was third down and you needed twenty yards, if you'd get the ball to Walt Garrison, by God, he'd get you five."

Garrison, who has often come back to Oklahoma State and still relishes his relationship with the school, is a member of the Oklahoma Sports Hall of Fame and is in the Oklahoma State

University Hall of Honor. He still wears a Cowboys hat and he still speaks and walks like a Cowboy.

26 Terry Miller

Four players in Oklahoma State history have factored into the Heisman balloting. Barry Sanders won the 1988 Heisman and his onetime teammate Thurman Thomas was seventh in the 1987 voting. Bob Fenimore was third in the 1945 Heisman voting. Terry Miller is the only runner-up for the Heisman from Oklahoma State, finishing second in the 1977 Heisman voting behind the great Earl Campbell of Texas.

Miller is one of the most versatile great running backs in Oklahoma State history. He came to Stillwater from Colorado Springs, Colorado, where he starred for Mitchell High School and was then recruited by most of the free world.

In 1974, Miller broke in as a backup for a very talented team that wound up beating Brigham Young in the Fiesta Bowl and finishing 7–5. The fleet, but also powerful, Miller had his break-out season in 1975 as he rushed for 1,026 yards, and he also lined up at fullback. Miller was fast enough to get outside and outrace opposing defenders for big yards, but he was as strong as a horse and could run inside the tackles. He was also such a good blocker he could lead smaller backs through a hole and allow them space to get going. Miller's longest run of his career was 81 yards and came in a win over North Texas in his sophomore season. That may have been Miller's longest run, but it would be far from his most memorable.

In 1976, Oklahoma State was battling with the Big Eight's behemoths, facing a very good Colorado team in Stillwater, and seemingly had the game won when the Buffs threw an interception in the end zone late. The Cowboys' Jerry Cramer picked off the pass, but instead of downing the ball in the end zone, he ran it out and fumbled, with Colorado recovering at the 2-yard line. The very next play, Colorado fumbled, and there are many, including the late Cowboys head coach Jim Stanley, who swear they recovered it. The Buffaloes went on to score and win the game. The next week, the 3–2 Cowboys were in Norman and Miller would have his most memorable run. Oklahoma was ranked No. 5 in the nation, and on a rainy and windy day at Owen Field, the Sooners won the toss and chose to take the wind. After the touchback, the Cowboys came out with a surprise, as Harold Bailey started at quarterback instead of Charlie Weatherbie. Bailey had Miller and Skip Taylor behind him in the backfield, and the Cowboys came out running the veer offense. After two straight gives to Taylor netted eight yards to set up a third-and-2 at the Oklahoma State 28-yard line, Bailey took the snap, faked to Taylor, and reversed out to the right, where he pitched outside to Miller, who juked the first defender, took advantage of a block on the cornerback, and then sped down the sideline for a 72-yard touchdown. Owen Field went silent, and Miller and the Cowboys weren't through, as they beat Oklahoma 31–24 on their way to a three-way tie for the Big Eight Championship.

Unfortunately, that loss to Colorado cost the Cowboys the tiebreaker and Colorado went to the Orange Bowl. OSU went to Florida and beat BYU 49–21 in the Tangerine Bowl.

Miller capped his Oklahoma State career with 1,680 yards and 14 touchdowns in the 1977 season, when he finished second to Campbell for the Heisman. Miller became one of just three players in Big Eight history to finish with more than 4,000 yards in a career, as Thurman Thomas had 5,001 a decade later and Nebraska

Heisman Trophy winner Mike Rozier had 4,780. Miller finished with 871 carries for 4,754 yards and 49 touchdowns.

Terry Miller was a first-round pick of the Buffalo Bills in the NFL Draft. He had some success in Buffalo, but his best year as a pro football player came when he was reunited with his college coach Jim Stanley in the USFL. The two helped guide the Michigan Panthers to that league's championship.

Terry Miller's No. 43 is retired, along with Bob Fenimore's No. 55, Barry Sanders' No. 21, and Thurman Thomas' No. 34.

27 Thurman Thomas

There probably shouldn't be a debate, but there often is, about which running back from the Pat Jones era was better—Thurman Thomas or Barry Sanders. Part of that debate stems from the head coach, who had two of the most gifted runners in the history of football. Both players are in the College Football Hall of Fame and both players are in Canton, Ohio, in the Pro Football Hall of Fame. There are many differences between the two, but each has a legacy in his football career the other would love to have, and you might find it surprising which one would covet the other more.

Barry Sanders won the Heisman Trophy. Thurman Thomas came close, as he finished seventh in the voting in 1987 behind the winner, Tim Brown of Notre Dame. Thomas had his best season as a collegian with 1,767 yards and 21 touchdowns, averaging 6.2 yards per carry. Thomas burst on the scene with a 1,650-yard season and 15 touchdowns in 1985, and finished tied for 10th in the Heisman voting, as Bo Jackson of Auburn won the award that season.

In the NFL, Thurman Thomas built a fabulous career with the Buffalo Bills, a long way from Stillwater and a long way from his childhood home in Missouri City, Texas. During his Hall of Fame career, Thomas was a force in the Bills' four straight Super Bowl seasons from 1991 to 1994 and Super Bowl XXV, a loss to the New York Giants. Super Bowl XXVI was a 37–24 loss to the Washington Redskins. The final two, Super Bowl XXVII and XXVIII, were back-to-back losses to the Dallas Cowboys. However, what an impressive feat it was to have made it to four straight Super Bowls; Barry Sanders has said that he was envious that his former Oklahoma State teammate had the chance.

"I would have loved to have played in one," Sanders once said. "I know Thurman's teams in Buffalo were saddled with losing those four Super Bowls, but what an achievement to have made it to the Super Bowl four straight seasons. That is something no other team has done and may ever do."

Sanders did look up to Thomas; when he arrived in Stillwater, Thomas had not only earned the respect of his teammates but was a huge favorite of head coach Pat Jones. Jones loved Thomas' work ethic and his practice habits of going full speed all the time.

"Barry had a lot of talent, but so did Thurman, and Thurman Thomas was a guy that gave so much effort in practice," Jones once said. "Thurman was going to go full speed every rep, every play. Barry didn't just love practice, but he showed over the years he really didn't need a lot of practice."

Jones is proud to be the only coach who has had two backs who made the college and pro halls of fame to overlap at one school.

Thomas is still the all-time leading rusher at Oklahoma State, and he burst on the scene as a freshman with 843 yards and seven touchdowns in Pat Jones' first season as head coach. Oklahoma State had Charles Crawford at the start of the season, but by the end of the year, the freshman was carrying the load and rushed for 155 yards on 32 carries, including the first touchdowns of the game, in the 21–14 Gator Bowl win over South Carolina. Thomas' second season was his breakout campaign, with 1,650 yards rushing, and the Cowboys lost to Florida State in a consecutive trip to the Gator Bowl.

Thomas struggled in 1986 after an off-field knee injury suffered playing pickup basketball held him up at the start of the season. Thomas finished with 741 yards and the Cowboys wound up 6–5 on the season. In 1987, not only was Thomas back at full speed, but Sanders was his backup and an All-American kick returner. Thomas finished off his career with 989 carries for 5,001 yards and 47 touchdowns. The Cowboys wound up 10–2 and beat West Virginia and star quarterback Major Harris in the Sun Bowl. The cardiac Cowboys came from behind for the 35–33 win in El Paso. Little did Thomas know on that afternoon that running in the snow would become a frequent occurrence for him in the NFL up in Buffalo.

28 Super Bowl Cowboys

Every college football program likes to brag about all the players it has put into the National Football League, as it is a source of pride and a valuable recruiting tool. Like most Power Five schools, Oklahoma State has produced a lot of NFL talent, including two of the greatest running backs to ever step into an NFL stadium, but oddly enough, one of those running back greats, a Pro Football Hall of Famer, doesn't make our list in this chapter. Oklahoma State has to be up there in number of players who have gone on to play in Super Bowl games. The Cowboys have seen 26 of their players go on to play in a total of 39 Super Bowl games.

Former Oklahoma State and Pittsburgh Steelers center Jon Kolb holds the Oklahoma State record for wins and Super Bowl rings with four, having won blocking for quarterback Terry Bradshaw, running back Franco Harris, and wide receiver Lynn Swann, playing opposite the Steel Curtain and company in Super Bowls IX, X, XIII, and XIV.

Running-back great and Pro Football Hall of Famer Thurman Thomas ties Kolb in appearances, but has no wins, as Thomas played with head coach Marv Levy, quarterback Jim Kelly, wide receiver Andre Reed, and defensive lineman Bruce Smith on the Buffalo Bills in Super Bowls XXV, XXVI, XXVII, and XXVIII.

Like Thomas, Marlow, Oklahoma's pride and joy, Terry Brown, knew the taste of more than one Super Bowl loss, as he was part of the back-to-back losses by the Minnesota Vikings in Super Bowls VIII and IX. Brown scored a touchdown on a blocked punt recovery in the end zone against the Pittsburgh Steelers in Super Bowl IX, and to this day is the only native Oklahoman to score a touchdown in a Super Bowl.

It was special to see native Oklahomans, such as tight end Billy Bajema from Moore, win with the Baltimore Ravens in 2013, Tulsa Washington product R. W. McQuarters with the New York Giants in 2008, and Oklahoma City John Marshall High School alumnus Antonio "Scobey" Smith with the Denver Broncos in 2016.

Cowboy through and through with Oklahoma State and Dallas, fullback Walt Garrison lost in Super Bowl V against the Colts but rebounded with his Dallas Cowboys for a win in Super Bowl VI against Miami.

One of the most famous Oklahoma State walk-ons, linebacker Matt Monger, was on the losing Buffalo Bills team in Super Bowl XXV, and all-time-great defensive end Leslie O'Neal was in Super Bowl XXIX with San Diego but lost to the San Francisco 49ers.

Other multiple Super Bowl participants not already mentioned include linebacker Jack Golden, who lost with the New

York Giants in Super Bowl XXXV and won in Super Bowl XXXVII with the Tampa Bay Buccaneers under Jon Gruden; Sherman, Texas, native and Oklahoma State tight end and offensive tackle Charlie Johnson, who won with Peyton Manning and the Indianapolis Colts in Super Bowl XLI and lost in Super Bowl XLIV; infamous defensive end Dexter Manley, who won with the Washington Redskins in Super Bowls XVII and XXI, but lost in Super Bowl XVIII; and offensive tackle Russell Okung, who won his first Super Bowl in Seattle in Super Bowl XLVIII and then lost in Super Bowl XLIX after that last-second interception by the New England Patriots.

You'll find Oklahoma State Cowboys involved all in and around Super Bowl history.

29 Walk-Ons

Under Mike Gundy, the walk-on program at Oklahoma State has taken off. It has also produced some celebrated players: current Dallas Cowboys kicker Dan Bailey and Houston Texans backup quarterback Brandon Weeden were both walk-ons. Weeden came directly out of professional baseball at the age of 25, and Bailey was a transfer from Arkansas, where he was also a walk-on.

Gundy started the walk-on tradition in his program with his very first class, which included a four-year starting deep snapper in Zach Allen, a holder and backup punter in Cole Reynolds, and a fullback and special-teams dynamo in Bryant Ward.

"Walk-ons have been very special to my staff and me," Gundy has said. "You know those guys want to play and you know they are going to work hard and do things the right way. They have been some of our very best players."

Over the years, Gundy has had more than 100 walk-ons, and many of them have played significant roles. Others have primarily helped on scout or demonstration teams in practice, but those are vital roles for the team.

Other prominent walk-ons include Cowboys backs Jeremy Seaton and Blake Jarwin, quarterback Taylor Cornelius, wide receiver Colton Chelf, wide receiver Kameron Doolittle, and defensive tackle Shane Jarka.

Gundy is so enthused about walk-ons and appreciates their contributions that he has a walk-on Hall of Fame designed on one of the walls outside the locker room and weight room on the field level of the west end zone. There are a dozen or so walk-ons honored there. On that list are Allen, Bailey, Ward, Weeden, and linebacker Seb Clements.

Most recently, starting center Brad Lundblade, who turned down some 11 Division I and FCS offers to walk-on at Oklahoma State, and senior captain for special teams in 2016 Keegan Metcalf have been highlighted in the walk-on program.

Prior to Gundy, there were many successful walk-ons, but the program wasn't as touted as it has become under Gundy. Two of the most prominent walk-ons in school history came during the Jimmy Johnson and Pat Jones days with linebackers Rick "Cowboy" Antle and Matt Monger, two Oklahoma kids who just wanted to play football and were willing to do it without a scholarship back in the days where most walk-ons truly were used as cannon fodder. Antle, from Foyil, Oklahoma, became a two-time All–Big Eight honoree, and Monger, from Tulsa, became an All–Big Eight player and had a lengthy career in the NFL with the Buffalo Bills and the New York Jets.

Jarwin caught a touchdown pass in his final game as a Cowboy in the 2016 Alamo Bowl win over No. 10 Colorado, and he is projected to have a productive career in the NFL. Walk-ons playing in the NFL have proved to be more than just a dream under Mike Gundy at Oklahoma State.

30 Rob Glass: Gundy's Most Important Hire

You've heard of the strong and silent type; count Rob Glass among them. Glass was not the first staffer whom new head football coach Mike Gundy hired in 2005 when he took over the program, but Glass was one of the first, and to this day he is the member of the staff who Gundy says has had the most impact in making Oklahoma State football the top-25 program it is now.

"He is the most important person in this program," Gundy said. "He is around the players more than any other coach because they lift and work out year round. This sport is now virtually 365 days a year and the one coach that is involved all the time is Rob [Glass] and his staff. I remember when we first got started and the change he made in a lot of our early players physically, and it still happens. I truly hope now that we are bringing him better, bigger, and stronger athletes to begin with. He coaches these kids almost every day and almost all year."

It is only right that Glass is there alongside Gundy building the program, because it was Gundy who had an influence in getting Glass to football and eventually strength and conditioning. Glass—who is the son Ike Glass, of one of Oklahoma's great education supporters and longtime State Regent for Higher Education—knew he wanted to coach when he made the way from high school to Oklahoma State. A baseball student-athlete, Glass became a student-coach for longtime and very successful Cowboys baseball coach Gary Ward.

Ward had recruited Midwest City standout two-sport athlete Gundy along with football head coach Pat Jones. Gundy was a quarterback in football and shortstop in baseball, and he crossed over and introduced Glass to the Cowboys' then young recruiting coordinator, Gordon Whitener, who eventually helped Glass move from baseball to a graduate assistant role in football.

Oklahoma State went through strength coaches fairly quickly in those days, and after John Stuckey left and Jerry Schmidt came in for about a year and left, Glass was the logical choice, as he had been assisting with the strength program. Pat Jones really liked Glass, and he asked Glass to take over the off-season conditioning program and supervise workouts in what was then a spartan and unimpressive Oklahoma State weight room. Right after that, seeing some of the players whom Glass had motivated and improved like Barry Sanders prior to his Heisman year, Jones made him the program's head strength coach.

Back then, the weight room was on the second floor, above the football locker room and where the wrestling room is now located. The equipment was a mixture of economic purchases and some homemade pieces.

"I remember that I would have to make some bars or get them made with welders around town," Glass said. "Also, I would paint the weight plates just so we looked professional up there."

Glass left Oklahoma State and went to Florida, working his way up the staff there for football coaches Steve Spurrier and Ron Zook. He finished as the coordinator for strength and conditioning with the Gators. In May of 2002 at Florida, he was named by the National Conference of College Strength and Conditioning Coaches Association as a Master Strength and Conditioning Coach, the highest honor that can be achieved in the business.

When Gundy was hired in 2005, he quickly went after Glass to bring him home to Stillwater, and, with the Mike Holder–managed and Boone Pickens–funded facilities improvements, Glass was able to move into a 20,000-square-foot weight room in the west end zone adjacent to the team's locker room. The facility is one of the best, if not the best, in Division I college football and it is exactly the way Glass wants it, down to a refueling and nutrition station built in one corner—one of the few in college and pro sports financed by Gatorade.

Glass is a well-educated individual about his business and motivation, which is a major factor in his world. He is also a man of few words outside his strength-and-conditioning domain, but he knows how to say thank you.

"We've really benefitted from a lot of gracious people, and [Pickens is] not the only one," Glass said. "There's a lot of people out there who have kind of helped the program, kind of trigger this movement."

31 Uniforms

When Oklahoma State University opened its doors as Oklahoma A&M College with Old Central, the school colors of Orange and Black, and the mascot Tigers, the school earned the nickname—and, by the way, wore it proudly—of "Princeton on the Plains." More recently, in college football Oklahoma State has been referred to as the Oregon of the Midwest. The reason is the Cowboys uniforms. Mike Gundy realized that, as coach, he needed to do anything and everything within reason to capture the attention of recruits. Nothing gets 16-, 17-, and 18-year-old football players going like bright and shiny helmets, jerseys, and pants. Oregon, with the power of Nike cofounder and then-chairman Phil Knight, was breaking out new uniforms nearly every week—not just using the Green and Gold, but about four different shades of green, highlighter yellow, gray, silver, black, and all kinds of combinations. Gundy could see Oklahoma State doing something similar, so on November 19, 2009, Oklahoma State broke out all-black uniforms. Oklahoma State had worn black uniforms before, but it had been a long time. The Cowboys beat Colorado that night in a come-from-behind game without their starting quarterback 31–28.

It was just the start, as gray soon made it into the color scheme in the pants and jerseys. The helmets began to get mixed in with black, orange, and a carbon fiber being used. Soon, people were recognizing that Oklahoma State had an almost unlimited mix-and-match uniform combination going that had fans and even players guessing what they would wear on Saturdays. It became a big deal to be the first to guess correctly or to see what the Cowboys were wearing that day.

The most exciting developments in uniforms came in the helmets during the 2014 and 2015 season. The program debuted an oversized Pistol Pete head logo on a chrome orange helmet, and then later on a white helmet, the head gears being dubbed the "orange Pete" and the "ice Pete."

The Oklahoma State equipment staff is headed by Matt "Chief" Davis as coordinator, Justin Williams as his assistant, and Len Magby as the third in charge, who also works with Josh Holliday's baseball program.

In 2014, Davis and Williams began working with Nike on the planning for a brand-new set of uniforms to debut in the 2016 season. Both Oklahoma State graduates, the OSU equipment duo wanted the new uniforms to represent the school and its history.

Nike's creative team seemed eager to go to work on the project and create highly customized jerseys that were unique to Oklahoma

State. The most interesting part of it, and somewhat reminiscent of the design on Florida State's uniforms, was the trim on the end of the sleeves and the neck of the jersey. The design pays homage to Frank Eaton, the original Pistol Pete; the Paddle People; OSU football's retired jersey numbers; and the train scene from the movie *Tombstone*. Much of the trim art on the neck and sleeves is presented using a custom paisley print inspired by a cowboy's bandana.

The numbers on the jersey, the word *Cowboys* on the leg, and the retired jersey numbers—21 for Barry Sanders, 34 for Thurman Thomas, 43 for Terry Miller, and 55 for Bob Fenimore—are all presented using a new barbed-wire typeface that serves as a reminder of the cowboys who drove their herds across Oklahoma along the great Chisholm Trail.

The word *Cowboys* appears on both legs of the pants and is stitched on using a reflective fabric that provides an ultramodern edge to the uniforms. The same reflective fabric is used behind the numbers on the black jerseys.

A new logo was inspired combining the brand OSU logo with a marshal's badge representing the badge worn by Eaton, who became a U.S. deputy marshal after single-handedly going out and getting justice by tracking down his father's murderers. The badge logo is on all jerseys at the base of the neck. The badge logo is also used on helmets, both white and black, and the entire design of the bandana and all the logos with it have been used on a helmet wrap that has created one of the most distinctive helmets in all of college football.

With all the creativity, Davis, Williams, and the designers at Nike stayed true to the primary colors of Oklahoma State. The jerseys come in orange, black, and white, and the pants come in orange, black, white, and gray. The orange jerseys feature white numbers outlined in black, and the black jerseys have orange numbers with a reflective gray background. New in the uniforms was the design of the road white jerseys, as they now have black numbers outlined in orange. All pants are adorned with the Shadow Pete logo and the word *Cowboys* on the side of the leg.

"It was great because Nike gave us a blank canvas and with Justin and I there was 35 years of pride in Oklahoma State football between us, we went here and this is our school, so we wanted to design something that was unique but special and meant something to all Oklahoma State people," Davis said of the process. "It was great because Frank Eaton [Pistol Pete] is one of the most unique mascots in all of college football, all of college athletics because he is a real person—not many schools can say that. We didn't want cookie-cutter uniforms, we wanted something unique for our players to be proud to wear and proud to win games in."

Oklahoma State's uniforms are built using Nike Mach Speed technology, which makes them 25 percent lighter than the uniforms worn by the Cowboys from 2011 to '15. The uniforms include the latest in lightweight-fabric innovation built for maximum speed, ventilation, and comfort.

Nike's Mach Speed Football uniform fabric construction features an articulated fit to match the athlete's motion of play. Ultimately this allows the athletes to move with the uniform fabrics, rather than against them.

32 America's Greatest Homecoming Celebration

The city of Stillwater and the campus at Oklahoma State are never more populated or crowded as they are on one weekend in the fall, usually in late October or early November, when close to 100,000 people descend on the area for America's Greatest Homecoming Celebration. Homecoming has long been a tradition on college campuses to bring alums back for a weekend to reminisce and relive their college days with friends and family by attending festivities and an athletic event. At Oklahoma State University, the weekend starts on Friday evening with Walkaround, easily one of the most popular events at Homecoming, as that is the night when the most people are on campus and on the streets.

Homecoming has been around at OSU since 1920, when the Oklahoma State Alumni Association began presenting the weekend. Current Alumni Association President and CEO Chris Batchelder is as enthusiastic as anyone who has ever been in charge at the Alumni Association when it comes to Homecoming. He has worked hard to help endow the event, and a major donation from Ron and Cindy Ward of El Reno, Oklahoma, went a long way in establishing that.

Preparation for the event begins with the start of classes in the fall, as fraternities and sororities, as well as other groups living on campus, plot their house decorations, floats, signs, and volunteers to represent them in all of the weeklong activities for Homecoming. By far the most work is put into the house decs (short for decorations) and parade floats. Hours upon hours of work are put into the engineering and mechanics, along with the skeleton of a frame for the projects. Computer design is used as well to come up with the proper design to bring the decorations and floats to life, primarily using chicken wire and tissue paper, along with some other materials. Think the Tournament of Roses Parade at the Rose Bowl, which uses all floral products in the design. At Oklahoma State, chicken wire and colorful tissue paper are in ample supply, and students put countless hours into the finished product. That is why so many people come from so far away to check out the elaborate designs. Several fraternities known for their skills, Alpha Gamma Rho, Sigma Nu, and Farmhouse, have become popular pair-ups with the sororities on campus.

Early in the week, the water in the Edmon Low Library fountain on campus is turned orange. There are sidewalk paintings and street paintings done on Hester Street through the heart of campus. The Walkaround, which shuts down the streets in and around campus on Friday night, is a highlight always followed by a pep rally and the Homecoming and Hoops event in Gallagher-Iba Arena, which really serves as Oklahoma State's answer to "Midnight Madness" events often put on by basketball programs at other schools. Oklahoma State football head coach Mike Gundy and some of his players often make an appearance at Homecoming and Hoops to rally the fans for the game the next day.

The parade, which goes right down Main Street from downtown Stillwater to Hall of Fame Avenue near campus, is held on Saturday morning. Then the Cowboys prepare to add another win to the record later in the day or evening with the Homecoming Game.

Homecoming has survived and thrived over the years, even through tragedy. The most recent came in 2015, when Adacia Chambers, a resident of Stillwater, drove her vehicle straight through a barricade at an intersection at the end of the parade into a crowd of approximately 50 people. Four people were killed and another 46 were injured, including former Oklahoma State fullback Robert Turner. One of the deceased was a two-year-old child. Chambers was charged with four counts of second-degree murder and 46 counts of felony assault and was sentenced to life in prison with the possibility of parole in January 2017.

In 1977, three members of the Alpha Gamma Rho fraternity were moving metal for part of the Homecoming float and the poles made contact with a high-voltage power line, electrocuting all three of the young men: Randal Logan, Merle George, and Kevin Wilson.

Both tragedies are remembered annually at Homecoming.

Even in the face of those tragedies, Oklahoma State University and its alumni, faculty, administration, and supporters recognize the contributions to charity and to the goodwill and spirit of the school, town, and state that the tradition of having America's Greatest Homecoming has had over the years. There are many homecoming celebrations in America, but none have the popularity and impact of Oklahoma State. It is a must-see for any college sports aficionado. Oklahoma State's record in homecoming games is 52–36–7.

33 Tailgating

Oklahoma began as a state with the Land Run of 1889 and now, more than 100 years later, that historic event is reenacted six to seven times each fall on the Oklahoma State campus. The official tailgating rules on the Oklahoma State campus allow for groups looking for tailgating space on campus, outside of the Oklahoma State Posse (official booster organization) parking lots, to stake out their spot Thursday evenings after 5:00 PM. There is a long list of rules attached to the tailgating scene at Oklahoma State, because it has become one of the most successful schools in all of college football when it comes to tailgating. Most tailgates at Oklahoma State have tents and comfortable lounging areas. Most of them come equipped with generators for power. It takes power to light up those big-screen televisions and the accompanying satellite receivers. Cowboys tailgaters love their team, but they have to keep up with the rest of the Big 12 and the country on football Saturdays.

Entertainment is a small part of it, because when it comes to food, Oklahoma State fans know how to come through like a linebacker shooting the A gap on a blitz. You can find plenty of grills with hamburger patties as big as a dinner plate, jumbo hot dogs, and every sausage known to man, including some really delicious bratwurst. Remember that Oklahoma State is an agriculture school and has a lot of graduates who go into the cattle breeding and raising business. You can find some really big pieces of meat on those custom-made smokers parked at tailgates all over campus.

"We like to do big cuts of beef, and we've even done a whole hog several times," said Steven Beam, long considered one of the champion tailgaters in the Oklahoma State community. Going

Oklahoma State enjoys one of the proudest college football tailgating traditions in the nation.

back a few years, there used to be an annual tailgating contest, and I even had the opportunity to judge a couple of times. It was impossible to really come up with a winner. There are too many talented tailgaters. Brisket, prime rib, and all kinds of cuts of steak, including the newly defined "Vegas strip," which was identified on the Oklahoma State campus at the University Meat Lab, can be found on grills and in smokers on game day. The aroma across campus is intoxicating for any barbeque aficionado.

Just as alluring are the various sides that accompany those smoked or grilled delights. I've seen award-winning deviled eggs and every version of coleslaw and potato salad imaginable. It gets even better when you start checking all the cookie, cupcake, cheesecake, pie, and homemade ice cream recipes.

You will find plenty of SEC and Big 10 schools that will brag about being the best tailgating school in the country. I've seen Michigan, Michigan State, and Wisconsin in person. I can tell you some of the best fried and smoked quail I've ever had was in Starkville, Mississippi, before an MSU game. LSU is really good, and you can't beat the Cajun cuisine, but when it comes to beef and pork and homemade delights you can't beat Oklahoma State. There are three kings of tailgating in the Big 12 and I will give Kansas State and Iowa State their due, as they are both really strong, but Oklahoma State is tough to beat. If you are a football fan who loves to eat, then you need to make it to Stillwater, because the best part of tailgating in Cowboy country is they all love to share on game day.

34 The Walk

During Les Miles' second season as head football coach at Oklahoma State he was looking for a way fans could celebrate the Cowboys team and allow the players to see their fans up close and realize the kind of spirit that they were bringing into Boone Pickens Stadium on game days. At Ole Miss, the players walk through the Grove on the way to Vaught-Hemmingway Stadium, and LSU players walk through their tailgating fans on the way to the tunnel outside Tiger Stadium that leads them to the home locker room. It didn't take a lot of thought to come up with The Walk.

Oklahoma State football teams had for several years begun staying on campus at the Atherton Hotel in the Student Union. It was easy, as they could eat on campus and the Student Union had ample meeting rooms, including a ballroom big enough for the Cowboys to use for walkthrough activities on game days. On days when the weather was excellent, the team could go outside on the library lawn and do their walkthroughs. The east side of the Student Union was on Hester Street and a straight shot for about two good-sized blocks from Boone Pickens Stadium, with easy access to the stadium and then on into the west end zone and the home locker room. Most of the area between the Student Union and the stadium was prime tailgating space and Posse (donor) parking lots. Once Miles decided that the team would take the walk down Hester, it wasn't hard to get the Oklahoma State fans to gather on either side of the street two hours before game time and create a great atmosphere for the team to soak up on their way to play.

"It's a special part of being a football player at Oklahoma State," 2016 graduate and Cowboys back Zac Veatch said. "We are able to share that time with our fans and look our fans in the eye on the way to the stadium."

"It was always special to me because right before we played, we had the opportunity to see the people we represented and that we were playing for," former Oklahoma State quarterback Zac Robinson said.

Most of the time, no matter whether it is the heat of September, the chill of November, or anytime in between—including rain— you will find the fans lined up on both sides of Hester as many as eight deep to wish the Cowboys well before the game.

It was a no brainer for Mike Gundy to keep The Walk going when he took over as head coach after Miles left for LSU in 2005. Gundy had been the offensive coordinator and assistant head coach under Miles, and he saw the impact that it had on the players.

The typical scenario is that the players meet in the Student Union Little Theater before leaving, and that is when Gundy gives the team a short address. After he finishes, Gundy leads the players out of the Student Union and they fall in behind the Oklahoma State Marching Band, OSU Spirit Squads, and Pistol Pete. Once the team arrives at the stadium, the players have developed a routine of going in the stadium and down to the field, where they circle up around the OSU logo at midfield and hear from several players and then have a team prayer before going to the home locker room and getting dressed for the game.

That ritual has been in place for some 14 years now, and it is hard to imagine that it will ever change. If you wonder how events become tradition, then The Walk is an excellent example.

35 Pistol Pete

As popular Oklahoma State football equipment coordinator Matt "Chief" Davis likes to say, our mascot is different because our mascot was a living, breathing, and honorable human being. Most sports fans know Oklahoma State's Pistol Pete as the cartoon character used for souvenirs. The big hat, big mustache, six-shooters, chaps, and boots all make the image powerful in representing the old-West Cowboy. But Davis is right, and a real picture of Frank Boardman Eaton will make anyone realize why students back around 1923 who saw Eaton marching in the Stillwater Armistice Day Parade asked him if he would volunteer to be the likeness for a new mascot at Oklahoma A&M.

Eaton ate it up and was more than willing to be around when asked. He loved to talk to students and folks in Stillwater about the old West and tell his stories about his days as a U.S. deputy marshal and a local sheriff.

Eaton is real, all right; he was born in 1860 in Hartford, Connecticut, but then at the age of eight moved to Twin Mounds, Kansas. His father, a vigilante, was shot and killed by six former confederates who had ridden with Quantrill's Raiders and later were part of a group called the Regulators. The legend has it that a family friend, Mose Beaman, started teaching young Frank to shoot in the hopes, even the challenge, that he would someday avenge his father's murder. At 15, Eaton was ready to strike out on his own, as he had become quite the gun handler and a master of trick shooting as well. He traveled into Indian Territory (Oklahoma) and went to Fort Gibson to further master gun handling. The commanding officer of the fort, Colonel Copinger, saw Eaton outshoot his soldiers and his best sharpshooters. He gave the young man a marksmanship badge and a nickname: "Pistol Pete." Eaton was too young for the Army, but at 17 he was made a deputy U.S. Marshal for Judge Isaac C. Parker, known as the "hanging judge" in the Indian Territory.

By the year 1887, Eaton had shot and killed five of the Regulators who had murdered his father, and the sixth had been shot by someone else after an argument over a poker game. The legend of Pistol Pete was on.

Oklahoma A&M first had the tiger as a mascot, as the school was nicknamed the Princeton of the Plains. Princeton had the Orange and Black and the tiger as a mascot. The students were never sold on the tiger, and that is why the group of students asked Eaton for permission to create a likeness in his image. Aggies and Aggie Cowboys were used but never made official. Oklahoma State entered the Big Eight Conference after residing in the Southwest Conference and later the Missouri Valley, but it was about the time that the school changed to Oklahoma State and entered the Big Eight that the Cowboys name and Pistol Pete mascot were adopted. The character was officially licensed in 1984.

The likeness is obvious when you compare the character and the real Frank Eaton, but Oklahoma State has had problems keeping the image of Pistol Pete to itself. Wyoming used the same character with the colors brown and gold and called him "Cowboy Joe." New Mexico State also used a similar likeness. Oklahoma State has since worked out agreements with both schools.

"Chief" was right in another way about Oklahoma State having a real person as a mascot. The Pistol Pete head, which was originally kind of homemade but then later constructed by artists at Walt Disney Inc., is worn by students at Oklahoma State as the mascot. Each year some 15 to 20 students audition and interview for the honor of becoming Pistol Pete. A panel of former Pistol Petes makes the decision and selects two new Pistol Petes. The selection is a huge honor, as the duo represents the university in many

The two students selected to portray Pistol Pete in an academic year can appear in their official capacity at up to 650 events a year.

highly attended and important events, including athletic events and Oklahoma State official events. The two students playing the role of Pistol Pete will often appear at some 650 events a year, including all of the OSU events, community parades and celebrations, corporate events, weddings, and birthday parties.

Pistol Pete always has been and continues to remain in high demand.

36 Paddle People

It is two hours before kickoff at Boone Pickens Stadium in Stillwater, and outside the stadium, The Walk is coming to a close as the football team has traveled from the Atherton Hotel and the Student Union, the team's home the night before football games, down Hester Street to the stadium. Behind the team are the Oklahoma State band, cheerleaders, and Pistol Pete. However, already inside the stadium are one of the newest and most popular student groups on campus, which forms and executes one of the newest traditions in college football. The nearly 300 members of the OSU Paddle People have already picked up their instruments and have started to warm up and play.

Paddle People? What the heck? Paddling has been removed from schools across America, and I'm not sure it was ever a form of punishment on college campuses unless you're talking fraternities, such as the scene from the classic movie *Animal House*. At Oklahoma State, the Paddle People first formed in the late 1990s. Oklahoma State football wasn't very good, as it was working to come back from one of the most devastating NCAA probations in the organization's history. A group of students, eight to ten in the beginning, started sneaking paddles into football games and then using them as noisemakers by pounding them on the padding that surrounds the inner walls of what was then Lewis Field. The stadium is very tight, so the walls are equipped with thick padding to form some semblance of protection for players crashing out of bounds. The padding also serves as a loud, smacking sounding board when slapped hard by the wood paddles.

Each season the group gained steam and members. In 2002, the Paddle People applied for and were granted official recognition as a student organization. They had grown to some 20 members. Over the next several seasons, the group grew to 35–40 members, and by 2008, the group was up to 60 members.

The instruments were becoming more sophisticated and more valuable; the group started fashioning paddles for each senior member of the football squad, and they were presented to the players at the Senior Banquet. I remember that the first group of players to receive paddles thought it was one of the coolest gifts they were given to commemorate their time as a player at Oklahoma State.

The group kept growing, and now before games in Boone Pickens Stadium there are more than 300 Paddle People there to make themselves heard. The Big 12 athletic directors, at the request of some of the league's coaches, tried to quiet the pounding noise in September of 2012, passing a rule outlawing artificial noise-makers at conference sporting events. The Paddle People weren't silenced, but they were contained. Now they were governed by the same rules that apply to bands and the public-address system with music and sound effects for the now-universally used jumbo video boards. They must stop when the offensive team comes to the line of scrimmage and is ready to snap the ball. Honestly, it hasn't really changed their impact.

"It is hard to think there in Stillwater," former Texas head coach Mack Brown once said. "Those dang paddles are pounding against the wall and you really don't realize just how much noise they make until you've been in there hearing that constantly for four quarters. It will drive you crazy."

Former Iowa State head coach Paul Rhoads once pounded his fist against the lectern at a news conference earlier in the week leading up to a road game against the Cowboys to try and simulate for the media a small sample of what he and his team deal with on the sidelines in Stillwater.

The paddles themselves have become more scientific and efficient in production and, like the uniforms the Cowboys wear, more colorful. In the beginning the one inch (thick) by four inch (width) by 16 inch (length) paddles were sanded and then painted orange with the word *Pokes* burned into the paddles and the letters painted black. Now, the paddle people have color combinations like the original, but also black paddles with orange letters, and white paddles with either orange or black letters.

Now, anytime an Oklahoma State home game is televised by the networks, there is almost always a camera assigned to the west end zone and the group that wraps all the way around the end zone and then down the north sideline toward the visitor's bench area. The Paddle People take up that entire area, most dressed up in crazy garb and all swinging in coordinated cadence the paddle design of the day. They have so quickly become ingrained into the Oklahoma State culture that crossed paddles appear on the trim of the new football uniforms and a swanky new wrap design on one of the selection of Cowboys game-day helmets. The Paddle People have branched out too. You will find them at Oklahoma State men's and women's basketball games, soccer matches, and wrestling matches.

37 Bullet

Another great symbol of the Western heritage that Oklahoma State rightfully embraces is the horse, and fans in Boone Pickens Stadium love to see Bullet and the Spirit Rider come cruising onto the turf either during pregame activities or after the Cowboys score a touchdown. A well-trained and selectively chosen American Quarter Horse, Bullet is trained to be used to crowds and comfortable with artificial turf. Still, football game officials are warned before every Oklahoma State game to be attentive after scoring plays in the west end zone to look out for Bullet.

The Spirit Rider program was launched in 1984, and for the few years that Oklahoma State used a live horse with rider on the field, the selected horsemen used their own horses to perform. In 1988, an American Quarter Horse named Stars Parr Money was donated to the school and the athletic department to take over as Bullet. Now a universal symbol for Oklahoma State almost to the level of Pistol Pete, Bullet is seen not only at football games but also at parades and events all over the state of Oklahoma. Bullet is a popular guest at schools, especially elementary schools, rodeos, horse shows, and other events, including the opening ceremonies each year of the Oklahoma State Special Olympic Games on the Oklahoma State University campus. Oddly enough, the longtime honorary coach of Oklahoma Special Olympics, who always takes a picture alongside Bullet and other dignitaries, is former Oklahoma Sooners football coach Barry Switzer. More than a few Cowboys fans have joked that Bullet needs to take that moment to take care of some necessary business.

The tradition of Bullet and the Spirit Rider goes back to Eddy Finley, who wanted to promote the school the "cowboy way"—on horseback. Since his inspiration, the school has received plenty of support for the Spirit Rider and Bullet program. The school has a custom horse trailer and special custom-tooled saddle, along with uniform dress for the Spirit Rider and assistants. There is a competition that is now held for the Spirit Rider position each year. Bullet has his own stall, complete with feed tub and tack box, underneath the west end zone at Boone Pickens Stadium, and, using the underground garage and ramp that takes you there from the parking lot immediately west of the stadium, it is easy to get Bullet to his game-day home safely.

In honor of the Spirit Rider and the tradition of Bullet, there is a bronze statue sculpted by Jim Hamilton that now sits in an open space where you can see it driving down Hall of Fame Avenue, between the practice home of the Cowboys in the Sherman Smith Training Center and the Wes Watkins Center for International Trade and Development.

38 Dave Hunziker and "Pistols Firing"

It was about 10 minutes to air time for the start of the pregame show on the Cowboy Radio Network. Oklahoma State was on the road to open the 2001 season, the first game for Les Miles as head football coach at OSU, and it was an overcast and steamy afternoon on September 1 in Hattiesburg, Mississippi. M.M. Roberts Stadium on the Southern Miss campus was two thirds full, and up in the press box it was the debut for another new member of the Oklahoma State family. Missouri graduate and longtime Big Eight and Big 12 enthusiast Dave Hunziker was about to call his first game as the new voice of the Cowboys. Before he could launch into his description of the game that day, he had to pay tribute to the man who had the mic before him and lost his life in his role as Oklahoma State's radio storyteller.

Hunziker picked up the phone and called Janice Teegins, the widow of former Oklahoma State play-by-play broadcaster and very popular statewide television sports anchor Bill Teegins. Teegins and nine others lost their lives when a small plane they were traveling on coming back from an OSU basketball game at Colorado crashed in the Flatirons outside of Denver. On one end of the phone, Hunziker calmly introduced himself to Janice and then proceeded to tell her how honored he was to be doing the same job her husband had cherished and excelled in doing. He told Janice he hoped that he could do a good job and do it well enough to honor his predecessor. A producer and engineer on the broadcast at the time and a close friend of Teegins', Joe Riddle, had given Hunziker the number, but it was Hunziker who chose that huge moment in his broadcast career to call Janice and try to comfort her before launching into a job he knew he was born to do.

It was as a youngster growing up in Kahoka, Missouri, near the Missouri–Iowa border that Hunziker discovered what it was he was meant to do: call sporting events on the radio. By the time he was 10 years old, he was doing public addresses at area softball tournaments, and he later landed a job at the local radio station and began calling games. He went on to the University of Missouri and was quickly spotted by the campus radio station and Mizzou baseball play-by-play voice Tex Little as Hunziker worked covering Missouri football and basketball games. He was also doing radio work on some of the other Mizzou sports. After graduating from Missouri, he went on to work at Columbia College doing publicity and broadcast work. Then he became the play-by-play voice at Radford University for eight years, and from there was the voice of the Hilltoppers at Western Kentucky for one year. It was while at WKU that Hunziker was contacted by then–Oklahoma State athletic director Terry Don Phillips off a strong recommendation from former University of Missouri associate athletic director and current athletic director at the University of Oklahoma Joe Castiglione. Oklahoma State needed a new radio voice, and it needed to be a special person.

It was a terribly sad situation that Hunziker was walking into in Stillwater. He was the right guy for it. Hunziker is unusual in the broadcasting business in that he doesn't carry around an inflated ego and is truly one of the nicest people you will ever meet. He thinks of his broadcast partners and the people around him before he thinks of himself. That goes not just every once in a while, but all the time. It was evident that first game when he prepared to call the Cowboys' opener at Southern Miss.

"It was difficult and certainly a hard time to come in, but it was a lot more difficult for the people directly affected," Hunziker said. "For those 18 months afterward, there was a lot of suffering still going on, and that was hard to watch."

Despite what was going on around him, Hunziker and his family—wife, Mary Beth, and daughters Mara and Grace—were welcomed warmly into the Oklahoma State and Stillwater communities. It is one of the reasons that Hunziker has ended up staying for what is now his sixteenth season as the Voice of the Cowboys.

"The way I looked at it was just to go and do my job to the best of my ability," Hunziker said. "The people [of Stillwater] were unbelievably kind to me and nice to me."

Hunziker left a permanent mark very early. He was known for some of his own colorful phrases, such as "Holy guacamole" or "Goodnight, Vienna." Some he would make up and some had ties to his youth in Kahoka. The phrase he launched at his first home football game in Stillwater celebrating an Oklahoma State touchdown had staying power. It has become one of the staple phrases used in Oklahoma State sports. It is so ingrained that it is on the trim of the football uniforms designed especially for Oklahoma

State by equipment coordinator Matt "Chief" Davis, his assistant Justin Williams, and the folks at Nike. It is on T-shirts, sweatshirts, coffee mugs, key chains, and anything else you can think of in souvenirs supporting a college team. Little did Hunziker or anyone else know what he started with that first cry of "pistols firing."

"Shocked. It was something I had given a little bit of thought to beforehand, but the first game [in 2001], I didn't say it," Hunziker explained to Bill Haisten of the *Tulsa World*. "It was the second week against Louisiana Tech.

"I thought, 'Well, let's just throw it out there and see if it sticks. See what happens. I'll find out if people don't like it, and I won't say it anymore.' Well, I guess they did. The biggest thing that had to do with that was, we were winning. Not so much [the 2001 season as a whole], but the last two games—Baylor and at OU—and just winning after that. The only reason it really took off was because this program was enjoying success at an unprecedented level."

Okay, maybe a little overly humble there, but I explained that Hunziker is not an ego guy. In Stillwater and at Oklahoma State he is one of us, and that makes him even more endeared. "Pistols firing" is something almost every Cowboys fan has said, but shaking hands with the man who first said it is something all Cowboys fans should do. You won't have to ask twice, because the Voice of the Cowboys is always there with a handshake and a good word. He's been that way from his very first day calling the Cowboys' games.

39 Cowboys "Ride with the Voice" Larry Reece

Oklahoma State has something that I'm pretty sure no other Division I school in the country has. It's very visible, but even more so, audible. The voice of Gallagher-Iba Arena and Boone Pickens Stadium, Larry Reece, is a senior associate athletic director for development in the OSU athletic department. He was behind the public-address microphone long before he became a primary fund-raiser for Cowboys and Cowgirls athletics. In fact, there have been past employers, including those in the athletic department, who questioned whether Reece could be effective at his "day job." Actually, it's his night and weekend job welcoming fans to "the rowdiest arena in the country" or asking if they are ready for "Big 12 Conference football" that has made him effective going to Cowboys fans and asking them to help pay the bills.

"Being the public-address announcer at Oklahoma State, and this is such a family, I think people feel like they know me even if they really don't," Reece said of his voice and presence over the speakers. "It helps me get into doors because I do the games. I think being the public-address announcer helps me with everything else I've done, including raising money for Oklahoma State athletics. You know we've raised over $400 million here in the last decade for facilities alone. It's amazing how far we've come."

Those facility projects include the two venues through which Reece bounces his deep, golden tones—Gallagher-Iba Arena and Boone Pickens Stadium. When he first started, it was Gallagher Hall and smaller, rusted-out Lewis Field. Reece came to Stillwater after attending NEO A&M Junior College in Miami, Oklahoma, for two years. It was just down the street from his house. Growing up in a smaller town afforded Reece the opportunity to follow in his dad's footsteps. He had always felt it was neat that his father announced on the PA at his Little League games, so when it was obvious Reece wasn't going Division I or pro as an athlete and he wanted to stay involved, he thought he could use his booming voice. He did some high school games around Miami, and then at Oklahoma State he enrolled in the class of his dreams, the Sports Practicum, a lab taught by Dr. Ed Paulin in the School of Journalism and Broadcasting.

"What a great opportunity because you got to call the game like you were on the radio, you have your demo tape, and everybody would critique, including Dr. Paulin," Reece explained. "You've got a little regionalism there, you sound like a hick, like you're from Miami, Oklahoma. You need to fix that.' All those little things you need to learn when you are going into broadcasting, but I still didn't think Dr. Paulin knew my name."

When the sports information director at Oklahoma State at the time, Steve Buzzard, approached Paulin as to whether he had a student he would recommend for public address at the women's basketball games, Dr. Paulin told Buzzard about Reece. Reece met with Buzzard and they soon found out they were near neighbors. Buzzard was from Quapaw, Oklahoma, just about 10 miles from Miami. Buzzard didn't even try him out; he just asked if he wanted the job.

"I went skipping out of there thinking I work for Oklahoma State athletics," Reece said of that meeting.

It wasn't long before Reece and his enthusiasm had the crowds excited at the Cowgirls' basketball games. Buzzard wanted to infuse the same enthusiasm into men's basketball and football games, so he got Reece the opportunity.

"There were a couple of faculty members that had been doing those sports for over 20 years; one had been doing football for 22 years and the other had been doing basketball for 25 years, so it was kind of a political deal to want this student to do it," Reece said about Buzzard's sticking his neck on the line. Even the president of the university at the time, Dr. John R. Campbell, inquired as to whether Buzzard was sure of his promotion. He was, and the enthusiasm has been building ever since. Reece is now in his 27th year as the public-address announcer for the major sports at Oklahoma State.

It was threatened and interrupted in the winter of 2015, when Reece discovered a swollen lymph node and finally got it checked out. It was cancer, but it was early and he had a good chance. The most assured form of treatment was an extended stay in Houston at M.D. Anderson. Reece arranged for fill-in public-address announcers, and he and his wife, Jimi, went to Houston. He did not go alone.

"I always knew I was part of the OSU family, but never was it more evident than when I had my cancer scare," Reece said of the group he called his "Prayer Posse." "When Tim 'the Mailman' Bays came up with the #Iridewiththevoice, first, I teared up, but then that became the way that I communicated and everybody else communicated with me while I was in Houston getting treatment. There wasn't hardly an hour that went by that I didn't get a message on Facebook or on Twitter or a letter in the mail or a care package. It got me through the toughest period in my life."

There were T-shirts sold that read I RIDE WITH THE VOICE. The proceeds went to Coaches vs. Cancer and now that Reece is completely cancer-free, he is active with that group, still bellowing his names and descriptions of athletic heroics, but also working hard to help fight the disease that threatened all the fun he's been having since being given a microphone.

40 1945 National Football Champions

It is most unusual to find out about a championship 71 years after it was earned, but that is exactly what happened at Oklahoma State on October 13, 2016. That is when the American Football Coaches Association informed Oklahoma State University and the football world that they were awarding the Coaches' Trophy representative of the College Football National Championship, which is currently won each year by the College Football Playoff champion ranked first in the Amway/USA Today Coaches Poll, to the Oklahoma A&M Aggies of 1945. The Aggies of two-time All-American and College Football Hall of Fame member Bob Fenimore and fellow two-time All-American Neill Armstrong, along with a group of 45 other tough guys and an outstanding head coach in Jim Lookabaugh, are the only unbeaten and untied team in school history. They navigated a schedule of five road games, a neutral-site contest, and only two home games on the way to a crushing 33–13 victory over St. Mary's in the Sugar Bowl.

Army won the 1945 National Championship according to the Associated Press poll, and the AFCA poll wouldn't begin until 1950. But the AFCA, which started in 1922, set out to go back and retroactively award national championships from the organization from 1922 to 1949, catching up with the year that the Coaches Poll was started. The organization established a Blue Ribbon Commission of coaches, including AFCA executive director emeritus Grant Teaff, a Hall of Fame coach from Baylor, former Georgia coach Vince Dooley, and several other outstanding former college football coaches. The committee used what video it could find and all kinds of data that was submitted by schools being considered and was available through the sources that have documented and kept alive the history of college football.

"After gathering all the pertinent information and doing our due diligence, it is the pleasure of our Blue Ribbon Commission of coaches to officially recognize Oklahoma State's 1945 championship season with the AFCA Coaches' Trophy," said AFCA executive director Todd Berry.

The Oklahoma State squad of 1945 (then referred to as Oklahoma A&M) had an average margin of victory of 23.2 points and still holds numerous school records, including fewest points allowed, fewest average points allowed, fewest first downs allowed, fewest rushing yards allowed, and fewest yards allowed per game. The 1945 squad also ranks in the top 10 in several more offensive and defensive categories, all of which is remarkable considering that season was played 70 years ago.

Coached by Jim Lookabaugh, the 1945 Oklahoma A&M roster included seven veterans of World War II. Bob Fenimore was a consensus All-American who led the nation in both rushing and total offense and also ranked in the top 15 nationally in rushing yards, passing yards, scoring, and punting. Teammate Neill Armstrong also earned All-America status that year from the Associated Press. In addition to Fenimore and Armstrong, J.C. Colhouer earned All–Missouri Valley Conference recognition.

The season started in Fayetteville, Arkansas, with a 19–14 win over a stingy Razorbacks squad, the only game in September. The Cowboys traveled to Denver to beat the University of Denver 31–7, met up with SMU in Oklahoma City at Taft Stadium for a 26–12 win, and then closed out October with back-to-back road trips, first to Salt Lake City to beat Utah 46–6 and then to Fort Worth and Amon Carter Stadium to beat the Horned Frogs 25–12.

On November 10, the Cowboys played their first home game at Lewis Field, beating a very talented Tulsa team in the Homecoming game 12–6. Texas Tech came in and was pounded in Stillwater 46–6 and the Cowboys closed out the regular season in Norman, beating the Sooners 47–0.

The Aggies capped their championship season with a resounding 33–13 win over St. Mary's in the Sugar Bowl, played in the old Tulane Stadium.

"We may have been the best team in the country that year," Armstrong said in December 2015. "We had a couple of All-Americans and a group of veterans who kept us in check. In practice, we scrimmaged every day. As hard as those scrimmages were, it's a wonder that we had anything left for the games, but those scrimmages toughened us and made us better. We had a lot of older guys who had fought in the war and understood that you don't win anything unless you do it as a team."

With the addition of the 1945 football national championship came several firsts. Oklahoma State (Oklahoma A&M) became the first college or university in Oklahoma to win a football national championship. The University of Oklahoma was awarded its first football national championship in 1950. Oklahoma State also became the only school to win a football and a basketball national championship in the same school year, as Henry Iba's Aggie basketball team won the title that winter in Madison Square Garden in New York City, beating NYC 49–45 for the NCAA Championship. Oklahoma A&M also won the NCAA wrestling national championship that same year.

In case you wonder how much a modern fan base will pay attention to a championship that is awarded retroactively 71 years later, the very next home game you could see T-shirts and sweatshirts honoring the 1945 accomplishment. The athletic department brought back one of the three remaining players still alive from the team to be honored at the game. A ceremony is planned for sometime in the 2017 season and signage outside and inside Boone Pickens Stadium will properly pay homage to the title and the men who earned it, even though many were gone before it happened.

41 1945 Cotton Bowl and 1946 Sugar Bowl

The first two bowl games in Oklahoma State—then Oklahoma A&M—history appear together because the overall impact of the games was an eventual national championship that would be awarded some 70 years after the unbeaten season was completed. The 1944 Oklahoma A&M team was unbeaten against college competition and the only loss was a 15–0 dropped game to the Norman Naval Air Station team, often referred to as the NAS Zoomers. The Aggies took care of the other team from Norman, OU, 28–6 at Taft Stadium in Oklahoma City. The 7–0 (against college competition) A&M team went to the Cotton Bowl and defeated TCU 34–0. After another eight straight wins in 1945, the Aggies were in New Orleans and beating West Coast power St. Mary's 33–13.

"I really believe that coming out of that Cotton Bowl in January of 1945 we felt different about our team," the star halfback of that team, Bob Fenimore, expressed. "We had a real confidence from that game that helped propel us into the 1945 season."

It was the war years, and like the loss to the Norman Naval Air Station, which also occurred in 1943 (20–0), many of the good young athletes were in the military. That is why Army (West Point) was such a dominant team in that era and won the Associated Press national championships in 1944 and 1945.

In 1944, Oklahoma A&M ran through West Texas A&M, Arkansas, Texas Tech, Denver, Tulsa, Texas (a huge win at 13–8), and Oklahoma before going to Dallas for the Cotton Bowl. Back then the now-popular bowl gifts that get publicized each season were being given. Each Oklahoma A&M player got a new suit of clothes and a Cotton Bowl watch. In the game, the first bowl appearance ever for the school, Fenimore was every bit of the All-American that he was billed to be. The "Blond Bomber" from Woodward, Oklahoma, scored on runs of one and eight yards and completed 6-of-13 passing for 136 yards. Fullback Jim Spavital ran for 120 yards and scored on a 52-yard run.

The Aggies defense limited TCU to five first downs, 74 yards rushing, and 31 yards passing. Later, in 2007, Fenimore would be inducted into the Cotton Bowl Hall of Fame.

"That we beat 'em as bad as we did, that surprised me," offensive and defensive end Neill Armstrong said. "We usually had pretty good games against TCU." Actually, the season before, TCU had beaten Oklahoma A&M 25–0 in Oklahoma City.

The Cotton Bowl held a dance later on that day after the game, and both teams were invited and attended.

"I think a bunch of girls [at the dance] chased us down," Armstrong said to the *Oklahoman* of the social event after the game.

The confidence built by the Cotton Bowl win showed up in the Aggies' next season as they opened with a 19–14 win at Arkansas. The team then won against Denver, SMU in Oklahoma City, at Utah, and at TCU before playing its first home game against a Tulsa team that may have been the best regular season opponent. The Aggies beat Tulsa for homecoming 12–6. Tulsa would finish 8–3 and ranked 17th in the final Associated Press poll. It lost to Georgia 20–6 in the now defunct Oil Bowl.

The Aggies finished with a 47–0 rout of Oklahoma, and it was on to New Orleans to play a St. Mary's team that had beaten California 20–13 and powerhouse Southern California 26–0. That team featured All-American and eventual College Hall of Fame member Herman Wedemeyer.

It was Wedemeyer who opened the scoring in front of the crowd of nearly 70,000 people in the old Sugar Bowl Stadium as he connected with Dennis O'Connor for a 29-yard touchdown, but Fenimore countered in the showdown of All-Americans with a 29-yard touchdown pass to Cecil Hankins. Fenimore would add two touchdowns runs, both of one yard. Jim Reynolds also scored a one-yard touchdown run and Reynolds threw a 20-yard touchdown pass to Joe Thomas.

The Aggies won 33–13 in New Orleans and outgained the Gaels 329 yards to 238 yards. It concluded a golden era of Oklahoma A&M football, as in 1946 the Aggies slid to 3–7–1.

42 Jim Lookabaugh

Did you know that Oklahoma State has two coaches in the College Football Hall of Fame? Jimmy Johnson did so much more after he left Oklahoma State (29–25–3), winning a national championship at Miami, Florida, in 1987. Then Johnson took over as the head coach of the Dallas Cowboys for his ultrarich teammate from the University of Arkansas, Jerry Jones. In Dallas, Johnson built the Dallas Cowboys through some creative trading and management of the salary cap and took the franchise to Super Bowls XXVII and XXVIII in 1992 and 1993. The other College Hall of Famer is Lynn "Pappy" Waldorf, who was inducted in 1966. In his time at Oklahoma A&M, Waldorf led the Aggies to four conference championships and was unbeaten (3–0–2) in his meetings with rival Oklahoma. Waldorf would later propel his legacy to Hall of Fame heights as the head coach at Cal with multiple Rose Bowl appearances.

Now, Jim Lookabaugh is not in the Hall of Fame—at least not the College Football Hall of Fame—but he has something that neither Johnson nor Waldorf does: he won a National Championship in Stillwater. In October 2016, the American Football Coaches Association bestowed a title on Lookabaugh's unbeaten and very deserving 1945 squad.

Lookabaugh coached at Oklahoma A&M for 11 years. He posted a winning record in six of those seasons, and in his final campaign was an even .500 at 4–4–2. Lookabaugh finished his Oklahoma State coaching career with a 58–41–6 record.

The highlight was that 9–0 season that ended with the 33–13 win in New Orleans in the Sugar Bowl over St. Mary's. Lookabaugh would have enjoyed lifting up that crystal football, just like we've seen with Nick Saban and Urban Meyer. What's even more amazing is Lookabaugh's best team were road warriors, as they won five true road games, two neutral-site games, and only two home games.

Born in Watonga, Lookabaugh was an outstanding high school athlete. He attended Oklahoma A&M and lettered in football, baseball, and basketball. He is one of just three coaches in football at Oklahoma State to be an alumnus of the school; later coaches Floyd Gass and current coach Mike Gundy also graduated from OSU.

Lookabaugh was a multiple state-championship coach in the prep ranks before taking over in Stillwater, as he won two high school state titles at Jet. He then coached for nine years at Oklahoma City's Capitol Hill High School and led the Redskins to legendary state championships in 1932–34 and '37. In 1933, Capitol Hill played Harrison Tech from Chicago, Illinois, for a national championship game and won 55–12.

Lookabaugh then moved on to Oklahoma A&M and went 5–4–1 and 3–1 in the Missouri Valley in his first season. Jim Lookabaugh was a coach. He had high standards, and it was those standards and not being able to meet them in his last several seasons that caused him to resign before the end of the 1949 season. Lookabaugh did not coach again and died in 1982 at the age of 79. Some 34 years after he was gone came his greatest accomplishment: a national championship.

43 Neill Armstrong

One of the most distinctive aspects of Oklahoma State as a university and its athletics is that it runs in the family. There have been so many families involved in the program, like the Woods family with brothers Rashaun, D'Juan, and Donovan all playing football at Oklahoma State, or the Smith family in wrestling with Lee Roy, John, and Pat all taking the mat for the Cowboys. One family in football skipped a generation, but was still really fun to see. Neill Armstrong is one of the all-time greats at Oklahoma State. A two-time All-American on the school's lone football national championship team in 1945, Armstrong was best friends with Bob Fenimore, the other smiling face shaking hands before kickoffs back in the mid-40s.

However, rather than recount his glory days and tell you all about how Fenimore, himself, and the other talented Aggies in that day rolled over opponents like TCU, Oklahoma, Tulsa, Texas Tech, SMU, Arkansas, and Utah; he'd rather tell you how far his grandson could punt and kick the ball. Armstrong's daughter had a son named Cole Farden, and once he committed to Oklahoma State and came to kick for the Cowboys, it was hard to keep Armstrong from showing up at every game.

The man who was once head coach of the Chicago Bears from 1978 to '81 was a top assistant at Minnesota during the Vikings' glory years under legendary head coach Bud Grant, and then went on to be a mainstay in the Dallas Cowboys organization, got chills down his spine when watching his grandson suit up and punt and kick for the Orange and Black. Armstrong; his wife, Jane; and Cole's mom, Gail, would line up on Hester Street before games for The Walk and then sit together to watch Cole play. In this case, grandson idolized granddad, but granddad relished in the success of grandson.

"I think Cole has done very well," Armstrong said back in 2003. "He just keeps getting a little better every game, every year. Now, I'm getting a kick out of watching OSU do as well as they're doing," Armstrong said. "They've been doing a great job there."

Armstrong passed away in August 2016, so he got to see his grandson follow in his footsteps: Farden currently coaches high school football in Texas. He also has lots of times to remember watching and talking football with his granddad. You could have learned a lot from Armstrong, as he had seen football through from the single-platoon days to the modern era of the National Football League.

Nicknamed "Felix the Cat" at Oklahoma A&M, the native of Tishomingo lettered four years for the Aggies and played end on both offense and defense, leading the nation in receiving, while his best friend, Fenimore, led the nation in total offense. His senior season, he caught 32 passes for 479 yards, which back then were monster numbers, as the forward pass was still in its infancy. Armstrong was also a ferocious tackler on defense—it was at defensive end he was named an All-American by the Associated Press in 1945 and the Central Press in 1946. Armstrong also kicked off for the Aggies. He was just as responsible for the great success in 1944 and 1945 as Fenimore.

Armstrong was a first-round choice by the Philadelphia Eagles in the 1947 NFL Draft, where he played from 1947 to '51. He also played briefly in the Canadian Football League, and that was where his path crossed with Bud Grant.

After playing he came home and joined the coaching staff at Oklahoma State, where he was an assistant under Cliff Speegle from 1955 to '61.

Armstrong moved on to become an assistant with the Houston Oilers of the AFL in 1962–63 and then went back to Canada and the Edmonton Eskimos from 1964 to '69, again linking up with Grant.

Armstrong coached on Grant's Minnesota Vikings staffs, from 1970 to '77, during which the Vikings made four Super Bowls. Unfortunately, like the Buffalo Bills would later, Minnesota lost all four—to the Chiefs, Steelers, Dolphins, and Raiders. Still, the success earned Armstrong the head coaching job with the Bears, and in his four years there, Chicago went 30–35.

He finished his coaching career on Tom Landry's Dallas Cowboys staff, then stayed over as a consultant when Jimmy Johnson became the Cowboys' coach.

The Cowboys' Super Bowl victory in 1996 marked Armstrong's last game in football. He spent his retirement enjoying his family, golfing, and watching football—primarily watching the grandson who followed him to Stillwater.

44 Pappy Waldorf

Oklahoma State's first inductee into the College Football Hall of Fame spent only five seasons on campus as head coach at Oklahoma A&M. Lynn "Pappy" Waldorf certainly proved his coaching prowess, as the Aggies had only moderate success at best, but under Waldorf they won four conference championships and their record against archrival Oklahoma was 3–0–2. Waldorf is the only coach in school history to go unbeaten against the Sooners.

Waldorf's first team in Stillwater went 4–3–2, but that was after a 1–7 season the year before. That 1929 group of Aggies tied Oklahoma 7–7 after the 1928 team had lost at home to OU 46–0. The 1930 team won a share of the Missouri Valley Championship with a 7–2–1 record. It ran the table in the final four games, beating Arkansas, Tulsa, Oklahoma, and Creighton, and allowed only seven points in the four games combined.

In 1931, the Aggies posted an 8–2–1 record with a tough trip to Minnesota to face a powerhouse team, and the Gophers beat the Aggies 20–0, by far the worst setback of that season and one of the few under Waldorf. In 1932 it was a Missouri Valley Championship and a 9–1–2 record with wins over OU, Drake, Arizona, and UTEP.

Waldorf's last season was a 6–2–1 campaign with a season-ending win over Oklahoma.

Waldorf was a three-time All-American tackle at Syracuse and graduated with degrees in sociology and psychology. His coaching philosophy combined toughness and lots of drills with humor, and it worked. He started out as athletic director and head coach at Oklahoma City University, a Methodist Church–affiliated school of which Waldorf was a member. After a year as an assistant at Kansas, he made his way to Oklahoma A&M. To further help out during the Great Depression, Waldorf was also athletic director at Oklahoma A&M. He went on to Kansas State, and, yes, he led K-State to its first Big Six Championship in his only year at the school. The bulk of his coaching was done at Northwestern and then at Cal, where Waldorf won 67 games. The year he came in he had followed a two-win season with a 9–1 season, the only loss being to powerhouse Southern Cal. His first team even beat Stanford in the Big Game, the first win by Cal over their rival in six years.

Waldorf would go on to lead the Bears to three Rose Bowl appearances.

45 1958 Bluegrass Bowl

You hate to refer to any bowl game as a novelty, but the 1958 Bluegrass Bowl was just that as Oklahoma State played in the game's first and only edition. The game was played in Louisville, Kentucky. It was the first time the school had been in a bowl game under the new school designation of Oklahoma State University. Only 7,000 fans turned out to Cardinal Stadium, the ballpark of the minor league baseball club in Louisville. The teams played on a field that was part baseball diamond, and both teams played on the frozen playing surface in tennis shoes.

Perhaps the biggest novelty of the game was the national telecast on ABC, which featured established play-by-play announcer Harry Wisner and a budding brash young broadcaster in Howard Cosell as the color commentator.

Oklahoma State won the game 15–6 over Florida State in the first meeting between the two schools. Duane Wood accounted for almost all of the Cowboys' points, as he scored in the second quarter on a 17-yard run. Jim Wood, an All-American defensive end, kicked the extra point. Duane Wood scored again on a one-yard run in the third quarter. The Cowboys defense was led by Jim Wood, Vandiver Childs, Jim Howard, Sonny Keys, John Calvin, and Fred Latham.

That Cowboys team finished 8–3 and ranked No. 19 in the nation, but it would be a long drought for Oklahoma State as far as bowls were concerned. Of course, the drought for the Bluegrass Bowl lasted forever after that frigid day in Louisville.

46 1974 Fiesta Bowl

Oklahoma State broke its 16-year bowl drought with a trip to Arizona and the Fiesta Bowl. I'm sure there have been bowl games that sold more souvenirs, but it seemed like everybody in Stillwater had purchased a shirt with the brightly colored sun logo of the relatively young Arizona bowl game. It was interesting that the Fiesta Bowl would grow to elite New Year's status and would, 37 years in the future, be the site of one of the school's greatest football wins.

The 1974 Oklahoma State team scored its greatest win in the second week of the season when it traveled to Little Rock and beat No. 10 Arkansas 26–7. The next week the Cowboys debuted in the Associated Press Top 20 at No. 12, only to lose to Baylor 31–14.

The Cowboys kind of plodded to a 6–5 record but, thanks largely to that win over Arkansas, got the invitation to play Brigham Young in the Fiesta Bowl.

By today's standards of wide-open, up-tempo, spread offenses, this Fiesta Bowl would have been used to cure insomnia. BYU kicked two first-quarter field goals, and just before halftime, halfback Kenny Walker took a pitch 12 yards for a touchdown and the Cowboys led 7–6.

Abby Daigle kicked a 42-yard field goal in the third quarter and then, in the fourth, on easily the most exciting play of the game, halfback Leonard Thompson, who would go on to a long career in the NFL with Detroit, took a pitch, stopped, and hit Gerald Bain for a 40-yard touchdown.

Oklahoma State beat the BYU Cougars 16–6, primarily on the strength of defensive linemen Phillip Dokes and James "Duck" White. Dokes decked BYU quarterback Gary Shiede late in the first quarter and Shiede never returned. Backup Mark Giles struggled.

Giles threw three interceptions and BYU fumbled twice. OSU was outgained 301 yards to 224. The turnovers were the difference, with Dokes named the defensive Most Valuable Player and Walker winning the same honor on offense.

47 1976 Big Eight Championship and Tangerine Bowl

Oklahoma State head coach Jim Stanley was in his fourth season, with three straight winning seasons behind him, albeit a slim 19–13–2 record overall. A coaching descendent of Paul "Bear" Bryant, Stanley was no-nonsense and could push his team pretty hard.

The 1976 Cowboys were talented with a veteran quarterback in Charlie Weatherbie, an All-American running back in Terry Miller, another All-American up front in guard Darrel Gofourth, All-American Phillip Dokes at defensive tackle, and a veteran kicking corps of kicker Abby Daigle and punter Cliff Parsley.

The season started with a 33–21 win at Lewis Field over Tulsa, and then in the seemingly annual trip to Arkansas, the Cowboys challenged but lost a last-minute opportunity to the No. 12–ranked Razorbacks 16–10.

Wins over North Texas and No. 8 Kansas set up an early showdown with unranked Colorado. The Cowboys led late in the game when Buffaloes quarterback Jeff Knappel threw a pass in the end zone that was intercepted by the Cowboys' Jerry Cramer, who made the mistake of running the ball out and fumbling the ball back to the Buffs. No dispute on that play, but a play later Colorado fumbled and, despite a Cowboys defender's holding up the ball, the officials ruled it Colorado ball. To his dying day, Jim

Stanley disputed that call. Colorado won the game 20–10 after scoring a touchdown off the Cowboys' desperation the next series.

The next Saturday Oklahoma State was in rainy Norman to play the No. 5 Oklahoma Sooners. At 3–2, the Cowboys seemed to be scuffling, but after Oklahoma won the toss and took the wind on the stormy day the Cowboys, who surprised everybody by starting running quarterback Harold Bailey and executing a split-back veer offense, pitched the ball to Terry Miller. Miller went 72 yards for a touchdown, and the Cowboys never looked back.

In the second half, Stanley and offensive coordinator Bill Turnbow turned back to Weatherbie at quarterback and the Cowboys threw the ball more to keep the OU defense off balance, as Oklahoma State won 31–24.

The Cowboys followed the win up with a 20–19 homecoming win over No. 10 Missouri. A loss to Nebraska would be the last negative result of the season. The Cowboys finished with wins at Kansas State, at home over Iowa State, and at UTEP.

Oklahoma State, Oklahoma, and Colorado all tied atop the Big 12, giving the conference triple champions. It was the first conference title for Oklahoma State since being Missouri Valley co-champs in 1953.

Because of the Big Eight tiebreaker, Colorado got the Orange Bowl bid and lost to Ohio State. The Cowboys got a Tangerine Bowl invitation to play BYU.

It was billed as a battle of the pass, with BYU's future NFL quarterback, Gifford Nielsen, and the run, with the Cowboys' star runner, Terry Miller. Nielsen flinched first, as OSU defensive tackle Chris Dawson picked off a pass and returned it 36 yards for a touchdown. Miller ran for 173 yards on 23 carries, including touchdown runs of 3, 78, 6, and 1 yard. As a team, the Cowboys ran for 375 yards and outgained the Cougars overall 402 to 255 yards. Nielsen threw four interceptions, one of them appropriately picked by Cramer.

Oklahoma State closed out a 9–3 season by beating BYU 49–21.

48 Jimmy Johnson

The other College Football Hall of Fame coach in Oklahoma State history can be seen on Sundays throughout the NFL season giving his honest—sometimes brutally so—opinions on Fox studio coverage of the NFL. Johnson is a big personality, and his first big stage in coaching was as head coach at Oklahoma State.

Growing up in Port Arthur, Texas, Johnson was an undersized but tough two-way lineman for Thomas Jefferson High School, later to become Memorial High School. Johnson sat by a famous classmate in school: rocker Janis Joplin. With family ties to Arkansas, Johnson went to the University of Arkansas to play for Frank Broyles. That is where he met Jerry Jones, which would later lead to his coaching the Dallas Cowboys, but before that would also lead to getting Johnson to Stillwater. Other classmates at Arkansas included future coaching great Ken Hatfield, College Football Hall of Famer Lloyd Phillips, and Ronnie Caveness. Young assistants there at Arkansas at the time included Barry Switzer and Johnny Majors, and all would play a role in Johnson's coaching career or life.

An All–Southwest Conference defensive lineman, Johnson helped Arkansas win a national championship in 1964. After he finished his playing career and graduated, Louisiana Tech was looking to come to Arkansas and learn the ins and outs of the Razorbacks defense. Broyles suggested instead of them coming to

Jimmy Johnson began his coaching career at Oklahoma State in 1979, helping turn around an inconsistent program.

Fayetteville that they just hire Johnson as an assistant coach, and they did.

He rose up the coaching ladder rapidly with stops at Wichita State, Iowa State, and Oklahoma before becoming defensive coordinator for his old coach, Broyles, at Arkansas. Then, when Broyles retired, he passed up Johnson for the head coaching job and hired Lou Holtz. Johnson left and hooked up with Johnny Majors as assistant head coach and defensive coordinator at Pittsburgh. Then, at Oklahoma State, after some success and a Big Eight Championship in 1976, the bottom fell out with an NCAA investigation and probation. Jim Stanley resigned after a 3–8 season. Johnson's old Arkansas roommate was in the oil business with an office in Oklahoma City, and Jerry Jones was in some circles with Oklahoma State supporters. Johnson was an obvious candidate, but Jones was pushing his name in the oil and business communities.

Johnson got the job—and it was obvious he was a coach unlike any Oklahoma State had employed. Johnson brought lots of swagger. He brought in assistants like Pat Jones, Paul Jette, Butch Davis, and Tony Wise, who would play big roles in moving Oklahoma State football from a backburner program to one that grabbed some attention. In Johnson's first season the Cowboys, on probation, turned the record around from 4–7 to 7–4.

"You think that was something, next season we will knock their eyes out," was the preseason statement from Johnson as he tried to pump pride into what had been a mostly downtrodden program.

It didn't work out so well, as Oklahoma State lost the opener at home 20–19 to lowly West Texas A&M. The next season, the Cowboys bounced back for a 7–5 record and earned a trip to Shreveport, Louisiana, to play Texas A&M on a frigid night in the Independence Bowl. A&M won the game 33–16, but progress was being made. The next season was another slip back, as the Cowboys lost three and tied two of their first six games.

The 1983 season propelled Oklahoma State into a strong decade and Jimmy Johnson's coaching career into high gear. Johnson, who, along with his staff, often held court at a Stillwater bar and steakhouse, the Ancestor, hit the high time. The Cowboys reeled off four wins to start the season, nearly upset top-ranked Nebraska in a 14–10 nail-biter in Stillwater, and then got beat by OU 21–20 on a fluky onside kick that bounced off the face mask of Cowboys cornerback Chris Rockins. That team beat a talented Baylor team 24–14 in the Bluebonnet Bowl.

Oklahoma State was loaded for a big season in 1984, but in June—really late for a coaching hire—Miami came calling and hired Jimmy Johnson. Pat Jones, with the support of staff members who wanted to stay in Stillwater, was named head coach. The Cowboys did have their big season that year, opening up with a 45–3 win over highly ranked Arizona State in Jones' first game as coach. Johnson fared okay as well, as he led Miami to a national championship. Eventually, Jerry Jones would hire him as head coach of the Dallas Cowboys after Jones bought the club. The two Super Bowl championships added to Johnson's coaching ledger, which as coach of the Oklahoma State Cowboys was a modest 29–25–3.

49 Pat Jones

There have been few individuals better suited to be the head coach at a particular school than Pat Jones. Jones was so perfect for the job that he, without knowing it at the time, groomed the future head coach who would later eclipse him in wins, success, and tenure in Stillwater. Jones had grown up in a well-to-do family in

Little Rock as a gym rat. Jones played all the sports and, although he was not a tremendous athlete, his effort and desire made him competitive. He especially loved football, and as a senior at Little Rock Hall he was named Honorable Mention All-State. Jones went on to play at Arkansas Tech before transferring to play at Arkansas for Frank Broyles. Jones, an undersized nose guard, got in with the vast array of coaching talent that was coming out of Arkansas at the time, including Jimmy Johnson, Barry Switzer, and Ken Hatfield.

Jones got into coaching in the Little Rock School District before moving into the college ranks as the defensive-line coach at Arkansas for then–defensive coordinator Jimmy Johnson. Jones was an assistant at SMU and then Pittsburgh before moving with Johnson to Oklahoma State as the defensive coordinator. As versatile a football coach as anyone could be, when Johnson was struggling to find somebody to take over and have success with the Cowboys offense, he moved Pat Jones over to offensive coordinator. Jones had become Johnson's right-hand man, and when Johnson took the Miami job in June 1984 he could have gone with his mentor to South Florida. Instead, Jones led a group of assistant coaches who wanted to stay, and he was the natural choice for Oklahoma State to promote to head coach. A few months later, when the Cowboys went to the desert and pummeled a highly ranked Arizona State team 45–3, it was clear Oklahoma State had the right guy.

The folksy Jones was popular with Oklahoma State fans, and his popularity grew with 10-win seasons in 1984, 1987, and 1988. Jones coached defensive stalwarts like Leslie O'Neal and John Washington. He had defensive backs who rocked opposing offensive players in Mark Moore and Rod Brown. On offense, he had two of the most prolific running backs in college and pro football history with Thurman Thomas and Heisman Trophy winner Barry Sanders. He also had an All-American and dominant pass receiver in Hart Lee Dykes. Jones' teams were famous for stars, but also well known for walk-ons and effort guys—blue-collar football players who filled in around the superstars. Jones was adept at handling all kinds of football players up and down the caste system built into a football program. He could make the biggest superstar feel guilty and the lowest scout-team player feel important.

Jones had a language and a delivery all his own; he was capable of combinations of words that would make a sailor blush, then could turn around and be charming enough to cause a nun to rethink her vows. That was the beauty of Pat Jones.

It is amazing that even to this day, after Mike Gundy has long surpassed his former coach in wins (Jones finished 62–60–3 in 11 years, and Gundy is 104–50 through year 12), you can still show up at an Oklahoma State practice and watch Gundy do his job, listen to Gundy talk to his team or to his assistants, and sometimes be reminded of Jones. Jones, who doesn't come back to Stillwater nearly often enough, has had a greater impact than he understands or maybe could even fathom.

Sure, the Cowboys program went into a tailspin that Jones could not pull it out of after the NCAA put Oklahoma State on probation after that terrific 1988 season that ended with Sanders' Heisman and a 62–14 win over Wyoming in the Holiday Bowl. It would be nice if you could have put a freeze on the picture of Jones being carried off the field in San Diego and also frozen in time the feeling all Cowboys fans were experiencing, but unfortunately there were the six seasons that resulted in no marks over .500 and no bowl games. Of course, that is what probation is supposed to feel like. Jones had benefitted from the likes of Hart Lee Dykes, Thurman Thomas, and Ronnie Williams, who had received illegal inducements, so now he and the Cowboys football family had to pay the price. It was steep, with the six losing seasons and an average of three wins per season, including an 0–10–1 campaign that Jones seriously symbolically buried in a grave outside the Oklahoma State dressing room.

Jones was always good for a great show, and after coaching at Miami and Oakland in the NFL, he came back to Oklahoma and now delivers good shows on radio every day as one of the most popular sports talk radio personalities in the state. Pat Jones is one of a kind, and it's a damn good thing that he put his football thumbprint on Oklahoma State because it is still a major reason for Cowboys football success. Jones really had an influence on his quarterback, and current head coach, Mike Gundy.

50 1984 Gator Bowl and First 10-Win Season

It has long been considered one of the most exciting football games in Oklahoma State history, and it capped a landmark season, as Pat Jones made his debut as head coach following his friend Jimmy Johnson—and did so spectacularly with a 9–2 record. The No. 9–ranked Cowboys were in Jacksonville, Florida, to take on No. 7 South Carolina in the Gator Bowl.

After South Carolina overcame a 13-point deficit with two third-quarter touchdowns to go up 14–13, the Cowboys thrilled a record 40th Gator Bowl crowd of 82,138 with an 88-yard drive to the winning score.

Running back Thurman Thomas rushed 32 times for 155 yards in the game, and he had several runs on that final drive, but quarterback Rusty Hilger, who was 24-of-41 for 205 yards, needed a big play on third down. He hit tight end Barry Hanna in the flat, and Hanna turned it upfield, tightroping the sideline and diving into the end zone for a 25-yard touchdown. It was Hanna's only touchdown of the season.

Thomas scored the other two OSU touchdowns, one on a run and the other on a pass from Hilger. Hilger also threw to his roommate, Jamie Harris, for a two-point conversion after the Hanna touchdown for a 21–14 Cowboys win.

The win clinched the first 10-win season in the history of Oklahoma State football.

51 1987 Sun Bowl and Second 10-Win Season

In Pat Jones' fourth season as head coach, he had the hero of his first season, running back Thurman Thomas; quarterback Mike Gundy; running back and kick returner Barry Sanders; wide receiver Hart Lee Dykes; and a salty defense helping him win games. The Cowboys finished the regular season 9–2 with the only losses being to Oklahoma and Nebraska.

Oklahoma State earned a bid to the Sun Bowl in El Paso and played West Virginia and its star quarterback Major Harris.

The game was absolutely crazy, both competitively and weatherwise. Thurman Thomas, who scored four touchdowns, opened the scoring with a five-yard run. That score was set up by a long Gundy-to-Dykes pass play. The Mountaineers were stout and scored 24 first-half points, including a 23-yard return for a touchdown off a rare Gundy interception.

The weather started off sunny and mild, but a cold front moved in during the first half and by the start of the second half, the two teams were playing in a heavy snowstorm that eventually covered the field.

Thomas, who rushed for 157 yards on 33 carries to earn the Most Valuable Player award in his last college game, scored his third and fourth touchdowns of the game in the second half. Gundy added a six-yard touchdown pass to tight end J.R. Dillard, but late in the game the Cowboys were only leading 35–27 when the Mountaineers scored a touchdown with 1:13 left.

On the try for two to tie the game, Cowboys linebacker Shawn Mackey tackled West Virginia's Keith Winn just shy of the goal line to preserve the win and the second 10-win season in school history.

52 1988 Holiday Bowl: The High Point under Pat Jones

The 1988 season, at the time, was considered by many the high point for Oklahoma State football. Sure, there had been the unbeaten season in 1945, but few remembered it and at that point the AFCA was many years away from even considering awarding retroactive national championships. Pat Jones had taken Oklahoma State to 10-win seasons in 1984 and 1987, but the 1988 season surpassed those years in a couple of ways. First, the Cowboys were expected to be national championship contenders and second, Barry Sanders was about to run loose and fans, even fans of other schools, were excited about seeing it.

Oklahoma State started with a 100-yard kickoff return for a touchdown the second season in a row, as Sanders took the first kickoff by Miami (Ohio) in the opener and went the distance, just like he had in 1987 against Tulsa. Sanders rushed for 178 yards against the Redskins. It was a modest start, as two weeks later all hell broke loose, the Cowboys took on the famed "Wrecking Crew" defense of Texas A&M, and Pat Jones coached against mentor and former boss Jackie Sherrill. The Cowboys stomped on Texas

A&M, as Sanders returned a punt for a touchdown and rushed for 157 yards, Gundy threw for a bunch, and Dykes had 122 yards receiving, much of it on a long touchdown pass over the middle where he reached out and snagged the Gundy pass from behind him. After the game, Jones anticipated Sherrill being critical in the postgame handshake, as Oklahoma State won 52–15. He wasn't, and even came back after the game to the Oklahoma State locker room to compliment Jones on how good his team was. Imagine that, because Jones was afraid Sherrill might take a shot at him.

The Cowboys ran through the schedule and were 4–0 going to Lincoln, Nebraska, when everything that could have gone wrong early did. Nebraska started sharp offensively and Gundy threw a rare interception that was returned for a touchdown. Before you could blink, it was 42–0 Nebraska—in the first half. Huskers coach Tom Osborne did not substitute and kept his starters in. At the time it looked like running up the score and poor sportsmanship, but by the end of the 63–42 game, you understood why. Sanders ran for 189 yards and Dykes had 125 yards receiving. The Cowboys were still an offensive nightmare, even for the Blackshirt defense. Two more wins in a row over Missouri and Kansas State and 474 yards rushing in those two games by Sanders, and the Cowboys were 6–1 playing Oklahoma in Stillwater. The Sooners' Mike Gaddis actually went toe-to-toe with Barry Sanders, as he rushed for touchdowns of 44 and 13 yards to burst the Sooners out to a 14–0 lead. Gaddis finished with 213 yards. Sanders had 215 yards and the Cowboys, thanks to fast-talking OU head coach Barry Switzer, who swayed the officiating crew into a well-timed unsportsmanlike conduct penalty, had to throw a desperation pass to Brent Parker that went through Parker's hands in the end zone as OU won 31–28.

Oklahoma State finished with three more wins in the regular season, the final win a 45–42 seesaw affair in Tokyo, Japan, against Texas Tech in the Coca-Cola Bowl. It was played the same day that Jones, the OSU offensive line (War Pigs), and fullback Garrett Limbrick joined Sanders in the CBS News studio in Tokyo to accept via satellite the Heisman Trophy.

All this time, the NCAA had been investigating Oklahoma State, like they had other schools, for the recruitment of Hart Lee Dykes. The NCAA had discovered some other violations against Oklahoma State football and was on the verge of delivering one of the worst probations in the organization's history.

The Cowboys went to the Holiday Bowl and got ready to cap off Sanders' Heisman and the Cowboys' 9–2 season against Wyoming. The 1988 Holiday Bowl went against the trend for the history of that bowl game. It was usually a barn burner, a game down to the wire and even into overtime. The 1988 game was anything but close. Oklahoma State led at halftime 17–7 after a pair of Sanders touchdown runs and a Cary Blanchard field goal. Then, in the second half, the Cowboys went crazy, with Gundy throwing a pair of touchdown passes, one to San Diego native Brent Parker and the other to Dykes. Gundy pitched to Sanders and Sanders threw it back to him downfield as Gundy got to the 1-yard line to set up one of three more Sanders touchdowns runs—five for the night and 222 yards rushing. Those numbers brought Sanders' total for the season to 2,850 yards and 44 touchdowns. Oklahoma State won the 1988 Holiday Bowl 62–14.

After the game, Sanders declared he was going pro and he would be drafted by the Detroit Lions. It was shortly after the Cowboys arrived back home that the NCAA announced the penalties, including two seasons of no bowl games and no television. It would lead Oklahoma State to a record of 18–45–3 the next six years under Pat Jones. The Cowboys would not enjoy a winning record again until 1997. The real consistent success started under Les Miles in 2002 and then, after a one-season cleansing of some players Mike Gundy didn't feel needed to be in the program, the Cowboys have had winning seasons and bowl games in 11 straight seasons.

2006 Independence Bowl

It came down to this: 13 seconds remaining and Oklahoma State sitting at the 13-yard line on the Alabama end of the field. Acting Alabama head coach Joe Kines was trying to ice anyone as he burned his timeouts, while the Cowboys' field-goal unit was huddled up around special teams coordinator Joe DeForest and head coach Mike Gundy. Off to the side was kicker Jason Ricks going through his motions. After three straight timeouts, the Cowboys went to work and the snap, hold, and kick were perfect. Oklahoma State led Alabama 34–31 with 8.9 seconds left. The Cowboys weathered the crazy kickoff return and then a crazier play from scrimmage and celebrated the first bowl win of Mike Gundy's coaching career.

In the locker room afterward, DeForest, the assistant head coach and the first assistant that Gundy hired, tossed the ball that Ricks had kicked and the Cowboys' managers had chased down in the end-zone bleachers of Independence Stadium to Gundy and said, "Coach, congratulations and here is the game ball from your first bowl win." Gundy, who has a keen sense of the here and now, almost without hesitation tossed the ball to billionaire T. Boone Pickens and told him that ball was his for all he had done for the program.

It was a happy locker room no matter who ended up with the game ball. Oklahoma State took the early lead on a one-yard touchdown run by Dantrell Savage. In the second quarter, the Cowboys added touchdown runs of four and seven yards by big back Keith Toston. At halftime the Cowboys led the Crimson Tide 24–14, and the win probably should have been more comfortable, as Savage and Toston combined to lead OSU to 207 yards rushing, and the Cowboys outgained Alabama 419 to 276 yards in total offense. Bobby Reid hooked up with Adarius Bowman for a fourth-quarter touchdown pass. It was an 86-yard punt return by Javier Arenas that pushed Alabama toward tying the game. A trick play throwing to an offensive tackle was part of the drive toward the tying score that was a two-yard run by Andre Smith.

It all led to that final Cowboys drive as Bobby Reid engineered the offense down the field and set up Ricks' winning kick.

Scratch and claw—that is what Gundy's team did in his second season as head coach as the Cowboys tried to get to a bowl game after missing the postseason in Gundy's first year with a 4–7 record and a lone conference win, albeit a good upset over No. 13–ranked Texas Tech. The Cowboys swept the first three nonconference games with wins over Missouri State, over Arkansas State in Little Rock, and at home against Florida Atlantic. Then came a rainy night in Houston and several really suspect calls against the Cowboys as the Art Briles–coached Cougars beat the Cowboys 34–25. Another loss on the road at Kansas State opened Big 12 play. The Cowboys won big at Kansas 42–32 before coming home and losing a heartbreaker in overtime to Texas A&M on homecoming. The highlight was a nationally televised win over Nebraska in the construction site that was then Boone Pickens Stadium. It was a 41–29 win over the No. 20–ranked Huskers. A loss at Texas and a 66–24 win over Baylor followed by a loss to Texas Tech and in Bedlam left the Cowboys at 6–6, good enough to go bowling.

The win over Alabama was special. The Crimson Tide would hire Nick Saban as their new head coach after the game, but in the history of Oklahoma State football the Cowboys have only played Bama once, and the all-time series has the Cowboys unbeaten at 1–0 versus the Crimson Tide.

54 2008 Win at Missouri: the "Program Changer"

Oklahoma State quarterback Zac Robinson came out for an early look at Faurot Field. The Cowboys had just arrived and Robinson slipped on his football girdle with pads and some shorts over that with a long-sleeved T-shirt and ran out onto the field to loosen up, throw a few passes, and get out of the sweaty, humid bunker that served as the visitors' dressing room. Once out on the field, Robinson found himself being quizzed by ESPN sideline reporter Erin Andrews. Asked if he needed any help getting away from the barrage of questions coming from Andrews, Robinson smiled and said, "No, I got this." That wasn't the last smile Robinson had on his face that night, and it wouldn't be the last time he found himself answering questions from Andrews.

Missouri had pasted Nebraska the week before and they were 5–0 on the season and ranked third in the country. They were sporting an offense that football analysts described as a video-game offense that could not be stopped, and it really hadn't been. Missouri came in having made a first down on every possession so far that season. In the first five games, quarterback Chase Daniel and his teammates had not gone three-and-out on any possession.

The Cowboys fell behind 3–0, but very early the Cowboys defense forced a three-and-out, proving that the Tigers could be stopped. Oklahoma State answered the Mizzou field goal with a 13-play, 71-yard drive that finished with Robinson going up the middle, shaking off a big hit, and landing in the end zone for a touchdown. The six-yard run and Dan Bailey's extra point made it 7–3. Midway through the second quarter, Missouri got great field position and went 36 yards for a go-ahead touchdown that came on a five-yard run by Derrick Washington, and at halftime the Tigers led the Pokes 10–7.

Oklahoma State had some issues to deal with at the half. The Cowboys defense had played well, but on offense Missouri was taking away their best receiving threat, as the Tigers had really banged up Dez Bryant. Bryant had even taken a few late hits and was struggling. Enter little-known, tall, skinny wide receiver Damian Davis from tiny Mart, Texas. Davis would come on in the second half and finish with three catches for 76 yards and two touchdowns.

To start the second half it was a familiar face and number, as running back Kendall Hunter got loose and went 68 yards on a second-and-6 on the Cowboys' first possession of the third quarter. What had been a noisy and wild nighttime Missouri crowd of more than 68,000 went as quiet as a country church preparing to pray. Missouri took the lead back as Chase Daniel, who finished 39-of-52 for 390 yards and a touchdown, led the Tigers offense 95 yards in 11 plays, as Jimmy Jackson scored from the 1. Mizzou led 17–14, but that would be it for Tigers leads that night.

Robinson finished a 66-yard drive in just four plays by hitting the Cowboys' secret weapon in Davis for a 40-yard touchdown in the back of the end zone on an acrobatic catch. It was now 21–17. The Cowboys defense came into play with three interceptions in the second half to nullify the success of Daniel throwing the ball around. Rickie Price grabbed the first and then his roommate Andre Sexton picked off the second of the game. Sexton's interception set up the second Robinson-to-Davis touchdown pass, this one for 31 yards and a 28–17 Oklahoma State lead.

"Our defense really did come up big with those interceptions," Robinson said after the game.

Still, another Daniel highlight with a touchdown pass to Danario Alexander with 4:27 left put the score at 28–23.

Missouri was driving toward the winning touchdown late when Cowboys linebacker Patrick Lavine cradled the third interception by the OSU defense. On the sideline, the coaching staff started computing the clock time with a Missouri timeout and trying to figure if they could run out the clock. It would be close. Oklahoma State still had to punt with some 10 seconds left. Matt Fodge did a great job of angling the ball, and the cover unit got the job done against one of the most dangerous punt returners in the country in Jeremy Maclin.

Oklahoma State knocked off the No. 3–ranked Missouri Tigers in Columbia on national television at night 28–23.

"That win changed our program. I truly believe that was the program-turning win. It was a really big win for us on a big stage that gave our players some evidence we can do this," Gundy would say several years later. "You have to win one to make people think you can do it, and I think that was a big game for our university and for our program."

"When I look back at my career, there's no doubt that was the biggest game in terms of putting the program on the map," Robinson said. "Everyone realized after that we were a legitimate contender."

55 Brandon Weeden

On the afternoon of March 3, 2016, the Oklahoma State Cowboys had gathered in their team meeting room for a prespring football team meeting, but it was actually a surprise, as the team was going to get a debut of the new football uniforms designed by the equipment staff and Nike. Head coach Mike Gundy had flown in some celebrity models from Dallas: Cowboys wide receiver and former Oklahoma State standout Dez Bryant, and former Oklahoma

State kicker and one of the best kickers in the NFL in Dan Bailey. Former Oklahoma State quarterback Brandon Weeden had driven up from his home in Edmond. While the team was in supposed meetings, those three broke through the doors in the back wearing the new threads and dancing to the loud music that was being

In his 2011 season at Oklahoma State, Brandon Weeden set records for passing yards (4,727), total offense (4,625), completed passes (408), completion percentage (72.3), and completions in a single game (47 versus Texas A&M), many of which surpassed records previously set by his head coach, Mike Gundy.

piped through the speakers of the meeting room. Okay—Bryant was dancing, jumping up and down, and getting the players crazy; Weeden and Bailey were trying. The pair can be excused, because dancing ability was not what earned them a spot modeling the new uniforms.

The story of how Brandon Weeden got to Oklahoma State is one of the most unusual in school history, but then again, having a starting quarterback at age 27 is unique. Brandon Weeden was a 24-year-old freshman. The former three-sport star at Edmond Santa Fe High School played football and basketball and then pitcher and shortstop as a major league prospect in baseball. He led Santa Fe to the state championship game and finished with 2,863 yards passing and 25 touchdowns. He was All-State in football and later his senior year in baseball.

With their first pick (a second-round selection) in the MLB Amateur Draft, the New York Yankees drafted Weeden and he signed out of high school. Weeden showed promise, but became part of a deal going along with Jeff Weaver from the Yankees organization to the Los Angeles Dodgers in exchange for All-Star pitcher Kevin Brown. Later, Weeden went to the Kansas City Royals in a Rule 5 draft. Weeden had battled injuries and was losing passion for trying to fight his way out of the minors to advance. In the spring of 2007, Weeden was let go in spring training by the Royals.

Sitting in Sky Harbor Airport in Phoenix and heading home to Oklahoma, Weeden made a couple of phone calls. He already knew what he wanted to do. He wanted to play college football. One call led to a friend calling a reporter who covered Oklahoma State. That reporter immediately called Cowboys offensive coordinator Larry Fedora and told Fedora that Weeden was coming back to Oklahoma and was available. Fedora told the reporter he would call back in a few minutes. The now–head coach at North Carolina went down the hall and grabbed a tape to watch Weeden in high school. Less than five minutes later Fedora called the reporter back and said, "Give me his number."

The next day Weeden was at Oklahoma State's Saturday practice during spring football and by the end of the practice, Weeden was heading to Stillwater.

With Zac Robinson setting records at quarterback, Weeden sat on the bench, but was always impressive throwing the ball around in practice. Then, in the 2009 season when Robinson was knocked out late in a win over Texas Tech on a hit by Tech corner Jamar Wall, a short week for a Thursday game with Colorado led to Alex Cate starting at quarterback and Weeden as the backup. Cate did not complete a pass the first half and threw one interception with Oklahoma State trailing. Weeden came on in the second half and led the Cowboys back, including an on-the-run laser throw deep to Justin Blackmon for the winning score in the 31–28 win.

Weeden was the starter the next season. Gundy brought in Dana Holgorsen to coordinate a more dominant passing offense, and the Cowboys won 11 games and finished with a 36–10 win in the Alamo Bowl over Arizona. About a week after that game, Weeden—now 27 years old—joined red-shirt sophomore receiver and his top target Justin Blackmon in a press conference to announce that the pair were coming back. Weeden opened the news conference.

"We're here and I want to announce that Justin Blackmon is coming back next season," Weeden said, and paused. "And so am I." Holgorsen had left to become head coach at West Virginia, but with Todd Monken coming in as offensive coordinator and Weeden showing him what they were doing on offense and what they had done the past season, including the Alamo Bowl, it was game on for 2011. Gundy felt his quarterback and receiver combination could trigger a huge season. Weeden admits he had to think about coming back as he explored his options, similar to but not exactly like Mason Rudolph did more recently in 2017.

"I was [exploring my options], just because I didn't know all the extra stuff. My situation was so different because of my age and I was kind of a late-on-the-scene-type guy," Weeden told the *Tulsa World* in 2016. "But I think [Gundy's] got a good point.

"I think, really, for me more than anything, I just kind of saw what promise we had as a team of the guys who were coming back for the following year, 2011," Weeden followed up. "I think we finished 10–2 in '10 and I think we brought back a lot of important pieces that kind of made the decision to come back pretty easy. I felt like we had unfinished business. We had lost to Oklahoma. Lost a close one to Nebraska in the middle of the year. I just felt like there was unfinished business that I wanted to be a part of. I wanted to be a part of something special and I felt like that gave me the best opportunity to do that. I knew we would have a pretty good football team in 2011."

Weeden got that opportunity and was a huge leader as Oklahoma State went 12–1, with the only loss a Friday-night matchup at Iowa State under some unusual circumstances. The team finished No. 3 in the nation and had the 41–38 overtime win over Stanford in the Fiesta Bowl—Weeden winning head up with the eventual first-round draft pick in Cardinal quarterback Andrew Luck.

Brandon Weeden was picked No. 22 in the first round of that NFL Draft and would play several years for the Cleveland Browns before spending a season and a half in Dallas. Weeden is currently a backup quarterback for the Houston Texans.

He still owns most of the career passing records at Oklahoma State, but those will be severely threatened in 2017 by returning Oklahoma State quarterback Mason Rudolph.

56 2011 Loss at Iowa State

As Oklahoma State entered the second-to-last game of the regular season, the Cowboys were 10–0 and ranked No. 2 in both major football polls. The Cowboys were heavy favorites over unranked, but always dangerous, Iowa State on a Friday-night game scheduled for national television on ESPN. The night before, the Cowboys had checked into the Des Moines, Iowa, Marriott and at around 6:00 AM on the morning of the game the word started to spread of what was going on back in Stillwater. It had been discovered early that morning that a private plane that had flown Cowgirls basketball head coach Kurt Budke and one of his assistants, Miranda Serna, over to Arkansas to watch a recruit had gone down, and both Budke and Serna, along with the two pilots, Olin and Paula Branstetter, were all dead. The Piper PA-28 Cherokee went down and was destroyed in a dense forest four miles south of Perryville, Arkansas.

Budke had been a regular visitor to watch Cowboys football practice and was friends with Cowboys head coach Mike Gundy. The Cowboys football players were often in attendance at Cowgirls games and were friendly with Budke, his entire staff, and the players. It hit the football team really hard. Athletic director Mike Holder, who was on the trip with the football team, chartered a flight and made his way back to Stillwater early that Friday morning. The two schools had discussions, but the decision was made to play the game.

On top of everything else, the Cowboys had one of their buses break down on the way from Des Moines to Ames for the game and arrived later than their normal two hours before game time. Gundy had lectured his team and had told them it was okay to be sad over the loss of the coaches and to be concerned for their friends on the Cowgirls basketball team, but it was not an excuse to play poorly and let their guard down against Iowa State.

The fans at Iowa State really get it. The vast majority of their fans are rabid without getting nasty or ugly. They have respect for opposing teams and the fans of those teams. That night, Oklahoma State fans in Jack Trice Stadium were greeted, sometimes hugged, and often told that they were in the prayers, thoughts, and condolences of Cyclones fans.

Then, as I remember describing that night on the radio broadcast, the Iowa State band played the national anthem, the official tossed the coin, and it was game on. Oklahoma State wasn't sharp, but scored first on a 70-yard interception return by linebacker Shaun Lewis off Iowa State quarterback Jared Barnett. It was one of those run-in-front grabs and before anybody knew it, Lewis was off to the races. Quinn Sharp added a field goal and then, just before halftime, Brandon Weeden connected with his favorite receiver and soon-to-be-All-American Justin Blackmon for a 27-yard touchdown and a 17–7 lead at halftime.

The halftime locker room was calm, but you could sense some concern over the team just not being as sharp as normal.

Oklahoma State opened the second-half scoring when Weeden hit Tracy Moore for a 30-yard touchdown, and it was 24–7 with Oklahoma State and Cowboys fans breathing easy. That would be the last Oklahoma State score in regulation, as Iowa State revved it up on both sides of the ball. Barnett at quarterback, who had been pedestrian as a passer throughout his playing time in the season, completed 31-of-58 passing for 376 yards in the game. James White had a 32-yard touchdown run for the Cyclones followed by a field goal, and then in the fourth quarter Barnett hit Albert Gary with a short touchdown pass to tie the game at 24–24 with 5:30 left in the contest.

Plenty of time, and Oklahoma State drove the ball down to give Sharp a 37-yard try at the game winner with 1:17 left. The kick went directly over the right upright. In the NFL, the kick is good by rule, but the NCAA rule is that the ball has to be completely inside the upright, and the official correctly signaled no good. I've seen that kick replayed hundreds of times, and every time in my best judgment it goes directly over the top of the upright. You'd love to see those uprights have been six to eight feet longer and you'd take a ricochet—a doink—because sometimes doinks deflect inside the upright.

Iowa State ran out the clock and went into overtime. Iowa State got the ball first and scored on the first play. The Cowboys drove the 25 yards required in overtime, and Weeden connected with Josh Cooper for a six-yard touchdown. The Cowboys had the ball next and turned it over on an interception. Iowa State scored in three plays with popular fullback Jeff Woody scoring from the four-yard line for the winner.

Mike Gundy had director of football operations Mack Butler screen the locker-room door—no assistant coaches, no support staff, but players only in the small dressing room. Once the final players were in, Gundy had the doors shut and he proceeded to tell his team that they had no idea how great an opportunity they had just blown.

"You will know tomorrow morning because the replays of this game will be on ESPN all day long," Gundy said. "Some of you will be going down the hall to speak with the media and I don't want to hear one word about how sad the team was about the deaths of Coach Budke and Coach Serna. Their families don't deserve that. Don't put this on them. We had the opportunity to win this football game and we didn't get it done. You give Iowa State credit because they worked for two weeks and came up with a great plan and executed it. I need to learn, our coaches need to learn, and all of you need to learn from them. We have two weeks and then we will play a very important game against a very good team. We need to use these two weeks the same way Iowa State used their two weeks to prepare for us."

I remember riding to the Des Moines airport in a rented SUV with Gundy. There may have been five or six words said the entire 40-minute drive, and that was with five people in the vehicle.

57 2011 Bedlam Football

Two weeks—actually, two weeks and a day—had passed since the crushing loss to Iowa State. Oklahoma State had recovered in the polls to be ranked No. 3 in one and No. 5 in the other, and here came Bedlam rival OU to Stillwater to battle at least for the Big 12 Championship and a BCS bowl game, if not for a spot in the BCS Championship Game.

Oklahoma made a mistake from the very start. The team came out onto the field from the ramp and entrance in the northeast corner, and several Sooners players decided to go the length of their sideline down to the northwest corner, where Oklahoma State was preparing to come out. There was some jawing, nothing serious, before the officials separated the teams, but the challenge was on and in this Bedlam Oklahoma State was the aggressor, the better and more talented team, and up for dealing out a butt-kicking.

The first touchdown was the end result of a four-play drive for 68 yards, with Jeremy Smith going the nine yards for the touchdown. Smith would rush for 119 yards on 10 carries in the game and Joseph Randle would run for 151 yards on 19 carries. Oklahoma State finished with 495 yards of offense and Weeden, while not throwing a touchdown pass for the first time in a game during the 2011 season, did complete 24-of-36 passing. After Quinn Sharp split the uprights on a 25-yard field goal, Randle had two consecutive touchdown runs of one yard and then two yards. Oklahoma State led 24–0. The first Randle touchdown was the result of a fumble forced by linebacker Alex Elkins as he punched the ball out of the grasp of OU quarterback Landry Jones. Defensive end Jamie Blatnick scooped it up and ran right down the Sooners' sideline 59 yards to the 1-yard line. Blatnick ran right past exasperated OU head coach Bob Stoops.

In the second half, with Oklahoma State up 27–3, the defense struck again, as the defensive end across from Blatnick, Richetti Jones, scooped another Landry Jones fumble and returned it the five yards needed to score a touchdown. The rout was on as Oklahoma State scored its second-most-emphatic win over OU with a 44–10 verdict, and the Big 12 Championship and berth in the Fiesta Bowl.

After the game, the field became a sea of orange as fans came down en masse. Some were injured in the jump over the wall onto the field, and some fans were trampled by the crowd. There were a few serious injuries and people taken to the hospital, but it was not a scene with which Oklahoma State fans had previously had much practice.

In the locker room, head coach Mike Gundy was presented the Big 12 Championship trophy and immediately let it be held by the stadium's namesake, T. Boone Pickens. The players enjoyed themselves and celebrated while Gundy went down the hall and spoke with the media, delivering a calculated message that Oklahoma State should get a break for a very unusual loss two weeks earlier and that instead of a rematch in the SEC between top-ranked LSU and Alabama, a team they had already defeated, it should be his Cowboys in the BCS Championship Game against LSU.

Gundy had one more go at it on Sunday before the BCS and bowl announcements were made, but the BCS computers and pollsters had LSU playing Alabama in the BCS National Championship in New Orleans and Oklahoma State, ranked No. 3, playing No. 4 Stanford in the Fiesta Bowl.

Now we have a committee—a human committee—that can use information from computers and look at polls, but also look at the games and come up with their own thoughts and opinions to decide the four teams that form the current College Football Playoff. Many believe, myself included, that you can thank Oklahoma State and the 2011 season as the major push to have the playoff, and the committee decide the participants.

58 2012 Fiesta Bowl vs. Stanford

It was the finishing touch on what—other than the undefeated season of 1945, which would be retroactively recognized as a national championship campaign—was the best season of football in Oklahoma State's history. It would finish as exciting as any bowl game. The showdown featured the high-powered Oklahoma State offense with the "triplets"—quarterback Brandon Weeden, wide receiver Justin Blackmon, and running back Joseph Randle—and the Stanford defense with the top-rated quarterback in the college ranks, Andrew Luck, who was just a few months away from becoming the top player taken in the NFL Draft. Just short of 70,000 people were there, and ESPN had the world watching from University of Phoenix Stadium in Glendale, Arizona.

It did not start well for the Cowboys, as Luck marched the Cardinals down the field and connected on a 53-yard touchdown pass to one of his favorite targets in Ty Montgomery for a 7–0 lead, and then Jeremy Stewart scored on a 24-yard touchdown run to make it 14–0. In the second quarter, the Cowboys battled back the best way they knew how, with the same two players who had kickstarted the season nearly a full year earlier in ultratalented Blackmon and bazooka-armed Weeden. Weeden hit Blackmon first for a 43-yard touchdown pass and then stretched the field for a 67-yard touchdown that became a highlight-reel play for the season.

The two teams traded touchdown runs late in the second quarter, and it was Weeden for two yards for the Cowboys as the halftime score was all tied up at 21–21.

Stanford scored a touchdown and Oklahoma State's Quinn Sharp kicked a field goal in the third quarter, so the fourth quarter started with Stanford leading 28–24. Stanford added a field goal from Jordan Williamson at the start of the fourth quarter, a 30-yarder to make it 31–24. The Cowboys had their work cut out for them, but as a veteran team they weren't fazed. Blackmon caught his third touchdown pass of the game, 17 yards from Weeden to tie the game, but then Stanford drove the ball 13 plays for 71 yards and methodically finished it off with a Steven Taylor touchdown run to go back up 38–31.

Less than five minutes remained, but this Oklahoma State team majored in quick scoring drives and big plays. It took just seven plays to go 67 yards, and Randle finished the drive and tied the game with a hard-driving four-yard touchdown run. Stanford had time and drove down the field, but Jordan Williamson missed a field goal at the end of the fourth quarter that was only slightly longer than the 30-yard field goal he had hit at the start of the final quarter. Regulation in the Fiesta Bowl ended 38–38.

The battle between No. 3 and No. 4 and between two soon-to-be first-round draft picks in Luck and Weeden was in overtime. Yet the overtime would be special, in that it was all about the kickers and a walk-on receiver who was there in part because his brother was the quarterback waiting on scholarship.

Stanford got the ball first, and the Oklahoma State defense, which had given up almost 600 yards in the game, picked a darn good time to get stingy. On fourth down, Jordan Williamson missed a 43-yard field goal. It was obvious that Stanford's road to victory needed to be driven by someone other than its kicker, as he was on the fritz.

For the Cowboys, the road to victory went right off Weeden's arm and into the hands of a walk-on receiver who had transferred from NEO A&M Junior College to join his younger brother, Clint Chelf, who was the backup quarterback and would soon have his own starring role in the offense the next season. In fact, Clint would be the player of the game in the Cowboys' 2013 Heart of Dallas Bowl win over Purdue. Older brother Colton Chelf caught the Weeden pass, and many feel he should have been credited with a touchdown. The official called it that way, but replay brought it back out to the 2-yard line and after a kneel by Weeden, Sharp came in and got a little redemption of his own for the kick over the upright in Ames two months prior. Oklahoma State beat Stanford 41–38 in overtime. The Cowboys finished No. 3 in the nation behind Alabama and LSU. Bama had beaten LSU in the BCS title game.

The Cowboys hauled home a huge winner's trophy from the Fiesta Bowl, but on the podium there in Glendale, Mike Gundy had a special helper there to hold it up in Shelley Budke, the wife of late Cowgirls basketball coach Kurt Budke. Gundy had personally invited Shelley and her kids to Arizona for the game. It was dramatic football season for the Cowboys and for Oklahoma State as a university. The ending wasn't all happy, but the right people were standing on that winning platform when it ended.

59 Justin Blackmon

Justin Blackmon's is one of the best stories of rising from humble beginnings to stardom, but also one of the saddest stories of a bright future tumbling down. Blackmon was a kid living in California playing roller hockey and all kinds of sports available on the West Coast before moving to Oklahoma. The son of a Marine Corps veteran and a kindergarten teacher, Blackmon came to Oklahoma State as an engaging and friendly person and a really underrated and talented athlete. At Plainview High School near Ardmore, Oklahoma, Blackmon had played football and basketball and run track and field, and he was amazing at everything he tried. His senior year, he worked on the high jump for the first time and took it to state. It wasn't long after he arrived at Oklahoma State that head coach Mike Gundy and his offensive staff knew they were looking at a very special player.

After a redshirt season, Blackmon broke out as a freshman and scratched the surface of what he was capable of. One of his most important catches that freshman season was an early glimpse of how well he would team up with quarterback Brandon Weeden, as Weeden came in for the second half of the Colorado game. Starter Zac Robinson was out with a concussion, and the Cowboys were down at the half after having not completed a single pass. Weeden came in and he and Blackmon started clicking, including on a winning touchdown pass where Weeden scrambled and hit Blackmon, who had made a route adjustment, for a long touchdown to save the night.

It was in 2010 as a sophomore that Blackmon went viral nationally as a receiver. He had 1,782 yards receiving, the most recorded by a sophomore in NCAA history. He also had 20 touchdown

In his three seasons at Oklahoma State, receiver Justin Blackmon won the Biletnikoff Award as the nation's top receiver twice. He was also the offensive MVP in the Fiesta Bowl win following the 2011 season.

receptions, the seventh most ever recorded. He was named an All-American and the Big 12 Offensive Player of the Year, and he won the Fred Biletnikoff Award as the top receiver in the nation.

In the 2010 Alamo Bowl, he was the offensive Most Valuable Player, catching nine passes for 117 yards and two touchdowns, one in which he caught some flak for imitating a move from the previous week in the NFL: he caught the pass and then, at the 5-yard line, ran across the field, taunting the Wildcats defenders. Blackmon wasn't mean-spirited, but he had some mischief in him. It was that part of his personality that may have eventually been his downfall.

The next season, as a junior, with defenders covering him and defensive coordinators drawing up all kinds of special coverages to stop him, Blackmon continued on his tear, destroying opposing pass defenses. He had 122 receptions for 1,522 yards and 18 touchdowns. His 122 catches represented the 13th most in NCAA history. He and Weeden were the top quarterback-receiver duo in Oklahoma State history. On many Saturdays, they simply could not be stopped.

Off the field, Blackmon was featured often, and one of the best stories of the year on *ESPN Gameday* was of how Blackmon befriended and become close with nine-year-old cancer patient and fighter Olivia Hamilton. They had met at an OSU Coaches vs. Cancer function and had immediately taken a liking to each other. Blackmon became close to Olivia's entire family, and the two made the effort to be together often. The Hamiltons came to as many games as they could and even stayed for the entire game in Tulsa, a contest that, because of weather delay, did not kick off until 12:20 AM local time and did not end until after 3:30 AM.

Blackmon was again an All-American in 2011 and won his second Biletnikoff Award as the top receiver in the nation. In the Cowboys' win over Stanford in the Fiesta Bowl, he was named the offensive Most Valuable Player, as he had eight receptions for 186 yards and three touchdowns.

That spring, he was the top pick in the NFL Draft by the Jacksonville Jaguars and a shoo-in to be an NFL star. He did start out well as a rookie, with 64 catches for 865 yards on a bad football team. Then the violations of the NFL substance-abuse policy began. Blackmon became a repeat offender and landed himself right out of football. To this day the Jacksonville Jaguars retain his rights, but he remains ineligible to play in the NFL.

It all makes you wonder. Blackmon had an incident his sophomore season where he was driving back from a Monday-night game at Dallas and was pulled over and ticketed for underage drinking. He admitted to the officer that he had two beers at the game. He was suspended for the Kansas State game the next week. Most everybody around the team thought it was an aberration. It is something that many people around the program continue to question, including what they could have done if they only knew or suspected more.

60 2010 Alamo Bowl

The story of the 2010 Alamo Bowl isn't what happened in the Alamo Dome in San Antonio, as Oklahoma State downed Arizona convincingly 36–10, so much as what happened a little more than a week later back in Stillwater. Twenty-seven-year-old quarterback Brandon Weeden and All-American wide receiver Justin Blackmon, keeping Cowboys fans in suspense about their immediate football futures, sat down together in the team meeting room in the Gallagher-Iba Athletic Center. Weeden spoke first.

"I'm here to tell you that Justin Blackmon is coming back next season to play at Oklahoma State," deadpanned the veteran quarterback into the microphones and the television cameras. Then, after a pregnant pause: "I am too."

That signaled what was to come in a Big 12 Championship season and a serious run at a national championship. Oklahoma State finished No. 3 in the major polls after the 2012 Fiesta Bowl win over Stanford and quarterback Andrew Luck.

Earlier, before the Weeden and Blackmon announcement, the Cowboys had torn through another Pac-12 opponent in Arizona. The Cowboys had finished the 2010 regular season with a 10–2 record. They had destroyed Washington State in the opener 65–17 as Weeden and Blackmon gave a preview of what would go on throughout the season. A narrow win over undervalued Troy was followed by another 65-point offensive output in a 65–28 win over Tulsa.

The Cowboys blew through Texas A&M, Louisiana-Lafayette, and Texas Tech before being beaten at home by Nebraska 51–41. Then it was another run of wins over Kansas State, Baylor, Texas, and Kansas before losing a seesaw affair with OU 47–41.

The Cowboys defense saved one of its better efforts for Arizona in San Antonio, as the unit held down future NFL quarterback Nick Foles and picked him off three times. The defense also forced a fumble, sacked Foles five times, and held the Wildcats to 90 yards on the ground.

Oklahoma State scored first on a six-yard run by Jeremy Smith and then, just minutes later, Weeden hit Justin Blackmon on a 71-yard touchdown pass. The Arizona defense would really never catch up with the Cowboys receiver. Blackmon was the offensive MVP in the game with nine receptions for 117 yards and two touchdowns.

Future Dallas Cowboys kicker Dan Bailey had three field goals of 40, 50, and 44 yards.

There is no doubt that the 2010 Alamo Bowl and the press conference just days later back in Oklahoma set the stage for one of the most spectacular football seasons ever in Stillwater.

61 Will History Repeat Itself with Mason Rudolph and James Washington?

Déjà vu—does it really happen? When it washes over you, should it cause expectations of history repeating itself...or maybe something even better? Oklahoma State was back in San Antonio at the end of the 2016 football season, and the last time the Cowboys were in the Alamo city they saw one of the most dynamic and productive quarterback-receiver combinations in school history destroy a Mike Stoops–coached Arizona team. The 2016 Oklahoma State Cowboys were preparing to meet up with an old friend in former Big Eight and Big 12 member Colorado, which had moved on to the Pac-12.

Just two days before the game, after the Cowboys had finished up their last major practice at San Antonio Alamo Heights High School, Cowboys quarterback Mason Rudolph, a true junior who had sent in his paperwork to get a draft evaluation from the NFL, and fellow junior wide receiver (and Rudolph's favorite target), James Washington, met Cowboys assistant athletic director and primary football media contact Gavin Lang underneath the stands of the stadium. Lang, armed with his smartphone, helped Rudolph and Washington tape the message that would delight Oklahoma State fans.

Much like Brandon Weeden and Justin Blackmon had back in 2011, Rudolph announced the pair was coming back—the primary difference being that Rudolph didn't pause like Weeden had.

"Yeah, I think it was a long-thought-out decision with both myself and James. We were in pretty similar positions," Rudolph said later in a press conference at the Alamo Bowl. "I think both of us, we know we can compete at that level. That's going to be next year. If we made the jump this year I think we would have both been ready, but we also know just what college means to us and what we've been enjoying, we've been enjoying these first three years, and we know the tremendous talent and opportunity we have next year coming back.

"We're both really looking forward to not only this game and capping off the season right with an Alamo victory, but also just a great off-season, just making sure that we are improving our game mentally and physically and then just kind of putting an exclamation point on both of our careers," continued Rudolph.

"Just basically like he said, just come back and have another year with our brothers," Washington said. "I look forward to coming back and having another year with him and everyone else, and plus we get degrees. It's worth it, so why not. But that pretty much covers it, what he said."

The Rudolph-Washington duo may have done their business in a different order than the Weeden-Blackmon combination, but a couple of days later in the Alamo Bowl the Rudolph-to-Washington connection helped destroy a Colorado defense and secondary that was rated one of the best in the nation.

Early in the second quarter, with OSU leading after a Ben Grogan field goal, Rudolph hit Washington in stride for what would have been at least a 50-yard gain and may have been a touchdown, but Washington dropped the ball. That almost never happened. That drive continued with Rudolph moving the chains on several completions to San Antonio native and senior receiver Austin Hays and a 24-yard completion to running back Chris Carson. Then Carson carried the ball 10 yards for the touchdown.

Washington, who may have as much pride in what he does as anybody in the football program, was seething over the drop, and that was the worst thing that could have happened from a Colorado standpoint. The next possession, Rudolph connected with Washington for a 42-yard gain down the sideline and then hit Washington on a five-yard slant to complete the drive for a touchdown.

Washington went on to catch nine passes—sound familiar? It was Blackmon with nine catches for 117 yards in the 2010 Alamo Bowl. Washington's nine catches added up to 171, and he was the Offensive Player of the Game in the Cowboys' 38–8 win over No. 10–ranked Colorado. Oklahoma State returned a lot of starters in the 2017 season who played in that Alamo Bowl win, with seven on offense and six on defense, as well as 30 others.

It was not lost on head coach Mike Gundy what the return of Rudolph and Washington meant and what the Alamo Bowl had represented in the past in setting up momentum for a huge season.

"They've been very fortunate to have each other. They're quality young men that work hard. They're very dedicated, they're humble. They understand the team," Gundy said of the quarterback-and-receiver duo. "What I've been most pleased with those guys is throughout their career, there's been times that we run the ball more based on the defense we see, and they're okay with it. A lot of times James doesn't get a lot of passes based on what we see. Neither one of them come to us and say, 'We need more touches.'

"Hopefully they can stay healthy," Gundy continued. "They've been great leaders for our team. Guys like that only come through every so often. All of you out there know, if you follow the game closely, Little League, high school, all levels of college ball, the NFL, if your quarterback is playing pretty good, you have a guy that is a tough guy that will take a chance, you got a chance to have a good team. That's really where they're at. So we were very excited about them making the decision to come back and be a part of our team next year."

Rudolph finished the 2016 season after the Alamo Bowl with 4,091 yards passing and threw 28 touchdown passes and just four interceptions. In his career, he has completed 597-of-958 passing for 8,714 yards and 55 touchdowns with just 17 interceptions. Washington had 71 receptions in 2016 for 1,380 yards and 10 touchdowns. In his career he has 152 receptions for 2,923 yards and 26 touchdowns. Rudolph is close to breaking a number of records currently held by Weeden. Washington could come close to several receiving marks, but Rashaun Woods' records will be tough to top.

Offensive coordinator Mike Yurcich is the coach who gets to make the offensive game plans, and having those two makes it that much easier. That said, you can tell the way Yurcich reacted that he respects not just the decision that Rudolph and Washington made, but all the reasons they took into account in making their decision.

"Well, I think they understand what's at stake. There's a lot to it, and you would have to ask them, but I would suspect they understand what all returns and what's at stake for us," Yurcich explained. "I think the biggest thing that James said is he said education, and that's a beautiful thing to hear. That's what you hope your son says if he's ever fortunate enough to be in that position. These guys know that—I think you have to credit our head coach and the fact that we keep things joyful to a certain extent. It's fun to play the game, it's fun to practice at Oklahoma State, and I think our guys, when we come out and when we go to practice, they play with joy, and I think that's a big deal. If it was a big grind-a-thon and it was just tough, as some of us do remember back in the day, maybe guys are more apt to come out [to the NFL]. But I think this is not the first time this has happened at Oklahoma State, so Coach Gundy, his experience, and I really feel that these guys enjoy playing together. We have really good camaraderie on our team, and that's a credit to the players. We all want as coaches, we all want to manufacture camaraderie and create camaraderie, but you can't. It has to come within the players and they have that. It's special, and I don't think they want to let it go. They're having fun."

62 2016 Alamo Bowl

Two days after junior quarterback Mason Rudolph and junior wide receiver James Washington alerted Cowboys fans via Twitter that they were going to be back for their senior seasons, they put an exclamation point on that message. Oklahoma State was playing No. 10–ranked Colorado in the Alamo Bowl and, like most Oklahoma State bowl games following a Bedlam loss to Oklahoma (the Cowboys lost in Norman 38–20), the OSU faithful were looking for something to raise their spirits. They got it, as the Cowboys dominated on both sides of the ball and destroyed Colorado 38–8.

The Cowboys were hot right out of the gate, taking the opening kickoff and driving 10 plays and 64 yards. Rudolph connected with Washington for 13 yards and then with Jalen McCleskey for 18 yards as two of the big movers on the drive. The Cowboys stalled, and senior kicker Ben Grogan added to his ever-growing school record for most points scored with a 28-yard field goal.

The first quarter ended with the score unchanged, as the Oklahoma State defense was playing aggressively and really limiting Buffaloes senior quarterback Sefo Liufau and talented running back Phillip Lindsay, the younger cousin of former Cowboys quarterback Tony Lindsay and former slot receiver Gabe Lindsay. By the end of the evening, Oklahoma State would have 200 more yards of total offense than Colorado, and the Cowboys defense picked off a pass, registered three sacks, and held the Buffs to 318 yards of total offense and just 4.7 yards per play.

The most important play of the game came early in the second quarter. It was an incomplete pass as Rudolph spotted Washington open on a vertical route down the sideline and hit him in his hands. Washington did something he rarely does—bobbled the ball—and it fell harmlessly to the turf. From that point on, until he suffered a compound fracture of his pinkie finger in the third quarter, Washington was on fire. Oklahoma State actually scored on the possession where Washington had his rare drop, as senior receiver and San Antonio Reagan High School graduate Austin Hays caught a key pass for 13 yards on a third-and-9, and Chris Carson finished the drive with a 10-yard touchdown run.

The next possession, Washington caught a 42-yard deep ball from Rudolph and then finished the drive with a five-yard slant for the touchdown and a 17–0 Oklahoma State advantage.

On the Cowboys' first possession of the third quarter, Rudolph hooked up with Washington again, this time for 46 yards, but the drive ended up empty after a missed field goal. Washington would get hurt later, ending his night, but not before he had nine catches for 171 yards and a touchdown, earning the offensive Most Valuable Player award.

Defensively, Vincent Taylor earned the Most Valuable Player trophy with seven tackles and a sack. Taylor was a real issue for the Colorado offensive line, and the next day the All–Big 12 defensive tackle announced he would be leaving early for the NFL Draft. He would be selected by the Miami Dolphins.

Rudolph finished with 22-of-32 passing for 314 yards and three touchdowns. Freshman All-American running back Justice Hill scored the final touchdown on a 37-yard run, and he finished with 19 carries for 100 yards. All the bowl stats added up to Oklahoma State being one of only two teams in the country to have a 4,000-yard passer (Rudolph), a 1,000-yard rusher (Hill), and a 1,000-yard receiver (Washington).

The defensive performance by the Cowboys was one of the top five defensive performances in bowl-game history.

The Start of Mason Rudolph and Bedlam 2014

If Mason Rudolph stays healthy in the 2017 season, he has a chance to finish his career with 40 or more career starts at quarterback. There is only one other member in that club, and that is his head coach, Mike Gundy. Gundy started 42 games during his career from 1986 to '89. Ironically, it was a decision that Gundy made in the 2014 season that gives Rudolph a chance to have 40 or more starts. Of course, that same decision could have delayed getting to 40, but given Rudolph more starts. It was a unique story that breathed new life into a program that was laboring at best.

Oklahoma State was struggling with a poor offensive line and even worse quarterback play, as an injury early in the year to starter J.W. Walsh had led to Daxx Garman playing quarterback. After losing to Texas 28–7 with total offense of just 192 yards and having been sacked seven times, Garman was dealing with concussion symptoms and questionable at best to play in the second-to-last game of the season at Baylor. The Cowboys appeared to be going nowhere, with a four-game losing streak and a 5–5 record with No. 6–ranked Baylor and No. 16 Oklahoma left—both games on the road. Should Gundy find somebody to take snaps or should he pull the red shirt off a promising freshman who had been red-shirting all season? Rudolph knew what he was giving up—Gundy really knew what he was giving up—but Rudolph wanted to play. Gundy couldn't stand the thought of sending a message to his team that they weren't trying to win. It was a difficult decision, but Rudolph played.

"When you're in a position like that, it's hard to ask the team to practice if you don't put out whoever you think gives them the best chance to win," Gundy said. "Because they know. You can say, 'Hey guys, I want you to practice hard and play hard, but Mason's a potentially good player, we're going to red-shirt him. The other guy's going to go play, but we want you to practice hard.' So that really wouldn't fly. But the ramifications of if it didn't work out, then you feel bad for Mason. There's a lot of things that could happen."

In the rain, in Waco, against a really good team, out marched Rudolph—but something his teammates noticed immediately and something Gundy, offensive coordinator Mike Yurcich, and the staff had noticed all week was that Rudolph didn't appear nervous. He didn't have that "deer in the headlights" stare. Rudolph came out and threw a pick early, but didn't let it intimidate or faze him. He led Oklahoma State to two first-half touchdowns, one an eight-yard pass to David Glidden.

Glidden would comment the next week on Rudolph:

"He really didn't seem nervous at all. He seemed very in control and confident. In fact, after a series or two I really kind of forgot he was making his first start."

Rudolph finished 13-of-25 for 281 yards, and he threw for two touchdowns, including a 68-yard bomb to the receiver who would become his frequent partner on the long ball, James Washington. There was a time you could feel the Baylor fans getting a little nervous about how close the game was, but they did go on to win 49–28.

Two weeks later, it was Bedlam in Norman and you knew if Oklahoma State could not win then Rudolph was going to have busted a red-shirt and an entire season for two games. The Oklahoma State streak of reaching bowl games eight seasons in a row was in jeopardy. Again, Rudolph looked really comfortable, and after OU took an early lead he led the Cowboys on a 77-yard drive to tie the game at 7–7. Future Green Bay Packers fullback Aaron Ripkowski was having a career day and scored two of his three touchdowns in the second quarter. The Sooners led at the half 28–14.

The third quarter was scoreless, but hope was renewed early in the fourth when Desmond Roland scored his second touchdown of the game to make it 28–21. Four minutes later, Ripkowski finished off an 83-yard drive and it was 35–21 Oklahoma.

Then Cowboys magic commenced as Rudolph connected with Brandon Sheperd on a 43-yard touchdown pass to make it 35–28. There was 4:51 left and Oklahoma ate up much of the clock until the Cowboys forced a punt. On the punt, linebacker Seth Jacobs was guilty of running into the punter. The penalty would not give Oklahoma a first down, but the Sooners could punt again and leave Oklahoma State even less than 45 seconds on the clock. Stoops chose to punt again, and current Kansas City Chiefs All-Pro playmaker and 2016 AFC Rookie of the Year Tyreek Hill took the punt and made a couple of moves to get in the clear. Hill turned on his jets past the last clearing block made by Jacobs as he mowed down the punter and finished the 92-yard punt return to tie the game.

"Those guys told me, 'Tyreek, we're going to block our tails off,' and I said, 'I got y'all,'" Hill said after the game. "We did everything we practiced, so it came out exactly how we practiced it. I was just happy that it all worked out in our favor."

In overtime, Oklahoma State stopped Oklahoma and, in fact, pushed the Sooners back. Michael Hunnicutt missed a field goal. The Cowboys drove the ball right down the middle of the Oklahoma defense with running plays down to the 3-yard line, and Ben Grogan kicked a 21-yard field goal for a 38–35 win over rival Oklahoma. More importantly, Rudolph and the Cowboys earned a trip to Arizona and the Cactus Bowl. Lost in the punt return and the overtime was that Rudolph, in his second start, was 19-of-35 for 273 yards and two touchdowns. He cut his interceptions down from two to one.

The Cactus Bowl was a celebration of the way the team had finished the season as two teams on the rise, Oklahoma State and Washington, met on one of the colder nights in the desert. Rudolph showed just how much he had progressed as he completed 17-of-26 passes for 299 yards and two touchdowns. He even performed a Mike Gundy tradition: catching a quarterback throwback for 22 yards. The offense got really fun, using defensive tackles James Castleman and Ofa Hautau in the backfield. Castleman scored on a one-yard run and then later caught a short pass in the flat that he made into a 48-yard gain to set up a field goal as the Cowboys won 30–22.

A tough decision in hindsight worked out as well as possible for Gundy and his young quarterback, who now has a chance to join him as the only quarterbacks in the 40-starts club.

64 Dez Bryant

Most football fans recognize Dez Bryant wearing the number 88 in Dallas and throwing up the X when he catches a touchdown pass. Bryant burst onto the scene in 2007 coming from Lufkin, Texas, where he was a highly rated prospect and one of the biggest recruiting wins for Oklahoma State under Mike Gundy. It would later become public that Bryant had a tough home life and his high school coaches, especially the late John Outlaw, the longtime head coach at Lufkin who died of a heart attack in 2011, helped tutor and raise him.

In something of a reversal from fellow Oklahoma State wide receiver Justin Blackmon, Dez Bryant's career at Oklahoma State was cut short when he was suspended in the 2009 season for violating an NCAA bylaw, but has gone on to a stellar NFL career with the Dallas Cowboys.

Mike Gundy would often say about Bryant, "Dez loves football. He doesn't do drugs, doesn't drink; all he wants to do is play football, but Dez never had anyone to teach him common sense and basics, so everybody thinks he's out of control."

Bryant came in as a freshman at Oklahoma State and caught 43 passes for 622 yards and six touchdowns. That was just the beginning; Bryant broke out as a sophomore with 87 receptions for 1,480 yards and 19 touchdowns. He also returned two punts for touchdowns. He was third nationally with a 17.9 yards-per-return average on punts.

The buildup to 2009 was similar to what it would later be at Oklahoma State with Brandon Weeden and Justin Blackmon, or in 2017 with Mason Rudolph and James Washington. The Cowboys had Bryant and quarterback Zac Robinson, not to mention an NFL-caliber running back in Kendall Hunter. Robinson and center Andrew Lewis were on one of the regional covers for *Sports Illustrated*'s college football preview. Bryant would make his own cover a few weeks later when he caught two touchdown passes, including the diving grab featured on the cover, in a 24–10 win over No. 13 Georgia in the opener. It would be one of the last memorable moments for Bryant.

There was no doubt that Bryant was going to the NFL after his junior season at Oklahoma State, but it turned out he would only play in two more games for the Cowboys: a loss at home to Houston and a win over Rice.

Bryant had gone to Dallas over the summer and had spent time with former NFL star Deion Sanders, who was "giving advice" to college athletes in the area. The speculation was that Sanders was doing some recruiting for his agent, Eugene Parker. The NCAA had questions for Bryant about the relationship and what had transpired in his meeting with Sanders. It turned out that there was likely nothing illegal that happened in the time Bryant spent with Sanders, but Bryant lied to NCAA enforcement representatives about the meeting, claiming it didn't happen. Meanwhile, Sanders had told the NCAA officials that he had Bryant over to his home and that they had worked out together.

"We are certainly disappointed, but we are moving forward as we would with any challenge during the season," head coach Mike Gundy said at the time.

"I made a mistake by not being entirely truthful when meeting with the NCAA. I sincerely regret my mistake and apologize to my teammates, coaches, OSU fans, and the NCAA," Bryant said in a statement.

Bryant was an All-American in 2008 and almost certainly would have repeated in 2009. He would have gone down as one of the all-time-great talents. He still is a tremendous source of pride for Oklahoma State fans, but so much of it is for what he has done in an NFL Cowboys uniform and not the Orange and Black.

He has had a strong career with the Dallas Cowboys, become immensely popular with Dallas fans, and represented the Cowboys in the Pro Bowl three times.

65 Dan Bailey

When he was in high school, Dan Bailey was much more likely to become a golf professional than the most accurate kicker in the history of the National Football League. At Southwest Covenant High School, a private school in Yukon, Oklahoma, Bailey had no goal post to practice on. When he finally did, it was a home-made wooden goal post. As an individual state champion in golf, Bailey was able to practice on a real golf course all the time. That situation alone leads you to believe he had a better chance in golf than kicking footballs.

Bailey had agreed to walk on at Arkansas, and was led to believe he would be getting an academic scholarship to help out with his expenses, but when he lost the competition for the kicking job, then–Arkansas head coach Houston Nutt told him he would have to pay his entire way. Bailey, frustrated and angry, left Arkansas and resurfaced at Oklahoma State. The Cowboys had a senior kicker in Jason Ricks, but Bailey looked to have the edge on getting the job when Ricks left. The clock sped up when, during his senior season, Ricks, normally steady, missed a critical kick late in a game with Texas that Oklahoma State had led almost throughout. Texas came back after Ricks' miss and hit a game-winning field goal, a huge disappointment. The next week Ricks struggled, his confidence gone. Bailey was inserted and never looked back.

Bailey finished his Oklahoma State career going 57-of-72 in field goals made, including making 13-of-20 between 40 and 49 yards and then making 4-of-8 from beyond 50 yards. Bailey had two makes from 51 yards and two from 52 yards in his career. His walk-off game winner in a nationally televised game against Texas A&M was one of his highlights. In 2010, with Oklahoma State's offense setting all kinds of records, he set a record at the time for the most points scored in a season by a kicker with 149. Bailey hit 27-of-31 field goals and 68-of-70 extra points. He was a 2010 Associated Press All-American and he won the Lou Groza Award as the top kicker in college football.

Bailey has only improved since joining the Dallas Cowboys as an undrafted free agent and beating out three competitors in training camp to win the job. In the second game of his NFL career, he missed a chip-shot field goal against the San Francisco 49ers. His career—any kicker's career—could have ended on that miss, but he came back and nailed a 48-yard field goal to tie the game and send it into overtime and then hit a 19-yarder to win the game. Later

Like fellow Oklahoma State Cowboy Dez Bryant, kicker Dan Bailey has also made his home in the NFL with the Dallas Cowboys.

that season, in an 18–16 win over the rival Washington Redskins, Bailey tied a rookie record with six field goals, accounting for all of the Dallas points in the win. He ended his rookie year making 32-of-37 field goals.

In his career, Bailey is 171-of-191 on field goals made through the 2016 NFL regular season, which is good for a career percentage of 89.5 and just barely trails Justin Tucker, current kicker of the Baltimore Ravens. Bailey is also a sensational 24-of-35 on kicks beyond 50 yards. He may have started on a wooden goal post, but it certainly didn't hold him back.

66 Rashaun Woods and the Woods Brothers

If you are looking for the first family of Oklahoma State football, there are several choices. Obviously, Mike Gundy qualifies as the winningest head coach in school history. You could opt for Barry Sanders and his oldest son, Barry J. Sanders, both of whom played for Oklahoma State—and the former, of course, won the Heisman Trophy. There have been combinations of brothers, such as Doug, David, and Daniel Koenig, who all came to Stillwater from Cape Coral, Florida, and all played on the offensive line.

I think most people would select the Woods family. For eight straight seasons, Lawrence and Juana Woods never missed an Oklahoma State game, home or away, to see their three sons play. It started with one of the greatest receivers to ever play college football in Rashaun.

A true technician, Rashaun Woods was an All-State player at Millwood High School before he came to Oklahoma State. After an injury-shortened freshman season of two games, Woods got a medical red-shirt. His real freshman season, he got his feet wet and caught 29 passes for 329 yards. The next season, Woods had the competition and the game measured and he was ready to dominate. He was also about to meet his soulmate when it came to the passing game.

Woods caught 80 passes in the 2001 season for 1,023 yards and 10 touchdowns, working primarily with quarterback Aso Pogi, but at the end of the season head coach Les Miles and offensive coordinator Mike Gundy made a switch, going with the younger quarterback in Stillwater product Josh Fields. Fields and Woods quickly developed a bond; Fields developed almost a sixth sense of where Woods was going to be or adjustments he would make to routes. The trust factor was extremely high, and after a win over Baylor in the next-to-last game of the season, the new passing combination led the Cowboys into Norman. With a key pass late from Fields down the middle to T.D. Bryant, a fabulous catch by Bryant set the stage for one of the most notable touchdown passes in Oklahoma State history.

Fields launched a fade into the southeast corner of Owen Field and Woods went up and high-pointed the ball over the OU defender, coming down with it for a 16–13 win. It was a win that launched the pair and the Oklahoma State football program into a new realm of success. Oklahoma was coming off a national championship season and the Cowboys rocked their world when nobody thought that was even possible.

The next season Fields and Woods ravaged opponents, connecting on 107 passes for 1,695 yards and 17 touchdowns in leading the Cowboys' season to a win over Southern Miss in the 2002 Houston Bowl. In the bowl, Woods caught nine passes for 164 yards and combined with Fields on a 51-yard touchdown pass, but the best was yet to come.

Opponents were stacked to stop Fields and Woods' air show in 2003, but they simply couldn't do it. The act hit its high point in a nonconference game at SMU, as the Mustangs defense set up to stop the run and tried to play Woods with man coverage. They never changed their defensive strategy all night, and Woods caught 13 passes for 232 yards and seven touchdowns, an NCAA record for touchdown catches in a game. Woods and Fields had broken a 34-year-old record. On the season, Rashaun finished with 77 receptions for 1,367 yards and 15 touchdowns. Woods was an All-American again. In the 2004 Cotton Bowl, Oklahoma State's first return to a traditional New Year's Day bowl game since the 1946 Sugar Bowl, Woods caught 11 passes for 223 yards and a 17-yard touchdown, but Eli Manning and Ole Miss fought back and won a 31–28 verdict. Woods' receptions and yardage marked a Cotton Bowl record, and he has since been voted into the Cotton Bowl Hall of Fame.

Away from the field, Woods was an avid angler. He absolutely loved to fish and still does. In fact, there were times that I was convinced that a four-pound largemouth bass on the line in some farm pond outside Stillwater was a bigger thrill for him than a touchdown catch. The catching, both fish and passes, was a little more special for him his last season because he shared it with his younger brother D'Juan. Also a receiver, D'Juan ended up a two-time All–Big 12 performer, first-team in 2003 and second-team in 2004. Rashaun is the all-time leader in receptions with 293, receiving yards with 4,414, and touchdown catches with 42. D'Juan is No. 5 all-time in receptions with 163, No. 5 in receiving yards with 2,751, and tied with Adarius Bowman for No. 6 in touchdown catches with 20.

While Rashaun had D'Juan join him for his final year in Stillwater, D'Juan had the youngest Woods brother, Donovan, join him for three seasons. Donovan came in as a quarterback, and in his first game as a Cowboy led the team in the Rose Bowl against UCLA to a 31–20 victory. Donovan quarterbacked the Cowboys through the 2004 season, completing 97-of-187 passing for 1,628 yards. Oklahoma State was more of a running offense that season, and Vernand Morency led the way with more than 1,400 yards rushing. The Cowboys finished 7–5, including wins over Colorado, Missouri, and Baylor, but they were swamped in the Alamo Bowl by Ohio State.

Donovan started the next season at quarterback, but by the third game under new head coach Mike Gundy, he had been switched to defense. Gundy and the staff felt Donovan would end up being a better defensive player. In 2005 and 2006 he tied for the team lead in interceptions with two each season. In 2007 he led the team in tackles with 81 stops.

All three Woods brothers would play in the NFL. Rashaun was a first-round draft choice of the San Francisco 49ers, but he never was able to duplicate his success from college and is now a successful high school coach at Oklahoma City's John Marshall High School. D'Juan spent a couple of seasons with the Jacksonville Jaguars, and Donovan Woods earned a Super Bowl ring with the Pittsburgh Steelers primarily playing special teams in 2008.

It is really hard to deny Lawrence and Juana's three boys the honor of being the first family of Oklahoma State football.

67 Leslie O'Neal

Absolutely one of the quietest and humblest star players ever to wear an Oklahoma State uniform is Leslie O'Neal. In 2016, O'Neal—who, by the way, went on following his Oklahoma State career to play 13 seasons in the NFL—was a three-time All-Pro, and named to the Pro Bowl six times. He was nominated to the College Football Hall of Fame, and while many nominees went on radio shows across the country, O'Neal politely declined and said that if he was deserving, he would get the votes. He didn't get in, and that is a shame.

When O'Neal arrived at Oklahoma State from Little Rock, Arkansas, he might have weighed about 215 pounds. He was not very big, but he was lightning fast and had a big frame, so as he pushed himself in Oklahoma State's somewhat antiquated weight room he started muscling up. O'Neal would have made a great before-and-after ad on the back of comic books for Charles Atlas or any other strength product on the market. The truth of O'Neal's conversion to a 285-pound—and eventually in the NFL, nearly 300-pound—defensive end was hard work and sweat.

The youngster from Little Rock played sparingly as a freshman in 1982 with a handful of tackles and a fumble recovery, but in Jimmy Johnson's last season O'Neal flourished, with 108 total tackles, 52 unassisted; 11 sacks; and 15 tackles for loss. Those are Emmanuel Ogbah and Vincent Taylor numbers, sort of, from their last season. That was O'Neal as a sophomore.

Many Cowboys fans believe that the best defenses in Oklahoma State history were in 1984 and 1985, and they were anchored by Leslie O'Neal. In 1984, O'Neal threw Big Eight quarterbacks around like rag dolls. He finished with 14 sacks; 17 tackles for loss; and 146 total tackles, 75 of those unassisted. He would add two more sacks in the Gator Bowl that were later added with the NCAA's approval to his regular season numbers, and that is a school record.

In 1985, O'Neal's efforts pushed the Cowboys back to the Gator Bowl, as he had seven sacks, 15 tackles for loss, and 112 total tackles. That season, he was double-teamed on virtually every play by opposing offenses. He was the quietest offensive backfield wrecker football may have ever seen. O'Neal finished with 34 career sacks and 47 career tackles for loss at Oklahoma State. He forced five fumbles and recovered six, most out of the hands of quarterbacks.

O'Neal spent 10 of his NFL seasons with the San Diego Chargers and became one of the most popular Chargers ever. At the end of his pro career, which concluded with the Kansas City Chiefs, he had 136 career sacks.

68 Hart Lee Dykes

His college head coach, Pat Jones, will tell you it doesn't matter that Hart Lee Dykes is the only student-athlete we know of who put four schools on some form of NCAA probation, or that he played at the same time the Cowboys had two of the best running backs ever to play the sport in Thurman Thomas and Heisman Trophy winner Barry Sanders. Jones will tell you Dykes may have been the most valuable weapon of them all, because he could make plays when no other player could. There are lots of reasons that every school in the nation was spending time in Bay City, Texas, recruiting Dykes. UCLA and USC came from the West Coast; Ohio State, Michigan, Illinois, and others came from the Midwest; Alabama, Florida, and LSU were all in from the SEC; and Texas A&M, Texas, Oklahoma, and Oklahoma State were among the closer schools to camp in the port city. Dykes was 6'4" plus, 220 pounds plus, and plenty fast, and had great hands.

Dykes once reached out behind him in a game with Texas A&M during the 1988 season, and even though the pass was significantly behind him he snagged it like a snow cone, pulled it in, and went the distance. Dykes did that kind of stuff all the time. He did so in practice so often that it became commonplace.

"We use the term *freaks* for our receiver group and we've had some. Just while I've been here you can count Adarius Bowman, Dez Bryant, Justin Blackmon, and James Washington is smaller, but he has some of that in him too," head coach Mike Gundy said. "However, Dykes was the original. He was so big, so explosive, and could catch so well with his big, big hands. I tried to be accurate throwing him the ball, but I really didn't need to. He was going to catch just about anything that I threw out there."

Dykes earned All-American honors in 1988, and that wasn't easy to do with the Cowboys so run-heavy with Sanders. His last two seasons as a junior, he caught 64 passes for 1,050 yards and eight touchdowns. Then, as a senior, he caught 84 passes for 1,441 yards and 15 touchdowns. His career numbers were 224 receptions for 3,510 yards and 31 touchdowns. But as Dykes and Sanders prepared to play their last games, with Sanders declaring early for the NFL Draft, a dark cloud developed over the Oklahoma State program. The NCAA was putting Oklahoma State on what to this day is the second-worst probation in history behind only the SMU death penalty.

Dykes, who would be picked No. 16 overall by the New England Patriots that spring in the NFL Draft, had remorse. For many years it bothered Dykes that Oklahoma State fans did not look at him the same way they looked at Thomas, Sanders, and Gundy.

"I've got to a point in my life where I'm comfortable with who I am," Dykes said to the *Daily O'Collegian*. Dykes' mother died, and he mellowed out and said he's begun not to be bothered by things that are out of his control. "If that's how OSU has accepted me, or I haven't received the recognition that other guys have received that were lesser players, then so be it."

Dykes said he is still close with Gundy. He called Sanders and Thomas the two greatest running backs ever to play, and he said it's okay if Oklahoma State fans aren't just as crazy about Dykes' contributions back then. He just isn't going to let it bother him. Dykes said he will still come back and he will still enjoy Oklahoma State football.

"I don't have to have the jersey retirement or the Hall of Fame induction," Dykes said. "I think what I did 25 years ago, people still talk about it. And I'm not talking about the stuff off the field. They're talking about performance on the field. It's amazing because whenever they catch a pretty decent player at OSU, people start calling me wanting to compare him to me," Dykes said. "I didn't play in an offense with four receivers. I played with two of the greatest running backs ever, and I was still able to perform at a high level.

"So imagine if I'd played in a four-receiver set," Dykes finished with the *O'Collegian*. "The records would be unattainable."

69 Remember the Ten

It was a normal road trip on a Saturday in January in the Big 12 as the Cowboys lost a hard-fought game in the Coors Events Center against an improving Colorado team 81–71. In those days, most college basketball teams, especially in conference play, would take several private planes, often donated for travel. The planes ranged from corporate jets to turboprop planes, such as Beechcraft King Air or Queen Air models. On this trip, Oklahoma State had two jets and a Beechcraft King Air 200 flying the team and the support staff, including the radio crew. After the late-afternoon game, the team bused out to Jefferson County Airport, now known as Rocky Mountain Airport, where they split up and boarded the three planes. The third plane, the King Air and the slowest of the three, was primarily support staff with a couple of players onboard. There was snow coming down, but the conditions were deemed safe for takeoff and flight back to Stillwater. That was the last time the basketball travel party would all be together. The King Air took off on its way to Stillwater and the two jets followed, but both landed in Stillwater a little more than an hour later; not unusual, as the jets were expected back earlier. However, as time went on and there was no contact with the King Air and the pilot, Denver Mills, concern heightened. It was clear something was wrong.

Every Oklahoma State fan, alumnus, and friend to the school remembers where they were and what they were doing on Saturday night, January 27, 2001, when they first heard that the plane had crashed and Oklahoma State had lost 10 men who were part of the university and basketball family. The plane had gone down in a field some 40 miles east of Denver, near Strasburg, Colorado. I remember the reactions from head coach Eddie Sutton, who took on the brunt of the burden of losing those 10 men. I remember athletic department spokesman and good friend Steve Buzzard and how compassionate he was in doing his job that night. More than that, I remember how that night changed both those men, and how they were never the same after that.

Sutton refused help from his staff and even his son, Sean, in calling wives, mothers, and fathers to inform them that their husbands or sons had been lost. He made every single one of the calls that had to be made. Sutton never once ducked responsibility in a situation where he would later admit he felt so much guilt, although he was not at the controls of the plane. It is really impossible to know exactly what happened at 7:37 PM MST when that King Air 200 went down. The FAA investigation could not find any mechanical failure at fault, and the crash was ruled a pilot error. Denver Mills was an experienced pilot and had a capable copilot in commercial aviator Bjorn Fahlstrom with him.

Those lost included Cowboys basketball players Daniel Lawson and popular walk-on Nate Fleming. Support staff on the flight were director of basketball operations Pat Noyes, student assistant Jared Weiberg, and athletic trainer Brian Luinstra. Talented sports information coordinator for basketball Will Hancock was lost on that flight. From the Cowboys Radio Network there were eight-time Oklahoma Sportscaster of the Year Bill Teegins and radio producer/engineer Kendall Durfey. The pilots, Mills and Fahlstrom, were also killed in the crash.

The days after the tragedy were filled with tears and almost more memorial services than the college town could handle, both emotionally and from a logistical standpoint. Sutton was the person out front, and you could see it wearing on him. Support and attendance for the main memorial service in Gallagher-Iba Arena came from all across college basketball, especially the Big 12 family. Colorado was especially giving in their help, as was archrival Oklahoma, throughout the mourning. Teegins' place on the radio was taken by different play-by-play announcers from across the conference for the rest of the season.

When Oklahoma State gathered itself nine days later and resumed the season, the Cowboys won an emotional game in Gallagher-Iba Arena over Missouri 69–66. The team would gather themselves to finish 20–10, then lost a first-round game to USC in the NCAA Tournament. It is one of the most devastating events in school history and one that Oklahoma State as an institution vowed never to forget.

Part of the substantial aftermath of the crash was an overhaul of Oklahoma State University team travel policies in the athletic department, and it pushed the rest of college athletics to look into travel policies across the board. Oklahoma State now has a manual that is very strict about how its student-athletes can travel, both in the air and on the ground. There is a system of oversight to make sure all decisions on team travel follow the guidelines created, which for air travel call for either regular commercial service or chartered air service for all teams.

A banner hangs from the rafters of Gallagher-Iba Arena with the names of the 10 men lost and above it the message WE WILL REMEMBER. The school has made good on that promise with a memorial in the lobby of the arena on the southeast side that honors the memory of each of the men and a kneeling Cowboy statue. In that field in Colorado where the plane came down, there is another equally impressive permanent memorial. Every year on January 27, 2001, the library bells toll for the men lost and there is always a memorial at the basketball game that is scheduled on the closest date possible, if not right on that very date. Each spring there is a 10-kilometer Remember the Ten Run, with proceeds going to counseling on campus, including grief counseling for students and OSU staff. Oklahoma State will always Remember the Ten.

70 Kurt Budke and Miranda Serna

Kurt Budke's first season as Oklahoma State Cowgirls basketball coach resulted in a winless campaign in the Big 12. That's right; Budke's team did not win a single game in Big 12 play! Yet, if Budke had registered to run for mayor of Stillwater he likely would have won in a landslide. Budke came in as a Hall of Fame junior-college coach who had made the transition to four-year schools by winning games at Louisiana Tech. In Stillwater, Budke knew he needed to cultivate not only players, but also support. Budke was visible throughout Stillwater, often having coffee in the morning downtown with Oklahoma State fans. He was the kind of person that Oklahoma State people just like to like. His teams got better as his second season resulted in a 20–11 record and an NCAA Tournament bid.

One of Budke's brightest assistants and an outstanding recruiter, Miranda Serna, was a former player of his at Trinity Valley Community College, She then played at Houston before later reuniting with Budke on his staff at Louisiana Tech and then Oklahoma State. Serna had developed the reputation as a good young coach and an excellent recruiter.

Serna and Budke were on their way to watch one of her recruits on November 17, 2011, when the four-seat Piper PA-28 Cherokee they were flying in went down in the hills of Arkansas near Perryville. The crash brought back the tragic memories of the 2001 plane crash in which 10 men, two players, four support staff, two radio network employees, and the two pilots died following an Oklahoma State basketball game at Colorado. That plane, a Beechcraft King Air 200, went down in a Colorado field some 40 miles east of Denver.

The news rocked the Oklahoma State community, including the football program, which learned of the crash on the morning of their scheduled Friday game at Iowa State. Athletic director Mike Holder quickly arranged a charter flight back to Stillwater. The team went on and played the game that night with heavy hearts. Mike Gundy would not blame the crash for the Cowboys' only loss that season in the upset at Iowa State.

Gundy really enjoyed his relationship with Budke and loved that the coach would often come out to Cowboys football practices before the women's season started, and would even come out for a few minutes before going in to conduct his practices. Gundy would later have Budke's widow and children with the team at the Fiesta Bowl. On the podium following the overtime win over Stanford, Gundy and Shelley Budke shared in accepting the Fiesta Bowl trophy from Reece Davis of ESPN.

Budke was an unbelievably spirited individual and seemingly always very positive. He would later coach the Cowgirls to one of their best seasons ever with a 27–8 finish and an NCAA Sweet Sixteen finish.

Following Budke's death, the Cowgirls missed their next two games but rallied to play well down the stretch in honor of Budke and Serna, and in their memory went into the Women's NIT, going all the way to win the tournament. The championship game was hosted in Stillwater and Gallagher-Iba Arena and allowed for Shelley Budke to assist in cutting down the net after the victory.

71 Alma Mater of the Founder of FCA

The Fellowship of Christian Athletes is an organization that is now recognized in 47 countries and all 50 United States, with a confirmed 12,758 Huddles (chapters). Last year there were 86,557 attendees at FCA camps. Countless young athletes have been influenced by people they've met and messages they've heard through the FCA. However, if you asked many of them where the organization got its start, they would probably give you a puzzled look.

Oklahoma is a state many people identify as the buckle of the "Bible Belt," but back in 1945, Don McClanen, a native of Trenton, New Jersey, who grew up in Morrisville, Pennsylvania, and a young sailor training to be a gunner's mate on submarine, was standing on a train platform when a naval officer made conversation.

"He said, 'Well sailor, what are you going to do now that you're out of the Navy?'" recalled McClanen.

He told him he was going to college, probably at the University of Pennsylvania near his hometown.

"Why don't you go to a good school?" the lieutenant asked.

"Where's that?" McClanen replied.

"Oklahoma A&M," the lieutenant said.

At that time Oklahoma A&M was *the* school. The football team was unbeaten and won the 1946 Sugar Bowl with Bob Fenimore and Neill Armstrong starring for Coach Jim Lookabaugh, and Henry P. Iba's basketball team was in a back-to-back run at the NCAA Championship. It was the "Princeton of the Plains."

The naval officer had a profound impact on McClanen. After he was discharged from the service in February 1946, he collected his childhood sweetheart and bride, Gloria Clark, and they moved to Stillwater, Oklahoma, where McClanen enrolled and joined Lookabaugh's football team.

Every day after football practice, McClanen would sit up in the bleachers of then–Gallagher Hall and watch Iba's basketball team run drills. He realized during those sessions in the bleachers that while football was good, his heart was really with basketball, so he spoke with Mr. Iba and the legendary coach offered him a job as manager of the basketball team.

While a student at Oklahoma A&M, McClanen was attending church in downtown Oklahoma City and as he knelt in the back pew of the large sanctuary he became a Christian and surrendered his life to God. That truly was the beginning of the Fellowship of Christian Athletes. McClanen began a hobby of clipping newspaper articles on Christian athletes and saving them.

McClanen soaked up the coaching prowess of Mr. Iba, and upon graduation in 1950 he jumped into education with teaching and coaching. He started at Norfolk and then became the athletic director and basketball coach at Eastern Oklahoma State College in Wilburton. In the spring of 1954, Louis H. Evans, a pastor and former college basketball player who was featured in one of the articles that McClanen had clipped, came to Stillwater. McClanen drove to his college home and met Evans for dinner. He told Evans about his hobby, and Evans encouraged McClanen to contact all of the athletes and personalities he had collected on newsprint.

Evans wrote 19 athletes and members of the sports community. Fourteen of those 19 men told McClanen they were interested. But Branch Rickey, the man who had signed Jackie Robinson when he was general manager of the Brooklyn Dodgers, didn't answer the letter. McClanen, however, pressed on for a meeting with Rickey, who was now the general manager of the Pittsburgh Pirates. He promised to drive to Pittsburgh to meet with Rickey on his own dime for a five-minute, face-to-face conversation. The meeting lasted five hours, and three months later and with a $10,000 gift from a Pittsburgh businessman, FCA became a reality, chartered in Oklahoma on November 12, 1954.

Two years after its beginning, FCA moved to new headquarters in Kansas City and it has remained there since.

A dream started at Oklahoma State and then later cultivated over dinner between two young Christians in Stillwater created an organization that has inspired millions of athletes over the years to use their talents and their influence for good.

McClanen was the first executive director of the Fellowship of Christian Athletes and never strayed far from involvement with the organization he founded all the way to his passing at 91.

72 Final Fours

In addition to the back-to-back national championships in 1945 and 1946, Oklahoma State has been to four other NCAA Final Fours, two under Henry Iba and two coached by his former player and pupil Eddie Sutton.

In 1949, Henry Iba found his team led by All-American Bob Harris and a strong supporting cast that included second-team All-American J.L. Parks and future All-American Gale McArthur back in contention for a national championship. The Aggies edged Wyoming 40–39 in the semifinals of the Western Regional in Kansas City before blowing away Oregon State 55–30 in the regional final. Then it was all the way to Seattle, one of two times the program would finish the season in the Emerald City.

A crowd of 10,600 packed Edmundson Pavilion on the University of Washington campus for a showdown of programs and coaches with Iba and the Aggies against Adolph Rupp and the Kentucky Wildcats. Poor shooting kept the Aggies out of it, and Kentucky star Alex Groza scored 25 points as the Wildcats won 46–36. Oklahoma A&M finished 23–5 and ranked second in the nation.

In the 1950–51 season the Aggies started on a 16–0 roll, but after climbing to the top of the polls, an upset loss to rival Oklahoma and a revenge effort by Bradley to win a game at Gallagher Hall led Oklahoma A&M to a 27–4 record heading into the NCAA Tournament. Led by junior Don Johnson and All-American Gale McArthur, the Aggies beat Montana State and Washington to start the Western Regional in Kansas City before a loss to Kansas State in the final at the regional 68–44. That still earned the Aggies a trip to Minneapolis and the Final Four for the third-place game against Illinois. The Illini were too tough and won 61–46, leaving the Aggies 29–6 for the season.

A drought of 44 years without going to the Final Four was ended, but unfortunately Mr. Iba did not live long enough to see Eddie Sutton get the Cowboys back there. The inside-outside combination of seven-footer Bryant "Big Country" Reeves and the three-point shooting of guard Randy Rutherford were difficult for opposing teams to defend. Oklahoma State started their run in Baltimore, beating Drexel in the first round and Alabama in the second game. The two wins came by a combined 38 points. It was on to East Rutherford, New Jersey, which would become a nice launching pad for Sutton's teams. Reeves battled Wake Forest star and future San Antonio Spurs Hall of Fame post Tim Duncan and Reeves, with 15 points and nine rebounds, held his own as the Cowboys beat the Demon Deacons 71–66. Then, in the East Regional final, Reeves had 24 points and 10 rebounds with 12 points and eight rebounds from Scott Pierce as they handled UMass 68–54.

The big noise for the Cowboys in Seattle came prior to the first game, as Reeves shattered a backboard in the Kingdome that sent souvenir seekers near the floor scurrying to grab a piece of the glass. The game with UCLA was close until the final two and a half minutes, as the Bruins used free throws and a fast-break escape from the OSU defense to win 74–61. Reeves finished his final game as a Cowboy with 25 points and nine rebounds.

One of the more fun teams to watch with defensive stopper Tony Allen, inside battler Ivan McFarlin, the brothers Joey and Stephen Graham, and John Lucas at point guard, the 2003–04 Oklahoma State Cowboys took a 27–3 record into the NCAA Tournament. They could have just stayed in Kansas City from the Big 12 Tournament, as they started the NCAA right there at Kemper Arena, beating Eastern Washington and Memphis by a combined 36 points. Back in East Rutherford, New Jersey, the Cowboys battled a physically tough Pittsburgh team and won 63–51 before taking on the "Cinderella" of that year's NCAA Tournament in Saint Joseph's and the national player of the year in Jameer Nelson. It was considered by some the game of the year in college basketball. St. Joe's led by six at the half, but the constant battle back and forth was decided with 6.9 seconds left when John Lucas nailed a three-pointer from the wing. Nelson came down and had a chance at the buzzer but missed, and Oklahoma State punched a ticket to the Final Four in San Antonio with a 64–62 win.

In San Antonio, the Cowboys met up with Georgia Tech and another tough game that was more inside-driven than outside was played out in the Alamodome. Australian center Luke Schenscher's 19 points and 12 rebounds, combined with a layup by guard Will Bynam with 1.5 seconds left, won it for Georgia Tech 67–65. The Cowboys finished the season with a 31–4 mark, Eddie Sutton's best record at Oklahoma State.

73 Byron Houston

When Eddie Sutton arrived back in Stillwater in 1990 to take over the basketball program he had once played in under his mentor, Mr. Iba, the wise, veteran coach was greeted by just the kind of player he needed to quickly revive the once-proud program. Byron Houston had come to Oklahoma State a year earlier out of Star Spencer High School, just outside of Oklahoma City. With a soft shooting touch, a 6'5" tight end or defensive end physique, and a tough mentality, he was perfect to blend in with Sutton's son and Cowboys point guard Sean Sutton and a freshman seven-foot post from the eastern farm country of Oklahoma, Bryant Reeves.

The burly Houston was such a physical force that one year at the Big Eight Tournament in Kansas City, a local writer dubbed him "Mount Crushmore." Houston was the leader of the Cowboys 1991 Big Eight Championship team. He was the Co–Big Eight Player of the Year as one of the league's top scorers and rebounders. He was named an honorable mention All-American after that season, which took Oklahoma State back to the NCAA Tournament after a seven-year absence.

The next season, Houston came back to Kansas City and this time was named the Big Eight Tournament Most Valuable Player, despite the Cowboys losing the championship game to Kansas. Houston led the Cowboys on to the Sweet 16 of the NCAA Tournament and a 75–72 loss to the Michigan Fab 5. Houston was named a first-team All-American, according to *Basketball Times*, and a second-teamer by virtually every other outlet.

The real contradiction with Houston was that, as tough and bruising as he was on the floor, he was so soft-spoken off of the court. He finished his Oklahoma State career as the school's leading scorer with 2,379 points and an average of 18.7 points per game. He was also the leader in rebounding with 1,189, blocked shots with 222, and field-goal attempts with 1,501. As many times as he put opponents at the charity stripe, Houston was Oklahoma State's all-time leader with 956 free throws attempted and 698 free throws made.

The Chicago Bulls, who at the time had the greatest basketball player ever in Michael Jordan, made Houston their top draft pick—the 27th overall pick in the first round of the NBA Draft. Houston was traded to the Golden State Warriors and played there for most of two seasons before playing one season in Seattle with the Supersonics and another with the Sacramento Kings before bouncing around minor-league and foreign basketball teams.

Houston was also a troubled man. Three times in the span of a year, he was caught exposing himself. Houston, it turned out, suffered from bipolar disorder that caused massive mood swings. He became an alcoholic. The reasons for the downfall of Byron Houston were multiple, as he also had seen his career come crashing down and his marriage was failing.

The sports hero was sentenced to a treatment center, where he got help. He also received support from former teammates and his coach Eddie Sutton, who knew something about addiction. Houston, thanks to help from his coach and former teammates, came back, got a job in construction, and got back on his feet. You can't keep a good Cowboy down.

74 Bryant "Big Country" Reeves

The legend of Bryant "Big Country" Reeves started right away with his freshman season, ranging from Mr. Iba stopping by practice and telling Coach Sutton that he thought the big freshman had promise but was going to take a lot of work, only to come back a week later and say that the big country kid was coming along quicker than he would have thought.

There was the fact that Bryant Reeves' first trip on an airplane came a few weeks later when the team boarded a commercial jet to fly to New York City for the Preseason NIT Final Four in Madison Square Garden, playing Pittsburgh and Georgia Tech.

"There were a lot of firsts for me that year," Reeves told *Posse* magazine. "New York City was shocking. First time on a plane, being on my own, first time to be out of eastern Oklahoma for more than a day or so. It opened up my eyes and was a whole new cultural aspect.

"Playing in Madison Square Garden. How do you top that for a first trip? Doing what I loved to do was huge!

"In the locker room, Byron [Houston] jokingly said that all of us white people looked alike. Then he said since I was from a real small place he would call me 'Big Country,' and it stuck."

Oklahoma State worked for Reeves, but more importantly, Eddie Sutton worked for Reeves. The seven-footer from tiny Gans, Oklahoma, was recruited by Oklahoma and its coach, Billy Tubbs. Gans nearly had a traffic jam, something most residents had deemed impossible, on the day that legendary Indiana coach Bob Knight came to town. Reeves said that current Kansas head coach and then–Oklahoma State assistant Bill Self was the coach who former OSU head coach Leonard Hamilton had sent to recruit Reeves. However, when Hamilton was fired and Sutton was hired, the recruiting was over. Reeves knew he wanted to play for Sutton. You see, in eastern Oklahoma they get a lot of Arkansas coverage, and Reeves had grown up on Razorback basketball and the legend of Sutton. He also knew that Sutton had coached Joe Klein at Arkansas, a big man that had gone on to a good NBA career.

"I had watched how Coach Sutton used the big man and I said yes, and arrived for Coach Sutton's second season," Reeves said.

It was all so new and different for Reeves, except for one thing—hard work. Now, Reeves may not have lifted weights, but he had lifted a lot of other things. Reeves had the size and natural strength that was maximized by his first time being involved in a weightlifting program. Reeves had big, soft hands, and he could shoot pretty well for a big man.

"With Coach Sutton practice was intense; everything we did was intense," Reeves said. "He expected so much out of everyone, a higher standard. Also, Coach had a lot of pride, and with Mr. Iba being there, there was pressure on Coach to turn the program around.

"Coach Self worked with us big guys; post moves, rebounding, the whole nine yards," added Reeves. "My freshman year I started 34 of 36 games. I had to believe I was good enough to be on the floor. That's the way I was raised."

Reeves was good enough, as he shot 52 percent from the floor, averaged 8.1 points and 5.1 rebounds a game, and was named to the Big Eight All-Freshman squad. He helped the Cowboys and the older starters, like Byron Houston and Sean Sutton, to a 28–8 record.

As a sophomore, the legend of Big Country grew a little more, as he shot 62 percent from the field, a school record at the time, and he averaged a double double with 19.5 points and 10 rebounds a game. He became the first player in Big Eight history to lead the league in those three categories—shooting percentage, scoring, and rebounding—since Wilt Chamberlain at Kansas. Reeves was the Big Eight Player of the Year and an honorable mention All-American. The team finished 20–9, losing to Louisville in the second round of the NCAA tournament.

As a junior, Reeves was a Playboy preseason All-American, and he lived up to those expectations on the court, averaging 21 points and 9.7 rebounds a game. He also recorded a personal-best 70 blocked shots. The team was 24–10, losing to Tulsa in the second round of the NCAA Tournament.

Reeves' senior season was the showstopper, especially when the team got to Seattle for the NCAA Final Four. Reeves scored a school-record 797 points, averaging 21.5 points a game. He was named the Big Eight Player of the Year for the second time and earned Big Eight Tournament Most Valuable Player honors. The team and Reeves beat Drexel and then Alabama to advance to the Sweet 16. They beat Wake Forest and Tim Duncan and then UMass to make it to the Final Four.

At the Kingdome on the practice day with a big crowd in the stands, Reeves went up for a dunk and brought the backboard down with glass spraying all over the floor, kind of the basketball version of *The Natural*. People immediately started collecting pieces of the backboard as souvenirs.

"Coach told me if I broke another one that he was going to put it on my bursar bill," Reeves said.

The Cowboys lost to UCLA to end the run, but Reeves was a first-round NBA Draft selection of the Vancouver Grizzlies, and he went on to average 13.3, 16.2, and 16.3 points his first three seasons in the NBA. After signing a $61.8 million contract for six years, Reeves had his best season in the league, but from that point on his career became increasingly plagued by injuries, including severe back problems.

Reeves is now a full-time rancher with 300 head of Black Angus in a calf-cow operation. His son Trey is now at Oklahoma State and a walk-on with the basketball team. At 6'4", Trey has earned the nickname "Little Country."

75 Desmond Mason

One of the most successful players under Eddie Sutton at Oklahoma State, in whom Sutton took such great pride, is Desmond Mason. The talented athlete from Waxahachie, Texas, came from a tough background, as his father was in prison during Mason's high school years. He was recruited to Oklahoma State, and Sutton became something of a father figure to Mason. One of his major weaknesses was his outside shooting, and Sutton and the Oklahoma State staff worked on that with great intensity.

As a result, Mason added the shooting touch to his athletic repertoire and became one of the most explosive players in the Big 12 Conference and across the country. He was a three-time All–Big 12 pick and made various All-American teams. In his final season at Oklahoma State, he averaged 18 points and 6.6 rebounds a game in leading the Cowboys to a 27–7 record and an Elite Eight appearance in the NCAA Tournament.

Mason was incredibly popular with the student section in Gallagher-Iba Arena; they would go nuts every time he launched one of his high-flying slam dunks or made one of his athletic moves on the defensive end of the floor.

As proud as Desmond Mason made Sutton and Oklahoma State fans in college, he went on to make them even prouder in his NBA career, as he finished with a career average of 12.1 points and almost five rebounds a game over a 10-year career with the Seattle Supersonics, Milwaukee Bucks, New Orleans/Oklahoma City Hornets, Oklahoma City Thunder, and Sacramento Kings.

In 2001 Mason won the NBA Slam Dunk Contest at the All-Star Game, and in 2003 he was the runner-up to Jason Richardson.

Now, Mason resides in Oklahoma City, makes frequent returns to Stillwater for events, is an NBA analyst for the Franchise sports-talk radio station, and is an abstract expressionist painter.

76 Tony Allen

What is the identity of Oklahoma State basketball? Try defense. It is the thread that runs from the father of the roundball sport at Oklahoma A&M, Henry Iba, to the return of true basketball at Oklahoma State with Eddie Sutton. Now, again after a drought of defense, here comes a descendent of the Iba coaching tree direct from playing for one of Mr. Iba's pupils at Kansas State, Jack Hartman. Defense is what engenders basketball being played the way Cowboys fans expect it. This is an arena full of fans who will cheer as loud, if not louder, for a shot-clock violation than a made three-pointer. A slam dunk gets much more of a roar when it starts with a steal, an opposing guard's pocket picked on the defensive end. That is why Tony Allen has such a cherished place in Cowboys basketball history.

Allen was a true Eddie Sutton reclamation project. He grew up in Chicago and played his high school ball at Crane High School.

Not exactly the kind of polished material that schools out of the Big Ten or even Big 12 schools like Missouri and Nebraska would take, Allen went to Butler County Community College as a freshman and then migrated back closer to home to Wabash Valley College in Mt. Carmel, Illinois, where he led his team to a 32–6 record and a fourth-place finish in the NJCAA National Championships. Though Allen was still rough around the edges, which contributed to his physical play on defense in the open floor, Sutton promised him a chance to improve his defense and gain the kind of offensive game that would give him a chance to make a career out of basketball.

Sutton also gave Allen something that he badly needed: a sense of belonging, a home, and a father figure whom he still calls on a regular basis. Sutton doesn't get around anywhere near as well as he did even a couple of years ago, but he will still make the trip from Tulsa down to Oklahoma City to see Allen when the Memphis Grizzlies are in OKC to play the Thunder.

Allen termed his treatment from Sutton "tough love." Sutton and his late wife, Patsy, both took on Allen as a cause. There were motivational talks; there were warm cookies just out of the oven and a glass of milk. Allen got a taste of Norman Rockwell's America, and Sutton and the Cowboys got one of the best defensive players college basketball has ever seen.

His first season in Stillwater, Allen started showing the propensity to score points—and he did, to the tune of 1,022 points in his two seasons, rising to No. 26 on the all-time career scoring list. Allen's defense was the key, as he always got the other team's top scorer or best offensive player. Allen could put the brakes on that player and still not let it affect his own offensive game. In his senior season, Oklahoma State won the regular season Big 12 Championship and then the Big 12 Tournament title and advanced to the Final Four in San Antonio, Texas. Allen shared the Big 12 Conference Co–Player of the Year Award with

Tony Allen transferred to Oklahoma State for his final two college seasons and became the first player in OSU history to score 1,000 career points in two seasons.

teammate John Lucas. He was also the Most Valuable Player in the Big 12 Tournament and an Associated Press honorable mention All-American.

Off the court, Allen fulfilled his dream of finishing with his degree in education. It was hard to tell, honestly, whether Allen was prouder of his accomplishments on the court or off the court.

"Tony was always thanking me and Patsy for what we did for him," Sutton said several years ago when asked about Allen. "He was tough and he was always needing guidance, but Tony Allen had a good heart and once he saw that was what could guide him, well, he didn't need as much help. He thanked us, but we were always thinking about how much he did for Oklahoma State basketball. I've always been proud of Tony for how hard he worked, on and off the basketball court."

To this day, Allen appreciates Sutton, and you get the sense that the at least once-a-month phone calls that Sutton told Allen that he needed to make didn't need the insistence. Sutton put his hand on Allen to guide him and it was as much a fatherly touch as it was a coach instructing.

"Once we get on the phone, we're on there for at least a good, solid 25 minutes," Allen said recently to the *Oklahoman*. "Like one time, he sent me a picture of him riding a bull. I thought it was funny so I called him right back. Had to make sure he was okay, didn't fall off it or nothing."

Now there is some coincidence. It was Sutton making sure when he got Allen to Stillwater from junior college that he stayed up and kept riding and didn't fall off. He never has, as Allen has now become a longtime career standout in the NBA. He's been riding well for the long haul, thanks to a leg up from his coach.

77 Doug Gottlieb

Doug Gottlieb is the answer to a personal trivia question—who's the only pro basketball player Robert Allen has ever roomed with? Through my experiences with the mile-a-minute talker and almost-as-quick thinker, I have an insight into one of the most interesting personalities in the history of Oklahoma State athletics. Just think of Gottlieb's range; though he was one of the most amazing passers and assist-heavy point guards in the school's illustrious basketball history, he was also one of the program's most infamous free-throw shooters. He was a teammate who was likeable but also capable of making you want to kick him in the butt, and the same feeling was prompted with his coaches. Gottlieb is one of the most sincere and caring people you could run across, but he is also capable of making that comment that makes you freeze in thought, or even anger. Gottlieb is a Californian with a little East Coast in him, and quite proud of being adopted as one of the best Jewish point guards to call the Midlands his home.

His story at Oklahoma State starts like a lot of Eddie Sutton's key players'—as a transfer. Gottlieb's father, who died of cancer in November 2014, was a former Sutton assistant at Creighton who had never lost touch with his former boss. Doug had been a tremendous high school point guard, one of the best passers in the country at Tustin High School in Orange County, California. Gottlieb signed with Notre Dame, and on the court, things went well, as Gottlieb started all but four games as a freshman and led the Irish in assists, with 154, and minutes played. Off the court, Gottlieb was charged with stealing credit cards from a roommate and two others and running up $900 in fraudulent charges. After paying back the charges, Gottlieb was able to leave Notre Dame and transfer without more serious consequences. His father knew that Sutton was an expert at giving second chances and making them work.

Gottlieb arrived at Oklahoma State following a year in which he sat out and attended class and helped coach at Golden West Community College, with a larger-than-life personality and the same game at point guard that was electric at Notre Dame. Playing for Sutton, he also enjoyed experiencing a greater appreciation for defense. Gottlieb immediately started at point guard and helped the Cowboys get to the NCAA Tournament as the Big 12 Newcomer of the Year. On the court, Gottlieb's brash play and quick mouth got him into some famous fights in practice, but he earned his respect and a reputation for never backing down.

His second season in Stillwater led to another strong performance in which he led the nation in assists with an average of 8.8 a game. The Cowboys went back to the NCAA and Gottlieb had busted the OSU career record for assists in only two seasons with 500. The previous mark had been from Matt Clark in four years with 432.

His final season was highlighted by a trip to the Elite Eight in the NCAA Tournament and an almost complete rewriting of the Oklahoma State record book's section on assists. Gottlieb was No. 2 in the nation in assists, with 8.5 a game, but he finished with 793 assists in his Cowboys career, 248 more than Byron Eaton, who is now No. 2. He finished with 34 games in which he had double-digit assists. The only single-season or career assists records he doesn't own are assist-to-turnover marks for a season and a career. He is No. 2 behind Scott Sutton, who did not play nearly the minutes that Gottlieb did.

Gottlieb's career mark on free throws is at Oklahoma State is 107-of-236 for .453 percent, and that may be one of the worst for a point guard in school history.

Academics were a strong suit for Gottlieb. He got his degree in marketing and was one of the better student-athletes. He also started doing some radio work as a fill-in and sometimes cohost on local sports-talk shows.

Gottlieb logged some brief experience with professional basketball both in the United States and overseas, including a championship season for Ural Great Perm of the Russian Basketball Federation. He was also the MVP for the winning USA team coached by former Tennessee and current Auburn coach Bruce Pearl in the Maccabiah Games in Israel.

His personality was magnetic, most of the time, and Gottlieb recruited and won the love of a Drumright, Oklahoma, native and Oklahoma State student, Angie, who became his wife. They now have three children.

While finishing up his pro career, he continued to dabble with doing radio and some color on the Oklahoma State game televised by Learfield. It soon blossomed, as he was hired full-time by ESPN Radio and went on to cohost college basketball programming and serve as an analyst on televised college basketball games. Gottlieb was eventually lured by CBS and CBS Sports with the opportunity to do games in the NCAA Basketball Tournament, to which CBS has long owned the rights. He is now doing his own daily show on the CBS Sports Network on cable and does regular season and NCAA Tournament games for CBS.

As for rooming with Gottlieb, I can say we had a lot of fun with the USBL Oklahoma Storm spending time in New York City and Atlantic City, and checking out the home of Bruce Springsteen in Asbury Park, New Jersey. I can also tell you he doesn't snore—that I know of.

78 The Shooters: Phil Forte and Keiton Page

How often do you see a player set a record—in this case, career three-point shooting—and then almost immediately, see another player come along and break it?

Usually records like that stand for some time. At Oklahoma State, current Cowboys director of player development Keiton Page was an outstanding three-point shooter as a Cowboys player. Page, who played for his father David in high school at Pawnee, came to Oklahoma State owning the national high school record for three-point shooting percentage in a career at 49.9 percent. He certainly didn't disappoint as a Cowboy, but after he completed his career (2008–12) along came Phil Forte. Another prolific three-point shooter, Forte (329-of-832) took aim at Page's Oklahoma State record.

"I've been very fortunate and blessed in so many ways," Forte said of the record. "To have the type of coaches and teammates that I've had here. I have had the best teammates in the country and they've made my job easy."

"Phil is ultradeserving of that [record]," Page said. "I've played with several gym rats and they were all good but I've never seen someone spend more time in the gym than Phil Forte. He's earned every one of those he's made."

Page, unbelievably stopped at 299, made three points as he passed Randy Rutherford, who made 279 between 1992 and '95. It is fair to say that Page hit 299-of-812 three pointers attempted for 36.8 percent.

An interesting aspect of this is that Forte gives Page a lot of credit for helping him to choose Oklahoma State and then for helping him to be successful once he was in Stillwater.

"KP has been great and I know he really helped me when I came in here as a freshman," Forte said. "So many things that I struggled with and he's helped me my entire five years. I watched him play and he's a big reason why I came here to Oklahoma State. Seeing the success he had here and just trying to follow behind him as he's gone down as one of the best players to ever play here. He's been great and someone that has helped me out."

Page has seen every three-point shot involved, being on staff the entire time Forte has played.

"It's been fun, like you say to watch all of them, and I've been here for everyone," Page admitted. "It's been fun getting to watch him and see him because he's in the gym before we practice and he stays after we're done getting up extra shots. He's been fun to watch."

More than 600 three-pointers made between two shooters who actually went about it the same way. It is a rarity you just don't come across every day.

79 Oklahoma State Wrestling Tradition

Pick a sport and you can almost automatically pick out a school that serves as a synonym for success in that sport. At Oklahoma State they like to refer to it as the "gold standard." If I say football, then you would probably respond with Alabama. The Crimson Tide has claimed 16 football national championships. If I tossed out men's basketball, then you would maybe say UCLA, as John Wooden had that run of 10 national titles in 12 years, including four unbeaten seasons, and the Bruins later added another NCAA Tournament Championship in 1995 under Jim Harrick. Okay, how about ice hockey? It is a lot more competitive, but the correct answer is the Michigan Wolverines, who have won the Frozen Four nine times and won six of the first nine NCAA Division I Hockey Championships.

In wrestling, it is unquestionably Oklahoma State, which has won 34 NCAA Wrestling National Championships, topping the number of championships won by any other school in any single sport. The banners representing each of the Cowboys' wrestling titles make up the vast majority of banners that ring the rafters of Gallagher-Iba Arena.

Oklahoma State, originally Oklahoma A&M, has dominated the sport of wrestling as its 34 titles leads Iowa, a proud program and worthwhile rival with 23 championships. Cowboys wrestlers have claimed 142 individual NCAA championships, with Iowa in second at 81. Oklahoma State has earned 458 All-America awards, with Iowa at 319 and Iowa State at 294.

To further illustrate the dominance of OSU wrestling, think of this. The father of college wrestling, Oklahoma A&M's initial wrestling coach, Ed Gallagher, delivered the first dual victory in school history in 1917, and in 2011 the current head coach and the winningest in school history, John Smith, coached the Cowboys to their 1,000[th] dual victory in the sport. Oklahoma State has better than an 89 percentage of wins in its wrestling duals.

You can go to professional sports and think of the best franchises and their accomplishments, like the Green Bay Packers in the NFL (13 World Championships), Montreal Canadiens in the NHL (24 Stanley Cups), New York Yankees (27 World Series championships), and Boston Celtics (17 NBA titles), and none of them can match the Oklahoma State wrestling program for championships won.

80 Myron Roderick

In all my time covering athletics at Oklahoma State, there are only a few men who I never ever called by their first names. No one ever called Mr. Iba either Henry or Hank. I certainly wasn't bold enough to try that one. Two other men I covered for a much longer period were Eddie Sutton and Myron Roderick, and to this day I still call Sutton "Coach Sutton." Roderick passed away in 2011, and right up until the last time I saw the man, he was Coach or Coach Roderick. Roderick's life can be summed up in one word: *competition*. Roderick was a competitor and, even after his days of wrestling, playing tennis, and coaching at Oklahoma State were over and he became the athletic director at his alma mater and then retired, he kept winning national championships.

Roderick is in two halls of fame: the National Wrestling Hall of Fame there in Stillwater and the Oklahoma Racquetball Hall of Fame. Roderick continued competing in his newfound sport and won 10 national championships in doubles in his age bracket with partner Dr. Bud Muehliesen. He also won two national championships in singles. Roderick could never stop competing.

Another word that describes Roderick is *fierce*. He was that as a wrestler and as a coach. He came to Oklahoma State from Winfield, Kansas, just across the state line, and in his time at Oklahoma State he won 42 of his 44 matches, and collected three national championships, one at 137 pounds, and then a pair at 130 pounds. He went on to earn a spot on the 1956 Olympic Team in Melbourne, where he placed fourth after losing a split decision to the eventual gold medalist.

Roderick as a coach was even more of a fierce competitor. Roderick jumped right out of wrestling in the Olympics to take over the tradition of Oklahoma State wrestling and, at 23 years old in 1958, he led the Cowboys to the NCAA team national championship, the youngest coach ever to lead a team to a title in NCAA history. In his 13 years as Oklahoma State head coach he led his alma mater to seven team NCAA Championships. They won 140 dual meets, losing only 10 and tying seven. One time they won 84 dual matches in a row.

Roderick's wrestlers collected 20 NCAA individual championships and four gold medals in the Olympic games. He was the head coach for Team USA in the 1963 World Championships and the assistant coach for the 1964 Olympic Games.

Roderick was also successful in business, and he used his business acumen to help his sport and his school. He was the first-ever executive director of the U.S. Wrestling Federation and he helped establish the foundation of USA Wrestling that is the sport's governing body to this day. He also saw the need for a National Wrestling Museum and Hall of Fame and helped establish that landmark in Stillwater on the Oklahoma State University campus.

When his school needed him, he came back and served as athletic director during a crucial time as the school fought off the negative impact of football probation. He hired Eddie Sutton and brought him home to coach the Cowboys, and also oversaw a remodel of Gallagher Hall into Gallagher-Iba Arena with chairback seating and a nicer exterior, restrooms, and concessions.

Roderick is also in another Hall of Fame and he is deserving of that honor: the Oklahoma Sports Hall of Fame.

81 Yojiro Uetake Obata

In Stillwater, Oklahoma, back in 1963, a young man from Japan who had won his nation's high school wrestling championship came to America to get his education. However, on the mat he ended up teaching lessons to a lot of collegiate wrestlers in the country and he made a great friend out of a bow-legged football fullback, who would go on to become pretty famous himself. Yojiro Uetake, or "Yo-Jo," took American college wrestling by storm. He won all 58 of his collegiate matches at Oklahoma State.

"I'll tell you Yo-Jo was one heckuva an athlete," Oklahoma State All–Big Eight fullback Walt Garrison said of his friend. "It only took me one time messing around with Yo-Jo in the dorm and I wasn't messing again. One of the nicest guys you'd ever know, but also on the wrestling mat one of the nastiest competitors. Yo-Jo wasn't ever going to lose, and once you got to know him he was funny, too."

Not very funny for opposing wrestlers, as after his sophomore season at Oklahoma State Uetake went home to Japan, made his country's team, and then won the Olympic Gold Medal in Tokyo. Four years later he went to Mexico City and went through the bracket in perfect fashion to become the first Japanese wrestler to win two Olympic gold medals. He was a combination of speed, strength, and tremendous smarts, so that he could call on any one of hundreds of holds and moves that he had in his repertoire and he did almost always on instinct. Rarely was he ever scored on.

"I don't know how good he was," his collegiate coach Myron Roderick once said, "because I never saw him seriously challenged."

Uetake, who in 2015 made a visit back to the Oklahoma State campus for the first time in a long time, has said he will always be in debt to Oklahoma State and the experience he had in Stillwater. He was back in Oklahoma in 2015 to be inducted in the Oklahoma Sports Hall of Fame, and it was Garrison who presented him. Uetake coached very well, too, just like his coach Roderick had gone from wrestler to coach. Uetake coached two seasons as an assistant at Oklahoma State and then headed up the freestyle program for Japan for the 1972 and 1976 Olympics.

82 Tommy Chesbro

There is no question that when it came time to be serious—time for a look that could stop a clock on the wall—Tommy Chesbro had the ability, but the rest of the time Chesbro was going to have fun. One of the most affable and easygoing (at the right time) wrestling personalities in Oklahoma State history, Chesbro started at Oklahoma State on the 1959 national championship team. He had been a state champion in high school and was solid as a wrestler for the Cowboys, but Chesbro's greatest success would be as a coach.

Chesbro was a Stillwater–Oklahoma State guy through and through. His father, Ray, had played guard in football at Oklahoma A&M and moved his family from Colorado City, Texas, back to Stillwater. At SHS, Chesbro played football and wrestled and was All-State in both. After graduating from Oklahoma State and wrestling on two national championship teams, starting on the one, he went into coaching and eventually was back in Stillwater as the Pioneers' head coach, leading them in 1969 to Stillwater's first team State Championship.

In eight years of coaching high school wrestling he had a record of 51–23–8.

In 1970 Chesbro was named the head wrestling coach at Oklahoma State. From that year through 1984, his Cowboys teams won 227 dual matches and lost only 26, a 90 percent winning record. He ended his career with a 43-match win streak. In 1983, his team won all 22 duals and shut out 10 of their opponents. In one dual win, the opponent posted a rare negative-one-point total, thanks to a penalty point on the coach. The Cowboys dominated Oklahoma and their coach Stan Abel in those days and Chesbro and Abel would routinely—along with the help of some very colorful wrestlers on both teams—put on a show that, while collegiate in style and technique, matched some of the more colorful wrestling shows on television.

His 1971 team won the NCAA Championship and his team was among the top four in the NCAA on a dozen seasons during that time. Chesbro had a strong relationship with his wrestlers. Current head coach John Smith, who wrestled for Chesbro, said it was like a father-son relationship. Smith was one of Chesbro's 20 NCAA individual champions and World and Olympic champions Smith and Kenny Monday, along with three-time NCAA heavyweight champion Jimmy Jackson, were among his very best.

In one of the best-ever fill-in performances, Chesbro, who after leaving coaching had become director of facilities for the OSU athletic department, jumped in to coach the wrestlers in a Bedlam dual in 1992. Head coach John Smith and assistant Kenny Monday were away training for the Olympic Games. Chesbro showed that his mastery of the Sooners was still in play as that Oklahoma State team won the dual 43–0, the largest margin of victory at that time in the history of the 72-year Bedlam series of wrestling.

One of Chesbro's sons, Doug, would later become the wrestling coach at Stillwater High School, continuing the legacy. His youngest son, Todd, would win three Big Eight Championships and was a three-time NCAA All-American. Chesbro died at the age of 66 of a heart attack while still serving as facilities director of the athletic department.

83 Kenny Monday

One of the most powerful athletes to ever compete in any sport for Oklahoma State, Kenny Monday is still teaching explosion, as he has taken his abilities and the coaching prowess to pass them on and is tutoring and training some of the top competitors in the newer combat competition of the UFC. Monday, had UFC been around when he finished his Oklahoma State wrestling career, may have been one of its greatest champions. Monday had all the tools, physical and mental, and used them to win an Olympic gold medal in the 1988 games, a silver medal in 1992, and a sixth-place finish in his third Olympics, virtually unheard of for a wrestler.

Monday came out of Tulsa's Booker T. Washington High School and won four straight state championships with a 140–0–1 high-school record. His four championships came at four different weights, as he started out skinny and filled out in high school. He came to Oklahoma State and settled in at 150 pounds. In Stillwater, he met back up with the only wrestler to tie him in high school in fellow Cowboys great Mike Sheets. Together the pair would combine for seven All-America seasons (Sheets with four), three NCAA individual championships (Sheets with two), and three NCAA runners-up (Monday with two). There teams never won the team NCAA title, but they were stout.

Monday's national individual title came in 1984 and he finished as the all-time leader in falls, with 51. Later he would be passed by Jordan Oliver, with 54.

He had a tremendous amount of success wrestling across the world as he and John Smith, who would later hire him as an assistant coach for the Cowboys, wrestled in almost every venue that sport offered. Monday won the 1988 Tblisi Tournament; 1989 World Championships; 1991 Pan American Games and the President's Cup in Turkey; 1992 Roger Coulon in France; and the 1996 Dan Kolov Tournament in Bulgaria. At the Tblisi, Monday won the coveted animal-skin cloak as the tournament's most outstanding wrestler. For many years it was on display at the National Wrestling Hall of Fame.

Monday is a member of the National Wrestling Hall of Fame.

84 Kendall Cross

Kendall Cross is one of the most logical and at the same time one of the most amazing Olympic gold medalists in wrestling history. Cross grew up in Mustang, Oklahoma, and was always talented. He finished his high school career winning a state championship and moved on to Oklahoma State, where he was a three-time All-American and in 1989 won the NCAA Championship. It all sounds good; sounds like that hard-working wrestler from the red-dirt state who rubs a little of it on his face and goes back to work.

Cross could find this unfair, or he could say, "You know, Robert Allen covered me and knows me pretty well." Cross could turn it on and off, but when he flipped the switch you had better not be in the way. His explosive and dominant manner was like a hurricane, or better yet, an Oklahoma tornado engulfing his opponent. He would often have a sheepish grin on his face, leaving an opponent wondering which Kendall Cross was about to appear on the mat.

In 1992, Cross was the only wrestler at his weight on Team USA who was not ranked No. 1 at the beginning of the year. He finished sixth in the 1992 Barcelona Olympics. Cross never had a paved road to success, and that was the case in 1996, as he had to battle former Iowa wrestler Terry Brands at the Olympic trials. Cross didn't waste his trip to Spokane, Washington, for the opportunity to go to the Olympics; he brought that tornadic style in beating the favored Brands.

In Atlanta, at the Olympic Games, Cross was dominant from start to finish in winning the gold medal, with one of the greatest wrestling performances seen by an American in the Olympics. He would go on to be named the USA Wrestling Athlete of the Year in 1997. Cross was a three-time Freestyle National Champion after graduating from Oklahoma State. He now tutors future tornadoes on the mat with the Kendall Cross Gold Medal Wrestling Club in Boston, Massachusetts. He is a member of the National Wrestling Hall of Fame and one of the most fun athletes in Oklahoma State history.

85 Pat Smith

In a family where it is very hard to top siblings who came before, Pat Smith found a way to top his brothers, NCAA champion Lee Roy and NCAA champion and two-time Olympic gold medalist John. Pat Smith made wrestling history from the time he arrived at Oklahoma State until the time he finished his collegiate career. You can start with the record Smith amassed—121–5–2 in his time in Stillwater—but it is how he finished each of his seasons at the NCAA tournament that really stands out. He finished on top and unbeaten in NCAA tournaments to become the first-ever four-time individual NCAA champion. He won the championships in 1990, 1991, and 1992, and, after a red-shirt season, came back and won again in 1994. His titles in 1990 and 1994 helped lead the Cowboys to team championships, the 1994 title with his older brother John as head coach of the Cowboys.

Since then, three other wrestlers have accomplished the feat. Former Iowa State wrestler and current Penn State coach Cael Sanderson was next, and then Cornell's Kyle Dake did it. Most recently, it was Logan Stieber of the Ohio State Buckeyes.

It was also that 1994 championship in which Smith was named the NCAA Outstanding Wrestler of the Tournament. Smith was just the third Oklahoma State wrestler to win four Big Eight individual wrestling championships.

Smith had success in his freestyle career, as he won the bronze medal in the 1997 World Cup, a second-place finish to fellow Oklahoma State wrestler and assistant coach Kenny Monday at the 1996 Olympic Trials. He was a two-time gold medalist at Olympic Festivals and had six All-America finishes at the U.S. National Open Freestyle Championships.

He went on to join his brother John as an assistant coach for the Cowboys. He is also enshrined in the National Wrestling Hall of Fame.

86 Johny Hendricks

Johny Hendricks is not in the National Wrestling Hall of Fame, and he was never the Outstanding Wrestler of the NCAA Tournament. However, Hendricks was really good as an Oklahoma State wrestler; in fact, his head coach, John Smith, may have thought of Johny as more of a son to him than a wrestling student-athlete. Close observers of the OSU program believe Smith saw a lot of himself in Hendricks, from the time he first recruited Hendricks out of Edmond Memorial High School. Hendricks' style in high school was to almost toy with his outmatched opponents and even experiment with different moves and holds before finally either pinning them or continuing to pile up points toward a technical fall. The thought was that Hendricks would finish his Oklahoma State career, which he did with two individual NCAA championships, and go on to work toward the Olympic gold medal many believe Smith saw him as capable of winning.

Something got in the way of Hendricks' Olympic future and Smith's Olympic vision for his pupil. It was a new sport movement—Ultimate Fighting Competition. Hendricks saw the rapid rise in popularity of the sport and opted to jump in. Smith tried not to be vocal about it, but it was obvious he was disappointed that Hendricks didn't pursue Olympic glory—but he sure found lots of gold—money, that is—in the UFC. Hendricks rapidly became one of the biggest rising stars in the sport that another former Oklahoma State wrestler, Randy Couture, had helped make popular. The UFC was overtaking boxing and even competing with the show that is pro wrestling.

Hendricks, an ethnic mixture of Dutch, German, and Native American ancestry, had an electric style and a personality that brought a lot of fans to the UFC and helped put up numbers on their big pay-per-view events. Hendricks started training in Las Vegas after leaving Oklahoma State, and in seven months fought his first fight and scored a third-round TKO at the Masters of the Cage 16 in Oklahoma City. Hendricks stayed on a roll and won twice more, including his television debut in 2008 in Tulsa. Hendricks moved up in competition and won three more fights. That was when Hendricks signed with the elite UFC. He won his first UFC fight in UFC 101 in Philadelphia on the undercard and the fight was stopped in 29 seconds.

Hendricks was 3–1 in his first full year of UFC, and then he went on a win streak, taking seven opponents in a row and finally earning his first shot at the UFC Welterweight Championship as he fought George St.-Pierre at UFC 167. He lost the bout in a controversial split decision that even UFC President Dana White questioned. About a month after losing, it was announced that St.-Pierre was going to take an indefinite break from MMA competition and vacate the belt, which immediately set up a fight between Hendricks and Robbie Lawler in March at UFC 171 for the vacant championship. Hendricks won the contentious fight by a unanimous decision.

Hendricks, most famous for—and dangerous because of—his explosive punch and his wrestling prowess, had to take a break when he had surgery to repair a torn biceps. He returned to training and in December 2014 fought Lawler in a rematch. After a strong start, his battle with cutting weight may have slowed him in later rounds and he lost in a split decision. Since then, Hendricks has been battling back, but cutting weight has continued to be a problem, as he has consistently missed weight and had to forfeit part of the purse to his opponent before even getting in the octagon.

Hendricks has recently made the move to middleweight and is working toward a title shot in that class.

87 Cowboys Wrestling and MMA

Johny Hendricks is arguably the most well-known and, maybe, the most accomplished Oklahoma State wrestler to move into mixed martial arts and the popular UFC competition, but the trailblazer was three-time All-American Randy Couture. Besides Couture, who really did use his military experience and his wrestling prowess at Oklahoma State to create an aura and develop a foundation that made him successful in the sport, we have seen Cowboys wrestlers like three-time national champion and four-time All-American Jake Rosholt and 2001 Oklahoma State NCAA All-American Daniel Cormier have success in the octagon.

Couture was born and raised in the state of Washington and won a high school state championship individually in wrestling his senior year. Couture then went into the U.S. Army after high school and attained the rank of sergeant in the 101st Airborne during his six-year tour from 1982 to 1988. He also did some wrestling and boxing during his time in the Army, including a stint on the Army Greco-Roman wrestling team.

After getting his honorable discharge from the military, Couture didn't mess around—he joined the Oklahoma State wrestling team and was a three-time All-American who finished as the runner-up his last two years at 190 pounds. In 1991, he lost to Paul Keyshaw of Cal State–Bakersfield, and in 1992 he lost in the finals in Oklahoma City to Mark Kerr of Syracuse. Couture was an Olympic team alternate for 1988, 1992, and 1996, and he was in the semifinals at the 2000 Olympic Trials. He had worked as a wrestling coach and in strength training at Oregon State University, and at that time in his life he gravitated toward the rising sport of MMA. He was really good, really fast.

Couture holds the UFC record of competing in 15 different title fights and he has been a three-time UFC Heavyweight Champion and a two-time UFC Light Heavyweight Champion. He became the first of what, to this day, are only three fighters to hold two UFC championship titles in two different divisions. The man is not only tough, but very resilient, as he fought 24 times in UFC, won a championship fight after being named to the UFC Hall of Fame, and is the only competitor to have come back and recovered a title he has lost—and he did it three times. He is the only man over 40 years of age to win a UFC Championship fight, and he did that four times.

Couture has partnered with several different people in developing several training centers and also a chain of gyms under the brand Xtreme Couture. He has also branched into acting, and is a popular villain or tough-guy guest star on television dramas.

Both Jake and Jared Rosholt have gone from Oklahoma State wrestling to MMA and UFC, although not with the degree of success of Hendricks, Couture, or Cormier. Jake was one of the greats at Oklahoma State, with a four-time All-American and three-time NCAA Championship career. The native of Sand Point, Idaho, who moved with his family to Ponca City in Oklahoma won the NCAA individual championships as a freshman, junior, and senior.

Younger brother Jared was a three-time All-American who finished as the runner-up in 2010 at the heavyweight division in the NCAA Tournament. Both have competed in MMA, as Jake started his career training in one of Randy Couture's training centers in Las

Vegas. He competed some in WEC before moving on and winning over Ultimate Fighter 1 alumnus Chris Leben at UFC 102. Since then, Jake Rosholt has dropped out of UFC competition and has seemingly retired. Jared is continuing to work at the sport.

The rising star and champion most recently out of the stable of former Oklahoma State wrestlers is Daniel Cormier. With a record of 18–1 with six knockouts, five submissions, and seven decisions, Cormier has been a natural at the sport, combining his wrestling talents with a strong punch and solid kicking ability. He has developed a rivalry in public, if not in the octagon, to the one fighter he has lost to, Jon Jones, who was suspended one year by the Nevada Athletic Commission. Cormier worked hard to get the shot and then become the Light Heavyweight Champion in UFC, and he is also considered the UFC's third-best pound-for-pound fighter.

Cormier took a different route to MMA, as he did invest in a freestyle career after Oklahoma State. He finished fourth in the 2004 Olympic Games and qualified for the 2008 Olympics, but had to scratch from competition as a result of kidney failure brought on by excessive weight cutting.

Cormier is expected to continue to be a top star in UFC events in the coming years, but at 38 years old he could be approaching retirement.

88 Oklahoma State Golf Tradition

Now going on more than 70 years, there are few athletic programs in the history of the NCAA that can compete with Oklahoma State golf. The Cowboys' golf program has competed in an NCAA-record 65 consecutive NCAA Championships from 1947 to 2011, winning the national championship 10 times and finishing lower than No. 5 just 14 times. After missing the tournament in 2012, the Cowboys' golf program has started a new streak from 2013 through 2016.

Eight Cowboys golfers have won the individual NCAA Championship—Earl Moeller (1953), Grier Jones (1968), David Edwards (1978), Scott Verplank (1986), Brain Watts (1987), E.J. Pfister (1988), Charles Howell (2000), and Pablo Martin (2006).

Oklahoma State has won 54 conference championships, including 36 of the 39 Big Eight Conference titles awarded. Oklahoma State has had 46 individual conference champions.

The Cowboys have seen 169 of their golfers honored as All-Americans, including at least one first-team All-American, in 41 of the last 57 years. Under Labron Harris, then Mike Holder, and now Alan Bratton, there have been 33 Academic All-Americans, as the term student-athlete is never a forgotten ideal in the Cowboys' golf program. Eight of those student-athletes have successfully crossed the honors of Academic All-American and All-American in the same season. That is more than any other NCAA golf program.

There have only been four head coaches in the history of Oklahoma State golf—the program's founder, Harris, who coached the first national championship team; the coach of champions, Holder, who coached eight of the 10 national championships in the program's history; Mike McGraw, who led the Cowboys to their 10th NCAA title in his first season as coach; and Bratton.

As far as the PGA Tour, Cowboys Michael Bradley, Danny Edwards, David Edwards, Dave Eichelberger, Rickie Fowler, Mark Hayes, Charles Howell, Grier Jones, Hunter Mahan, Doug Tewell, Bo Van Pelt, Scott Verplank, Bo Wininger, and Willie Wood have won tournaments on the main PGA Tour in North America. Bob Tway not only won eight PGA Tour events, but he won the only major won by a Cowboy to this date in the 1986 PGA Championship.

The most amazing statistic of all is this one: through the 2015–2016 academic year, Oklahoma State golfers had competed in 567 tournaments during the regular season and the postseason, and they won 214 of those events for an unbelievable 38 winning percentage. Oklahoma State is often in events where only the best teams in the country are entered. If you only won 38 percent of your football games or basketball games, well, that wouldn't be so good, but in the sport of golf that is one of the most amazing statistics you could imagine—much less actually write as fact.

89 Scott Verplank

Bob Tway may have won the PGA Championship, but it is fair to say that the most decorated of all Oklahoma State golfers during his time in Stillwater and his amateur and PGA events is Scott Verplank. It is not uncommon at all these days to see Verplank at a football practice shooting the breeze with Cowboys recruiting coordinator Johnny Barr or strength-and-conditioning coordinator Rob Glass. Verplank is often on the sidelines at Oklahoma

State football games. The Dallas native is a huge fan of all that is Oklahoma State. Then, there are Oklahoma State folks who have been and will always be fans of the Edmond, Oklahoma, resident.

Verplank is also known for his courageous battle against diabetes and how he has played successfully despite having to deal with being diabetic. Verplank has always had to watch his blood sugar and how he eats and hydrates. He has had to give himself insulin shots on the course during a match or a tournament. He is really an inspiration to the millions of Americans, and especially youngsters, who have diabetes as to what can be accomplished despite having the disease.

At Oklahoma State, Verplank was a first-team All American in 1984, '85, and '86. He was a second-team All-American as a freshman in 1983, and finished second in the NCAA Championship, losing in a playoff to Jim Carter of Arizona. That finish to his freshman season set the stage for a strong sophomore year. Verplank won the Kansas Fall Invitational, his first collegiate tournament win, and then in the spring he finished second in the All-American Classic with rounds of 70-68-70 for a 208 total. He also won the Big Eight Championship. That summer Verplank was busy, as he won the Western Amateur and then won the United States Amateur in front of his home crowd at Oak Tree in Edmond. He also took the other major amateur tournament, the Sunnehanna, which he would win again in 1985.

In the 1984–85 season, the hits just kept on coming as Verplank won the Crown Colony, the Rafael Alarcon International, named for former OSU golfer Rafael Alarcon. He was No. 2 in the Jackson Invitational and the Big Eight Championship, and No. 16 in the NCAA Championship. The big event would come that summer, when Verplank became the first amateur in 29 years to win a PGA event since Doug Sanders won the 1956 Canadian Open. Verplank defeated tour veteran Jim Thorpe in a playoff to win the 1985 Wastern Open.

In his final college season, he played in four tournaments, including the 1986 NCAA Championship with rounds of 68-68-73-73 for a total of 282. He was a Walker Cup Team member, was the Big Eight Athlete of the Year, and won the Fred Haskins Award as Player of the Year.

After joining the PGA Tour, where he could win tournaments and cash the checks, Verplank won the 1988 Buick Open, 2000 Reno-Tahoe Open, 2001 Bell Canadian Open, and 2007 Byron Nelson Classic. The Byron Nelson was extremely emotional for the Dallas native, who grew up attending the Byron Nelson and knew the great Dallas resident legend personally. Verplank is also a Ryder Cup veteran from 2002 and 2006.

90 Labron Harris

The Oklahoma State golf legacy has been written by many, but only one can start the process. That man was Labron Harris, who initiated the golf program in 1947 and was the only head coach until 1973. Harris' first team in 1947 at then–Oklahoma A&M won the Missouri Valley Championship and finished No. 5 in the NCAA Championship. Harris' teams, which practiced at the current Lakeside Golf Course, were always prepared and competitive every time they showed up. In a series of firsts, Earl Moeller in 1953 won the first NCAA individual national championship. In 1958, Oklahoma State joined the Big Eight Conference and won its first team title of 36 the program would win in the Big Eight, 15 of those under Harris. They also finished second that year in the NCAA Championship, their highest finish to that point.

The real breakthrough, and the greatest accomplishment of Harris' coaching career, other than simply molding a top-flight program from its infancy, came in 1963 when the Cowboys won their first NCAA team championship, beating Houston by one shot.

Harris coached Mike Holder as a golfer and student-athlete at Oklahoma State and, at some point, realized that he was grooming his successor. That was part of Harris' success; he knew people, what they were capable of, and what their talents were. He could see in Holder a leader who would take the Oklahoma State golf program even further than he could.

Harris, in retirement, watched the program's accomplishments with delight and pride as he lived to the age of 86, passing away in 1995. Harris saw seven of the eight NCAA championships to which Holder coached the Cowboys, including 1995, just a couple of months before he passed away.

91 Michele Smith

There are likely three former Oklahoma State student-athletes who would have a hard time walking down the street in Tokyo, Japan, without being mobbed for pictures and autographs. Current PGA golfer and pop culture icon Rickie Fowler and Olympic wrestling champion John Smith would be two of the three, but actually, the third might be the most popular, as Michele Smith still lives part of her year in Japan to take advantage from a business standpoint of her popularity there.

Smith has been an eight-time Japanese Professional Softball Champion and an MVP for the Toyota Shokki, and she also came back and played professionally in the United States for the New

York/New Jersey Juggernaut. But she was so successful in Japan that she was doing endorsements and serving as the star teacher and attraction at a number of softball clinics and academies.

Smith has been a longtime announcer for ESPN and its college softball coverage, including annual coverage of the NCAA Women's College World Series at the National Softball Hall of Fame in Oklahoma City. Smith has stayed connected with Oklahoma State and is not only a member of the Oklahoma State Athletic Hall of Fame, but also a trusted advisor to athletic director Mike Holder on the sport and an enthusiast of Oklahoma State softball.

A large part of her rise to stardom in Japan and in her home country was her Olympic softball experience, as Smith was a major force for the United States teams that won the gold medal in the 1996 and 2000 Summer Olympic Games. The left-handed pitcher was devastating and could really dominate from the circle.

Her career could be considered something of a miracle, because after starting out early in life loving softball and playing the sport, an accident almost took it out of her life. Just after her 19th birthday, while she was home in New Jersey for the summer, her father was driving her home from an oral surgeon's appointment. Sleeping in the truck, she was thrown out when her unlocked door opened while the truck was turning. Smith fell into a roadside post that chopped off part of her elbow bone and tore the triceps muscle from her left arm. There was muscle and nerve damage to the arm.

"It was like losing my identity," Smith said about the threat of not playing and pitching again.

Smith, as she has proved throughout her life both on the field and off, came back better than before. Nine months of intense rehab and strength-and-conditioning work, all at OSU, saw her come back and pitch the softball 3 mph faster than before the accident.

Smith finished her Cowgirls career as a two-time first-team All-American, winning the honor in 1988 and 1989. She was a three-time All–Big Eight selection and also made the All–Big Eight Tournament Team on three occasions. She was named to the Women's College World Series Tournament Team in 1989 and helped guide Oklahoma State to a third-place finish. She still holds the Oklahoma State record for most no-hitters thrown, with nine, and two of those were perfect games. Smith won 82 games in her career, which is still the record. She is second all-time in shutouts with 46, and on the offensive side is tied for third all-time with 10 triples. She finished with 26 pitching victories in two different seasons (tied for third most in a season),

Smith is also known for her work in baseball broadcasting for TBS with both the Atlanta Braves and Major League Baseball. While fellow softball star Jessica Mendoza at ESPN gets much notoriety as an MLB announcer, it is Smith who is credited with being the first woman to serve as a color announcer on an MLB broadcast. She did it in 2012. If you want to sell a lot of cars in Japan or softball bats and gloves, well, Smith is your spokesperson.

92 1959 Baseball National Champions

Gary Ward's teams were dominant during the 1980s and into the 1990s, but with 10 trips to Omaha the Cowboys could never bring back the national championship trophy. It sure would have been nice, but it wouldn't have been the first. Any trophy brought home in the future will join a baseball national championship trophy earned by the 1959 Oklahoma State Cowboys. Toby Greene's team that season had a future big-league pitcher in Joel Horlen, who would pitch for 12 seasons with the Chicago White Sox and Oakland Athletics. Multisport standout Dick Soergel was a pitcher in the spring, a quarterback in the fall, and a forward for Mr. Iba in basketball. The team also featured a brother combination who could turn a double play in their sleep, they knew each other so well, in Bruce (second base) and Bob (shortstop) Andrew.

Back then, baseball seasons weren't nearly as long at the college level as they are today, and the Cowboys won the Big Eight championship, finishing with a 17–3 record and series wins late in the season over Iowa State and Missouri.

The Cowboys had to go to Peoria, Illinois, for the District V Championship in a two-out-of-three series with Missouri Valley Conference winner Bradley. Oklahoma State wasted no time with the Braves, as it swept a doubleheader the first day to win the series and move on directly to Omaha and the College World Series.

Horlen showed his prowess on the mound in the opener in Omaha as he pitched a five-hit gem for a 10–2 win over Western Michigan. In the next game, the Cowboys had to rally with three runs in the seventh inning and picked up an insurance run in the eighth inning for an 8–6 win over Penn State.

The next game had the Cowboys against the team they would eventually have to beat to win the College World Series, but Arizona was tough, handing the multitalented Soergel his first loss on the mound in college in 12 decisions. The Wildcats won the game 5–3 as the Cowboys' bats were mostly silent.

In the losers' bracket, the Cowboys eliminated Penn State 4–3 as Horlen threw a complete game to get the win. That same day, Fresno State handed Arizona its first loss and three teams were left with one loss. Arizona won the coin toss and got the bye and sat back to see who would win between the Cowboys and the Bulldogs. The third of three starting pitchers, Roy Peterson, got the ball for the game, and the right-hander pitched a four-hit gem and complete game shutout to send the Cowboys back against Arizona for the title.

Little did anybody back then know, but some 57 years later in Omaha, the Cowboys and Arizona would battle in a College World Series to see who would play Coastal Carolina for a championship. Oklahoma State would win the first meeting, only to lose the next two.

In 1959, it was all the Cowboys. Trailing 3–2 in the seventh inning, Bruce Andrew got his only hit in the game to spark a three-run rally, and the Cowboys made it stand with 5⅓ innings of relief pitching from Soergel to win 5–3.

After the game and in accepting the trophy, the mostly quiet Cowboys coach Toby Greene said to the Rosenblatt Stadium crowd, "Tonight, these young men around me have made an old man very happy. Thank you."

93 The Best Pitching Coach in College Baseball and a Father-Son Story

When Josh Holliday was hired as the Cowboys' head baseball coach in 2012, he was up against some stiff and familiar competition. Athletic director Mike Holder had interviewed former Oklahoma State pitcher and very successful Oral Roberts University head coach Rob Walton for the job. Walton, ironically, had been recruited to Oklahoma State by Tom Holliday, Josh's dad, and Josh grew up as a kid watching Walton and the Cowboys of that day dominate the Big Eight and make so many trips to Omaha that Josh and younger brother Matt simply thought it was a summer vacation destination. Someone else grew up not experiencing the trips to Omaha, but instead hearing all the stories about them. Donnie Walton knew his dad had pitched for the Cowboys and had pitched in the College World Series. Donnie, a talented shortstop at Bishop Kelley High

School in Tulsa, was all set to head to play for the program he had grown up around in Tulsa at ORU. Then Holder and Holliday discussed an idea and put it into action. The pair went to Tulsa to talk Walton into coming back to Oklahoma State as pitching coach. The crazy thing is, it worked, and now Donnie was heading to play for his dad at his alma mater and for a coach who knew just exactly how Donnie had grown up, because that is the way Josh grew up—around a college baseball program.

"I think it was easier for Donnie and I to connect and relate to each other because we had grown up around the same situation," Holliday said once early in his time as head coach and Donnie's time as a player. "You know they call some kids 'gym rats;' well, we were diamond or dugout rats. Just always around baseball and baseball players."

Rob Walton had to give up being a head coach, but he saw some possibilities with the move that might prove unforgettable.

"This is really a special opportunity for me and my family," Walton said when he made the decision. "My wife and I went to school there, and it's our chance to come back to our alma mater and help Coach Holliday get the program going in the right direction. Hopefully, we can bring it back to prominence."

They certainly have, and it has been on the strength of Holliday's enthusiasm and Walton's tremendous ability to coach and develop young pitchers. The first season under the new coaching staff, the Cowboys made the NCAA Regional in Louisville and went to the final two teams before losing to the host. In 2014, the Cowboys hosted an NCAA Regional and won and then hosted Cal–Irvine in the Super Regional, losing the first two games of the best of three format. In 2015, the Cowboys again hosted an NCAA Regional and lost. However, last season the Pokes went on the road and blitzed through a regional at Clemson, beating the host team twice before going to South Carolina for the Super Regional and winning in two games. On to Omaha, the Cowboys made the final four before losing to Arizona.

A huge part of the success goes down to pitching. Rob Walton has had back-to-back Big 12 Pitcher of the Year winners in Michael Freeman and Thomas Hatch, and the Cowboys' team ERA, 3.21 in 2016 as a CWS final four team, has been in the NCAA Division I top 25 in three of the four seasons Walton has coached the pitchers in Stillwater. In 2016, the Cowboys pitchers wore T-shirts with Walton's likeness on the body of *Harry Potter* wizard Dumbledore. Walton's nickname with his pitchers and about everybody around the program is "the Wizard."

"He can fix any pitcher on the staff," son and shortstop Donnie Walton said.

Baseball America named Walton its 2016 Baseball America/American Baseball Coaches Association Assistant Coach of the Year.

However, that was just part of the reward for Walton and his family in a special season. Famed radio journalist Paul Harvey used to have a daily series when he was alive and broadcasting titled "The Rest of the Story."

In his senior season at Oklahoma State, Rob Walton helped lead the Cowboys to Omaha and the College World Series. While there, he was the primary part of the Cowboys' last shutout in a CWS game as the Pokes blanked Indiana State 4–0. Growing up, Donnie had heard those stories, so in his senior season he hit .337 with 16 doubles, three home runs, and a fielding percentage of .969 at shortstop, which is amazing.

"Yes, this is really special because my Pops played there. I've always wanted to do it and now we get to do it together."

As a result, father and son both got to experience a College World Series together—and how about this: in the first game in Omaha, Big 12 Pitcher of the Year Thomas Hatch shuts out Cal–Santa Barbara—the first shutout for Oklahoma State in the

College World Series since the one Rob Walton pitched in as a player in 1986. Now, Paul Harvey would say, you know the rest of the story.

94 Inky and the Home Run Record

Pete Incaviglia was one of those California imports that Oklahoma State brought into the baseball program. You could call it a reverse *Grapes of Wrath*. Lots of baseball talent—more than the West Coast schools could all accommodate—and Tom Holliday is just the kind of guy who would hit it off with a young man like Incaviglia. Nicknamed "Inky" at Oklahoma State, you combine his quick hands and strength with the convictions and discipline of Gary Ward—and, believe this—the lessons weren't always completely adhered to—and they were a dangerous combination for opposing pitchers and outfield fences. Incaviglia had power, but he was also athletic and led the team in doubles in his junior and final year as a Cowboy.

That season, 1985, was also his magical year, as his assault on the NCAA record book was a major story. Back then, ESPN was not yet in the business of televising Major League Baseball, and it had turned college baseball into a major property with games every weekend and a national Monday-night college baseball game, usually featuring a top nonconference matchup between power teams. College baseball had a larger stage, and everyone knows that home runs are highlights. Incaviglia was the Babe Ruth of campus baseball. He finished the season with 48 home runs. His career mark of 100 home runs is also an NCAA record, as were his 143 runs batted in, total bases with 285, and slugging percentage of 1.140. The home run records still stand, and with the changes since in the aluminum bats used in college baseball, those records are likely to always stand.

Talk to his teammates during those years and they will tell you that "Inky" was one of the guys. He loved cards and was often involved in poker games on road trips. He loved to have fun and if there was a fight going on, he was going to show up for it. School was not something he enjoyed, but he kept his academics up enough so he could still play baseball for three years.

Home runs haven't been measured officially at Allie Reynolds Stadium, but old-timers swear that Incaviglia hit the longest home run in school history on a ball that left the park in right-center field, cleared a house across the street on Duck, and landed in the backyard.

Another important aspect of Incaviglia's career is that he led the Cowboys to the College World Series in all three of his seasons in Stillwater.

Incaviglia was drafted after his junior season by the Montreal Expos, but he refused to play in Canada, and his rights were traded to the Texas Rangers. He was one of, at the time, just 15 players to go straight into the major leagues without playing a day in the minors, and Incaviglia hit 20 home runs in each of his first five seasons with Texas. His playing time diminished, and he spent single seasons with Detroit and Houston before seeing his career rise again after a trade to Philadelphia. While with the Phillies in 1993, he hit 24 home runs with 89 runs batted in for a team that came up just short of winning the World Series.

"The bottom line was we were going to do whatever it took to win ballgames," Incaviglia told MLB. "Go out and grind. We were kind of a blue-collar team, and I think the fans enjoyed the way we played baseball. We were a bunch of nuts. We slid hard and took people out and got dirty. We played for each other. We played for that dream of putting a ring on our finger. I know we didn't, but every one of those guys who was in the dugout feels like a champion."

That really sums up Incaviglia, who to this day is still involved in baseball managing an independent team. He played till he couldn't anymore, even doing a stint in Japan and a year in Mexico. Pete Incaviglia is a baseball lifer and a part of Oklahoma State history that will never be forgotten.

95 Robin Ventura and the Streak

Another of the Californians who came to Oklahoma State, Robin Ventura, was quite different from most of the players on Gary Ward's teams recruited by Tom Holliday. Ventura was quiet—very quiet. All he wanted to do was go out and play baseball, but as his exploits on the diamond grew and he captured more attention it wasn't nearly as much fun for him. Ventura finished his Oklahoma State career with a Big Eight–record 329 hits.

Amazingly, in two of his three seasons as a Cowboy he led the team in at-bats, runs scored, doubles, runs batted in, and batting average, and he led the team in hits three straight seasons. Ventura was one of the best hitters the game has ever seen, and in the 1987 season he captivated America by getting a hit in nearly every game the Cowboys played that season.

It started on March 18 in a 23–1 win over Missouri Southern at Allie Reynolds Stadium. Everybody in the lineup got a hit that day, but for Ventura it was the start of a record.

Still not paying a lot of attention to it, even though the streak had grown to 29 games in a row, Ventura was up against it in Lawrence, Kansas, as the Cowboys led the second game of the series

12–1. But Ward, while replacing most of the starters, left Ventura in. He still didn't have a hit in the game.

"I was down to my last at bat and hadn't gotten a hit," Ventura told Jeff Williams of the NCAA. "It was a 3–2 count and the guys in the dugout were yelling that I had to swing. It hadn't even crossed my mind that I had a hitting streak going. But I got a hit on the next pitch and it became a bigger deal after that."

Ventura passed the mark of 47 by Wichita State's Phil Stephenson to set a new NCAA record, but now the media was tuned in to what Ventura was doing. Even so, he was doing it at a completely different level, and it was being compared to the major league record of Yankees Hall of Famer Joe DiMaggio: his 56-game hitting streak. Playing in an NCAA Regional in Starkville, Mississippi, the Cowboys had to win a doubleheader against Texas A&M to advance—and they did 7–4 and 11–9. Ventura had the game-winning hits and RBIs in both games and, after the second, his hitting streak matched that of Joltin' Joe's at 56.

In Game 1 of the College World Series, the Cowboys defeated Arizona State 8–3 and Ventura ripped an RBI single down the right-field line at Rosenblatt in his third at-bat to run the streak past the MLB record to 57.

Three days later, thanks to weather, Oklahoma State played LSU and Ventura was hitless with a walk after three trips to the plate. The rains came again, and the game was stopped and the finish moved to the next day. LSU came back with future big-league pitcher Ben McDonald on the mound, and Ventura came through with an RBI double for an 8–7 OSU win and his 58th straight game with a base hit.

Game 3 was huge, as unbeaten Oklahoma State (2–0) took on Stanford, also unbeaten. In those days, the winner of that game was automatically moved into the College World Series Championship Game. Ventura and the Cowboys were up against the Cardinals' ace and Ventura's future teammate with the White Sox, Jack

McDowell. Ventura was struggling against McDowell, but after a slow start, his teammates weren't. The Cowboys came up with a huge third inning, sending eight men to the plate and scoring six runs to go up 6–2. In the top of the ninth, with Oklahoma State still leading 6–2, everyone in Rosenblatt Stadium and most in the national ESPN cable audience knew Ventura was 0-for-4 at the plate and the streak was in dire straits. Facing another future major league pitcher in reliever Al Osuna, and thanks to a single by teammate Ray Ortiz, Ventura got one more chance. He hit a hard ground ball to second, where Stanford's Frank Carey had the ball bounce off the script STANFORD lettering on his chest and then rushed a sloppy throw to first that Ventura beat out and advanced to second on.

Now, all eyes were on the stadium scoreboard, and after reviewing a replay of the ground ball and throw, longtime CWS official scorer Lou Spry ruled the play an error on Carey and Ventura was 0-for-5—the streak ended at 58. As always, Ventura, who was never happy about the extra individual attention that the streak focused on him, was classy about the decision. In fact, being there to cover the event, those of us around him could tell he was glad it was over.

"It doesn't matter that my streak was broken, because we're now playing for the national title," Ventura said during the post-game news conference. He also had no problem with the scorer's decision. "It was an error. My only question was the fact that it wasn't two errors. Jack McDowell is a good pitcher and I swung at some pitches I shouldn't have."

The much larger disappointment in the end was that Oklahoma State lost to Stanford 9–5 in the CWS Championship Game. Ventura, a three-time All-American, went on to win the Dick Howser Award and the Golden Spikes Award as the top college baseball player that season. He would later be inducted into the first class of the College Baseball Hall of Fame.

Ventura went on to have a tremendous major league career with the Chicago White Sox, primarily, as well as the New York Mets and New York Yankees. He finished with a career .267 average and 294 home runs, including 18 grand slams, tying him for fifth all-time. He had 1,182 RBIs in his career, and was known as a classy player and good teammate. One of the few differences in that overall perception of Ventura and something that many of us that know him thought was out of character was the night in Arlington, Texas, when he was hit by a Nolan Ryan fastball and he charged the mound, only to find Ryan ready and willing to throw some punches.

That is not to say Ventura didn't play with fight. He always played hard, and there were many examples over his career to point to in that regard. Several years after retiring and doing some broadcasting and coaching of high school and youth baseball, Ventura was called on to manage his old team, the Chicago White Sox. Despite no previous professional coaching or managing experience, he stayed with it for five seasons, going 85–77 in his first season and finishing with a record of 375–435.

Ventura lives in California with his wife, Stephanie, and three daughters and one son.

96 John Farrell and the Red Sox

John Farrell came to Oklahoma State from Monmouth Beach, New Jersey, and Shore Regional High School and played for the Cowboys for four seasons. He had a strong finish in his senior season, winning 12 games while pitching the most innings (111) and tying on the pitching staff for strikeouts with 87. Farrell made an impact as a player, but after a major league career that spanned nine seasons he came back to Stillwater and rose to become one of the top managers in the big leagues.

When he finished his senior season at Oklahoma State in 1984, Farrell was drafted and signed with the Cleveland Indians. He made his big-league debut for the team in 1987 and pitched three strong seasons before he developed arm issues. He wound up pitching some for the California Angels, going back to Cleveland, and then finishing with the Detroit Tigers. His major league record was 36–46 with a career 4.56 ERA and 355 strikeouts. Farrell came back to Oklahoma State in 1996 after his big-league career ended to be the pitching coach for his old pitching coach at Oklahoma State, newly named head coach Tom Holliday. He was back in Stillwater for four seasons before being called to the major leagues again, this time as an administrator. Farrell took over as director of player development for the Cleveland Indians and did such a good job that the Indians were twice honored as the Organization of the Year by *USA Today Sports Weekly*.

Farrell's next move was to join his former Indians roommate Terry Francona as the pitching coach for the Boston Red Sox and together, they helped the Red Sox win the 2007 World Series.

In 2010, Farrell was hired as the manager of the Toronto Blue Jays and showed he had the stuff to head up a team, and then in 2013 the Red Sox came back and hired Farrell to take over as manager. He was very consistent—one of his personality traits—as he took the Red Sox to the 2013 World Series.

Farrell had an operation in August of 2015, during the season, for a hernia, and it was then he was discovered to have Stage 1 lymphoma. He announced he would step aside to get treatment but would be back to manage the Red Sox in 2016. The cancer was discovered early and treatment was successful, allowing Farrell to be back with the Red Sox. It is safe to say that Farrell is one of the most successful Oklahoma State graduates to go on and coach or manage in professional sports.

97 Dave Smith's Building Dynasty

If you are going to dream, then you might as well dream big. Oklahoma State women's track middle distance runner Kaela Edwards dreams big. She wants to make it to the Olympic Games, win a medal, and then run professionally for as long as she can. Kaela loves to run. There was a time when athletes could come to Oklahoma State University and use it as a stepping stone to the Olympic Games. The school had a powerhouse track program for many years in the '40s, '50s, and '60s. Then, the track facility at Oklahoma State became obsolete. It was run-down and the configuration was not up to par to host college meets. For years, the Cowboy Jamboree in the fall was a highlight event in the sport of cross country. The meet is the oldest continuous cross country collegiate event west of the Mississippi. In the spring, the Cowboy Relays was a major event in the midlands. That changed as the track program and cross country, to a lesser degree, were ignored.

Enter Dave Smith, who came in as head coach for cross country and a middling track-and-field program and has risen to be assistant athletic director for track and field and cross country. The rise has coincided with national championships and the men's program winning the Big 12 Indoor Championship in 2016. Smith has been named the NCAA Division I Men's Cross Country National Coach of the Year three times, the Big 12 Men's Cross Country Coach of the Year eight times, and the Big 12 Women's Cross Country Coach of the Year once—and really special is the Big 12 Men's Track and Field Indoor Coach of the Year last spring with that championship.

A former distance runner and cross-country competitor, four-time All–Big Ten performer, and champion in 10,000 meters at Michigan State, Smith spent a year as a volunteer coach at the University of Washington while earning his master's degree and then took over as head coach for cross country and track and field at Texas Tech for four years before coming to Oklahoma State. The winning seemed to start immediately, and the recruiting kicked in, too.

Smith very quickly brought in a rock star among runners in America when German Fernandez signed with Oklahoma State and went on in his first year to win the NCAA outdoor 1,500 meters. Smith has coached seven NCAA individual champions, including women's outdoor 1,500 meter champion Natalja Pilusina and 2015 men's 1,500 meter outdoor champion Chad Noelle. He has coached 129 All-Americans and 101 Big 12 Champions.

Oklahoma State has a new track-and-field facility, built near the Michael and Ann Greenwood Tennis Center and next door to where the university plans to build the new baseball stadium. The track includes areas for all of the field events, a full locker room, and offices for the program.

The Cowboy Jamboree Cross Country event is back to being one of the premier events in that sport, with schools from coast to coast asking to be included. Oklahoma State does not currently host a track meet, but with the new facility it is possible it could in the future.

As for Kaela Edwards, who won the NCAA championship in the indoor mile, and her goals of being a champion, being an Olympian, and moving on to the professional ranks? She is well on the way. On January 13, 2017, in Lincoln, Nebraska, Edwards headed the trio of runners from Oklahoma State in the women's 1,000 meters in the Holiday Inn Invitational. The trio did not disappoint, finishing 1-2-3. It was Edwards who finished ahead of Savannah Camacho and Chelsea Jarvis. Edwards didn't just win— she broke the collegiate record in the event with a time of 2:40.79. It was the fastest time by a full two seconds.

"It was awesome to see," Dave Smith said. "She went out and led wire-to-wire and looked up with about a lap to go and realized she had a chance to break it, so she turned it up. She got it by about three-hundredths of a second, and a collegiate record is a great accomplishment for her and a great way for her to start her season."

These are the things that seem to keep happening now that Dave Smith is in charge of the running that is going on in Oklahoma State athletics.

98 Bedlam

Bedlam is the word used to symbolize the series between rivals Oklahoma State University and the University of Oklahoma. Broadcasters and writers seem to love it as much as some of the other names of college rivalries out there, like the "Iron Bowl" for Alabama and Auburn; "Holy War" for Utah and BYU; "Backyard Brawl" for Pittsburgh and West Virginia; "Clean Old-Fashioned Hate" for Georgia and Georgia Tech; "the Big Game" for California and Stanford; and "the Civil War" for Oregon and Oregon State. In my mind, the difference between Bedlam and these other names is that, in so many cases, the names for other collegiate rivalries are more for one sport or event—mostly football, but in some cases basketball. Bedlam often describes anytime the Cowboys and the Sooners compete in anything.

Bedlam started with wrestling, at least as the story that has been passed down over the history of the rivalry goes. According to old-timers, there was a wrestling match between the two schools, and the noise was easily heard outside the field house. As a spectator emerged outside, he was asked what was happening inside, and his response was, "It's bedlam in there."

That is one explanation; another, from the *Tulsa World*, is that the phrase *bedlam* was used to describe the 1917 football game between the two schools, the first that was won by Oklahoma A&M 9–0. The phrase was then not used in print with the series again until 1943. It is used virtually every time the two schools meet. It is usually pretty accurate, but in some sports the series are lopsided. Oklahoma State has a massive lead in the wrestling series between the schools, and Oklahoma is proud of its more-than-healthy edge in football. Other sports are fairly close, such as women's basketball, which has seen each school have its time of dominance. Men's basketball has been very competitive, as has baseball, which in terms of extracurricular activity has seen as much true bedlam as any sport.

One sport that has been dominant since the beginning is one that is fairly new to both schools. Oklahoma State and Oklahoma, like all NCAA schools, have battled with coming up with sports for women that will help balance out the scholarships in Division I football and help with gender equity and Title IX mandates. Both brought in women's soccer, and in Stillwater, where original head coach Karen Hancock and early assistant and now head coach Colin Carmichael have been on staff and part of every Cowgirls soccer team, they have dominated their rival, Oklahoma.

The Cowgirls, who have also become a consistent NCAA Tournament qualifier, have a 20–8–3 edge in bedlam competition, and some of the wins have been amazing, like the "thrill on the hill" comeback in 2002. With many in a full-house crowd having left and the Cowgirls down 2–0, they stormed back in the final six minutes with three goals and a 3–2 win. All three goals were scored by defender Jeni Jackson, who until that night had never scored a goal for the Cowgirls and never scored another after that night. However, on November 1, 2002, Jeni Jackson represented exactly what bedlam is—the amazing, the unimaginable, and sometimes the uncontrollable.

99 The Rant

Oklahoma State head football coach Mike Gundy has successfully found ways to stand out over the years; most recently, during the 2016 season, the Cowboys football mentor let his hair grow starting back in the summer to, by midseason, a legitimate mullet hairstyle. The media attention started in the summer when Gundy showed up in Dallas, Texas, at the Big 12 Conference Football Media Days event with his hair working on that style.

"That's not a real mullet," one of the Fox Sports camera people told Gundy after an interview. "Coach, that's an Arkansas waterfall."

Gundy joked that he was inspired to let his hair grow when his middle son insisted that he go get a haircut. Gundy said he was just showing his son a little defiance. He also was clear that defiance was not something he would allow to be reciprocated.

The mullet was interesting, but Gundy, a popular and successful quarterback, assistant coach, and offensive coordinator prior to his being named head coach at his alma mater, first made a huge national splash with "the Rant."

On that day, Oklahoma State was in a furious contest at home in Boone Pickens Stadium with the Mike Leach–led Texas Tech squad. The game seesawed back and forth, and Oklahoma State came back late on a touchdown pass from Zac Robinson to future Detroit Lions tight end Brandon Pettigrew. Pettigrew dived into the corner of the end zone to make the score 49–45, and then Texas Tech drove down the field only to see a pass intended for Michael Crabtree in the end zone be tipped ever so slightly, but enough to throw Crabtree off, by safety Rickie Price.

The screaming by coaches following that game could be heard on both ends of the Athletic Center portion of Gallagher-Iba Arena. Tech's Mike Leach railed about the lack of performance by his defense and dropped several profanities in his postgame discussion with the media.

The histrionics on the Tech end were nothing compared with what Gundy launched in his press conference.

The game had been the first start at quarterback for Zac Robinson, as incumbent Bobby Reid had struggled with Oklahoma State losing at Georgia to open the season and at Troy the week before the Texas Tech game. Oklahoma State had come into the game 1–2. That morning the *Daily Oklahoman* had a column in its sports page on the quarterback situation and how Reid had underachieved. The story was written by sports columnist Jenni Carlson, and featured what seemed to be an eyewitness account of Reid being comforted by his mother after the loss at Troy. She was seen feeding him chicken out of a box dinner players had in their lockers or that was passed out following games. It was not a flattering portrayal of Reid. The interesting aspect was that Carlson had not been in Alabama the week before and had not covered the Cowboys' loss to Troy. Still, those seeing the story recognized that it might cause issues.

It was so potentially disturbing that Oklahoma State football's director of operations at the time, Jimmy Gonzales, pulled the newspapers off the tables at the team's pregame meal. He pulled all the copies of the *Daily Oklahoman* and only left the copies of the *Tulsa*

World. Gundy had not seen the story, but after the game there was a copy of the sports page sitting in the coach's dressing room. Right after the game, Gundy came into that room before coming back out to address the team. He had seen the story and quickly read it, and his blood started a rapid simmer to boiling by the time he entered the meeting room in Gallagher-Iba to meet with the media.

Gundy never discussed the game and the win over Texas Tech, and what he launched into upon seeing Carlson, who had covered that game sitting on the front row, was one of the greatest rants in sports history. It is one that is still quoted nationally to this day.

"I want to talk about this article right here. If anybody hasn't read this article—I don't read it—this was brought to me by a mother of children," Gundy started as his voice climbed higher throughout the delivery. "I think it's worth reading. Let me tell you why I want to talk about this article. Three-fourths of this is inaccurate. It's fiction. And, this article embarrasses me to be involved with athletics, tremendously. And that article had to have been written by a person that doesn't have a child. And has never had a child that's had their heart broken and come home...upset. And had to deal with the child when he is upset. And kick a person when he's down.

"Here's all that kid did: he goes to class, he's respectful to the media, he's respectful to the public, and he's a good kid. And he's not a professional athlete, and he doesn't deserve to be kicked when he's down.

"If you have a child someday, you'll understand how it feels," Gundy was looking right at Carlson. "But you obviously don't have a child. I do.

"Your child goes down the street, and somebody makes fun of him, because he dropped a pass in a pickup game, or says he's fat, and he comes home crying to his mom, you'd understand. But you don't have that. But someday, you will. And when your child comes home, you'll understand.

"If you want to go after an athlete—one of my athletes—you go after one that doesn't do the right things. You don't downgrade him because he does everything right and may not play as well on Saturday. And you let us make that decision.

"That's why I don't read the newspaper, because it's garbage. And the editor that let it come out is garbage. Attacking an amateur athlete for doing everything right. And then you want to write articles about guys that don't do things right and downgrade them—the ones who do make plays.

"Are you kidding me? Where are we at in society today? Come after me! I'm a man! I'm 40! I'm not—I'm not a kid. Write something about me, or our coaches. Don't write about a kid that does everything right that's heartbroken, and then say that the coaches said he was scared. That ain't true! And then to say that we made that decision because Donovan Woods, because he threatened to transfer. That's not true! So get your facts straight.

"And I hope someday you have a child and somebody downgrades him, and belittles him, and you have to look him in the eye and say, 'You know what? It's okay. They're supposed to be mature adults, but they're really not.' Who's the kid here? Who's the kid here? Are you kidding me?

"That's all I've got to say. Makes me want to puke."

Gundy stormed out of the room and back to the Oklahoma State locker room. One of the most amazing aspects of the Rant is that Gundy, who delivered it almost immediately after reading the story and without any rehearsal of what he wanted to say, delivered a well-structured message that did not use a single cuss word in the entire monologue.

There is no doubt—and Gundy has said as much when discussing the Rant—that it came up in homes with parents as he was recruiting and he was known as the coach who stood up for his player. Reid, who had been was a highly regarded recruit coming out of Galena Park North Shore in the Houston area, never regained his starting job and finished his career at Texas Southern University. He blamed Gundy for some of the issues he had and blamed the Rant, but he came back and served as a graduate assistant coach on Gundy's staff before moving on to be an assistant coach for Chad Morris at SMU.

The Rant has lived on and is always mentioned in discussion of great sports or coaching rants. It also comes up every year on Mike Gundy's birthday, to update his age and restate that he is a man.

100 Underwood Departs Abruptly, Enter Boynton as Basketball Coach

One of the greatest things about college athletics and the fun of being a college fan, and the roller-coaster ride that passion takes you on, is change. For this author, writing about the history, current events, happenings, and landmarks of a powerful university is certainly an adventure that can change at a moment's notice.

Enter chapter 100, certainly a great spot with an eye toward the future. This is the second writing of chapter 100. The first centered on a revival of a season in 2016–17 under a coach with a pedigree made for Oklahoma State. The second documents a tumultuous week that landed Oklahoma State a new leader to put the hoops program in the place fans of this school feel it should always occupy.

As you read this, the dust has settled a little, the anger has subsided some, but the end of the basketball season in 2017 was one volatile weekend for Cowboys fans, and it turned into a full week of finger-pointing, sadness, anger, disbelief, and a conclusion that nobody really saw coming, including the rookie head coach who, a year earlier, thought he was a slam dunk to become a first-time head coach at a mid-major.

The story starts with the events of a year before, as Gallagher-Iba Arena, once the rowdiest arena in the country, had gone mostly quiet with the mediocrity of teams produced by head coach Travis Ford. It wasn't bad basketball; it just wasn't the aggressive man defense and high-flying offense that Eddie Sutton's teams had spoiled Cowboys fans with.

Ford was a good coach, but after a terrific first season and being rewarded by athletic director Mike Holder with a huge contract in years and compensation, Oklahoma State and Ford had kind of become stuck with each other.

Holder brought in Brad Underwood from Stephen F. Austin, where he had dominated the Southland Conference and even scored a big NCAA Tournament upset in 2016 over one of his mentors, Bob Huggins, and West Virginia.

Underwood, the native of McPherson, Kansas, almost came to Oklahoma State for school, but instead went to Kansas State, where he played for Jack Hartman, a former Oklahoma A&M great in basketball for Henry Iba and also a quarterback in football. Underwood has that direct tie to the Iba coaching tree. He also came in talking the talk. He spoke of how he wanted to bring back the sellout crowds, the great expectations, and the end-of-the-season NCAA rewards that are associated with Cowboys basketball.

"Certain areas of it have been everything I knew it could be and I thought it would be," Underwood said before beating Arkansas in a sellout game at Gallagher-Iba Arena and then a win in his first Bedlam game at rival Oklahoma. "Certain areas we've got to continue to fight the battles, but we have to get back to growing. There is a reason that this place is so historic and so great. It is one of the top college basketball programs in America and we're not far off."

Fast-forward to the last weekend of the season, and the most exciting first-round game in the NCAA Tournament, as No. 10

seed Oklahoma State lost a 92–91 thriller to No. 7 Michigan in Indianapolis. Negotiations to bump Underwood's first-season pay, a relatively low $1 million, had turned sour—even adversarial—earlier in the previous week. As a result, Underwood's agent was speaking with other schools, and as the Cowboys' team charter jet flew back to Stillwater on Friday evening, March 17, 2017, a private jet carrying Illinois athletic director Josh Whitman was trailing just behind.

The next morning, Whitman and Underwood took a now-infamous picture for OSU fans of the two men wearing orange Illinois pullovers in front of Underwood's fireplace in Stillwater. It was done; Underwood, a coach Cowboys fans had so quickly and so closely identified with, was gone. Oklahoma State forward Mitchell Solomon told the media that the hastily called good-bye meeting that afternoon lasted all of 10 minutes, and Underwood said his good-bye to his players in about three minutes.

It was a Twitter event, with that photo of Underwood and Whitman being the social media centerpiece that truly rocked Cowboys fans and the Oklahoma State nation.

The aftermath included finger-pointing at Holder for not paying Underwood the kind of money he was looking for, by most accounts the kind of money paid to coaches who have taken their teams to Final Fours or at least major conference championships. There were also the reports of things said in negotiations that angered Underwood and that Underwood fired back to anger Holder. A mess, to be sure.

The new hire needed to be quick and popular; former Oklahoma State point guard and national broadcaster Doug Gottlieb, with the pedigree of his late father and brother being college coaches and his own basketball acumen, tossed his hat in the ring again. This time, he got an interview with Holder, the Board of Regents, and University President Burns Hargis.

Much of the Oklahoma State fan base was now pulling for the zero coaching experience but all-out passion and enthusiasm of Gottlieb. Doug is a convincing person. However, in the other four interviews conducted that first day of interviews, just five full days after the tremor of Underwood's jetting away to Illinois, Holder and the panel discovered Oklahoma State's next head coach.

New York City is a hotbed for basketball. Rucker Park, over in Harlem, is well known for monster pickup basketball games, but Michael Boynton learned to value his runs on the courts at Jackie Robinson Park and Jesse Owens Playground in his native Brooklyn neighborhood of Bedford-Stuyvesant, an area with roughly 153,000 residents.

"You learn to fight out there, play really hard," Boynton said of his playground days. "Because if you lose, there a long line before you get a chance to play again."

Boynton came up a Brooklyn and New York basketball product, the son of a loving family that included two older sisters and one younger. He started going to the basketball gym at a young age with his father at 6:00 AM on weekends, a time where the old guys could have the court. Getting to the right court for the right instruction was worth whatever effort it took.

"I played my eighth-grade year at a school in Harlem, and I took a train and a bus every day to and from school to play in a very competitive middle school with some very good players that have gone on to have great success in several areas," Boynton explained. "It was part of what prepared me for this because it gave me not an arrogance, but a confidence that I played against the best guys every day and there is no other place that can make you tough like New York City can. I was a pretty good point guard and I was probably better in high school than I was in college. I was an okay college player. [Former NBA star] Mark Jackson was a pretty good point guard at my high school. I did break a few of his assists records, but I probably played with a little more talent [around me] than he did."

This is that Boynton, one of Underwood's assistants and a coach who was hands down the favorite to succeed Underwood at SFA when he left for Oklahoma State. Instead, the Lumberjacks tabbed a former Oklahoma State assistant under Eddie and Sean Sutton, Kyle Keller, as head coach.

This time, Boynton wasn't as positive going in on his chances to land the job, but he certainly felt he was more prepared for the interview, thanks to his experience the year before.

"I felt good about it," he continued. "I really did after going through the process last year. To be honest, [last year] I felt I was ready for the job. I don't know if I was ready for the interview process, so that gave me an opportunity to grow and I've already thanked the administration there for that. Those are great people down in Nacogdoches, but to be here and Coach Holder believes in me."

Boynton points to Underwood and current South Carolina coach Frank Martin as influences on his coaching career. He also talks of the coach who recruited him to South Carolina, Eddie Fogler, and the coach he primarily played for with the Gamecocks, Dave Odom, as influences, and other coaches he worked for, like Buzz Peterson and Michael Young. When it comes to someone who had perhaps the deepest influence, it goes back to high school and his coach at Bishop Loughlin in Brooklyn, Bob Leckie.

"You come to work every single day and you do your job to the very best of your ability," Boynton said when asked what he learned most from the 13-time Brooklyn Coach of the Year, who later went on to coach at his college alma mater of St. Peter's and led them to the MAAC Championship Game. "Coach Leckie was a really hard coach to play for because he was extremely demanding, especially for high school. He taught me how to think about the game through the lens of a coach as a high school player. People now ask about my lack of experience as a head coach. It goes back to leadership for me, and Coach Leckie will tell you he never had to worry about if he had to miss practice. Sometimes as a high school coach you have another job and in an extreme circumstance you might have to miss practice. He never worried about that because I could run practice as a 15-year-old, 16-year-old."

Boynton wasn't kidding, as his high school coach, who can't seem to retire, is back assisting at the same Bishop Loughlin where Boynton and many other future college standouts and some NBA players got their primary education.

"You've got to be able to trust your point guard because he is an extension of you out there on the court. In certain circumstances, I could easily trust Michael to start practice and even run it all," Leckie said, admitting that he has owned a bar and restaurant and that even though he's retired from basketball several times, "it keeps drawing me back in. I tell people I keep coaching so I can keep the bar and restaurant open."

Boynton, after a year assisting Underwood to wake up the rowdy and get the Cowboys going, understands what he is responsible for now. He enters as the head coach of a school that, despite its great tradition, particularly in his sport, also has challenges and needs the enthusiasm and support of all who proudly wear Oklahoma State Orange. As an unknown, there are some skeptics that he has to win over.

"I'm 35 years old and I've never been a head coach before; Coach Holder and the Board of Regents have just named me as the head coach of Oklahoma State University. What kind of person would I be to dismiss that? That means a lot to me," Boynton said just a day after accepting the job. "We will have the recruiting base covered. I have to get the people that buy tickets, the fans, to understand that the sky is not falling. It rained a little bit, but the sky was a little cloudy and the sun is coming back. Our current players are the priority always. I'm as committed to this place and I am proud to lead this program. I am not thinking about anything else than doing the job really, really, well for as long as they will have me here."

Oklahoma State and Stillwater, Oklahoma, may have a population of 45,000, but on football Saturdays there are close to 60,000 in Boone Pickens Stadium. The sea of orange also swells on basketball nights, and another chapter in Cowboys lore never seems too far away.

Sources

Media Guides

2016 Oklahoma State Football Media Guide
2016 Oklahoma State Alamo Bowl Media Guide
2016–17 Oklahoma State Basketball Media Guide
2016–17 Oklahoma State Wrestling Media Guide
2016–17 Oklahoma State Golf Media Guide
2017 Oklahoma State Baseball Media Guide

Newspapers

Oklahoman
Tulsa World
Daily O'Collegian

Books and Other Publications

Allen, Robert. *More Than a Championship: The 2011 Oklahoma State Cowboys*. Oklahoma City: Oklahoma Heritage Association, 2012.

Dellinger, Bob. *The Cowboys Ride Again!: The History of Wrestling's Dynasty*. Stillwater: Oklahoma Bylines, 1994.

Websites

AFCA.com
Alamobowl.com
Big12sports.com
ESPN.com
Gopokes.com
KUathletics.com
NCAA.com
Okstate.com